Reckoning with
Social Media

Reckoning with Social Media

Edited by Aleena Chia, Ana Jorge,
and Tero Karppi

ROWMAN & LITTLEFIELD
Lanham • Boulder • New York • London

Published by Rowman & Littlefield
An imprint of The Rowman & Littlefield Publishing Group, Inc.
4501 Forbes Boulevard, Suite 200, Lanham, Maryland 20706
www.rowman.com
86-90 Paul Street, London EC2A 4NE

British Library Cataloguing in Publication Information Available

Library of Congress Cataloging-in-Publication Data

Names: Chia, Aleena Leng An, editor. | Jorge, Ana, 1982– editor. | Karppi, Tero, editor.
Title: Reckoning with social media / edited by Aleena Chia, Ana Jorge, and Tero Karppi.
Description: Lanham : Rowman & Littlefield, [2021] | Includes bibliographical references and index.
Identifiers: LCCN 2021037893 (print) | LCCN 2021037894 (ebook) | ISBN 9781538147405 (cloth) | ISBN 9781538147429 (pbk.) | ISBN 9781538147412 (epub)
Subjects: LCSH: Social media.
Classification: LCC HM742 .R433 2021 (print) | LCC HM742 (ebook) | DDC 302.23/1—dc23
LC record available at https://lccn.loc.gov/2021037893
LC ebook record available at https://lccn.loc.gov/2021037894

Contents

Introduction

Reckoning with Social Media in the Pandemic Denouement

Aleena Chia, Ana Jorge, and Tero Karppi

Once celebrated for connecting people and circulating ideas, social media have been problematized as a necessary evil for getting by and getting on in platform capitalism, especially during Covid-19 disruptions to workspace and social life. Criticisms and moral panics about social media's hold over individuals and leverage over society have always accompanied their rise to dominance. In 2016, these criticisms burst into public consciousness in what became known as the 'techlash'. Su, Lazar, and Irani (2021) inform that the techlash normalized critique of big tech and public demands for accountability for their platforms' anticompetitive reach, extractive-addictive design, and toxicity to democracy. Galvanizing questions and criticisms by journalists, users, politicians, and tech workers, the techlash reckons with social media by asking platforms to account for being too big, too engaging, too unruly. Scaffolding public debates and affects, techlash documentaries such as (Amer and Noujaim 2019) and *The Social Dilemma* (Orlowski 2020) often weigh strategies to regulate how platforms operate technically, economically, and legally against individual tactics to manage the effects of social media by disconnecting from them.

These disconnection practices—from restricting screen time and detoxing from device use to deleting apps and accounts—often reinforce rather than confront the ways social media organise attention, everyday life, and society. *Reckoning with Social Media* challenges the prevailing critique of social media that pits small adjustments against big changes, that either celebrates personal transformation or champions structural reformation. This edited volume reframes evaluative claims about disconnection practices as either restorative or reformative of current social media systems by beginning where other studies conclude: the ambivalence and complicity of separating from social media, which has been compounded in the pandemic's state of exception.

1

As we write this introduction, the vaccine's steady roll-out in North America and Europe stands in cruel contrast to the virus's ravage of communities in India and Brazil. In Canada and Portugal where we are based, social media feeds loop from the reserved gratitude of vaccine selfies to the utter devastation of mass cremations, keeping users glued to their screens in states of suspended affective animation. As countries battle waves of Covid-19 infections and its variants with domestic confinement, commercial suspension, and physical separation, social media platforms have further entrenched themselves as a basic infrastructure for work and leisure (Neves and Steinberg 2020). The pandemic's cascade of crises—from the public health breakdown of cities to the economic ruination of communities—has spun ambient anxieties into a state of perpetual disorientation (Means and Slater 2021) that has arguably disrupted the momentum of the techlash. The crises of Covid-19 have hollowed out the techlash's criticism into satire and its radicalism into resignation. Joseph Masco (2017, S65) explains that because of its media saturation and eschatological associations, 'crisis' has lost its power to shock and mobilize: 'It is thus a predominantly conservative modality, seeking to stabilize an existing structure within a radically contingent world.'

While the spread of social media—if we follow the viral metaphor—has been pandemic, worldwide, border-crossing phenomena affecting the many, the forms of reckoning are endemic: localized forms of resistance actualized through connectivity. How do these everyday practices and meanings of restricting and rejecting apps and devices constitute cultures of connection that iteratively configure social media platforms? How can we mobilize such iterative processes of constitution and configuration towards more ethical social media ecosystems? This volume tackles these questions by addressing how disconnection practices imbricate across regulatory, collective, and individual levels.

By grounding critical inquiry in the analysis of interpretive meanings, the chapters in this book situate the conspicuous non-consumption (Portwood-Stacer 2013) of disconnection practices within the politics of networked visibility (Banet-Weiser 2018) and the ambivalent dependence on social media platforms. The chapters put user anxieties about the techlash in critical conversation with civic exigencies about platform economics and surveillance capitalism (Zuboff 2019). Drawing from media and cultural studies, contributions to this volume cut through the scandals of big tech and the outrage of the techlash to examine how everyday resistance to and negotiation of apps and platforms impede and invigorate changes to social media's modulation of what we do, how we think, and how we relate to each other.

Reckoning with Social Media engages with critical debates and pressing issues in a growing corpus of book-length studies on disconnection (Light 2014; Karppi 2018; Brennen 2019; Syvertsen 2020; Stäheli 2021a) that predominantly address resistance to social media either by making sense of the meanings of disconnection from user studies or by mapping out the imperatives of platforms through political economic and media-theoretical analyses. The proposed volume does not just illustrate the multiplicity, normativity, and contradictions of disconnection practices. The edited chapters go further to interrogate the meshwork of individual and collective practices, personal and structural agency, and restorative and transformative resistance towards social media that make up the dialectics of disconnection. The contributions investigate common themes through complementary methodologies ranging from qualitative interviews and quantitative surveys to textual approaches such as discourse analysis and critical theory. This edited volume puts established digital media scholars in conversation with emerging researchers across Nordic, European, British, North American, and South American case studies and field sites.

How we name the processes of reckoning with social media matters. Nonuse (Selwyn 2006) and abstention (Portwood-Stacer 2013) direct the attention to the systematic exclusion of connectivity; detox (Sutton 2017; Syvertsen 2020) evokes the context of well-being; opting out (Brennen 2019) speaks of user choice; unfriending (John and Dvir-Gvirsman 2015), undoing (Stäheli 2021b), and disconnective practices (Light 2014) bring us to the activity of managing connections where avoidance is one choice among others (Lingel 2020). This limited example of the conceptual cornucopia illustrates the elusiveness of our object of study and the different approaches developed to make sense of it. We locate practices and discourses of reckoning in the context of disconnection studies, which provides a conceptual register for synthesizing the aforementioned arguments and commitments.

This edited collection is thematically structured around defining the stakes of disconnection for users and researchers, beginning with laying the conceptual groundwork of disconnection studies and its conceptualization of subjectivity. The book proceeds by politicizing desires to disconnect through qualitative and textual analyses of how social media users make sense of their practices and how mobile device designers and artists mobilize imaginaries of disconnection.[1] The book concludes with the temporal politics of disconnection, which provides an analytical lens to understand the nostalgia for communicative immediacy, the leisure of bike touring, and pandemic work-life balance. *Reckoning with Social Media* highlights the disjuncture in scales of inquiry between the interpretive focus at the level of individual users and the critical and theoretical focus at the level of platform regulation. This translation between experiential and infrastructural scales and between

---

[1] The image on the cover of our book is from the IP/Privacy collection by fashion designer Nicole Scheller. Scheller designs ways to live with and resist automated facial recognition technologies and forward-looking infrared cameras tracking our identities. Photograph: Franz Grünewald; Model: Christina Dalbert; Design: URBANPRIVACY by Nicole Scheller.

empirical and theoretical approaches is vital to understanding and politicizing disconnection.

DEFINING DISCONNECTION

In 'Defining Disconnection,' Magdalena Kania-Lundholm's chapter 'Why Disconnecting Matters? Towards a Critical Research Agenda on Online Disconnection' maps different approaches in this field of study in the past 17 years. She examines 72 academic texts and shows how studies of disconnection have transformed in tandem with changes in our digital environment. Kania-Lundholm maps the dominant narratives of disconnection studies from the early framings of non-use and digital and social exclusion to different forms of disconnection such as detox, temporary breaks, and the overall interest in the management of connectivity. She points out that in the postdigital era the narratives are again changing. Based on this existing scholarship Kania-Lundholm initiates a critical research agenda for our time, which challenges normative ideas of connectivity, usage, and participation, and asks readers to consider disconnection as both contingent and contextual.

Annette N. Markham's chapter 'The Ontological Insecurity of Disconnecting: A Theory of Echolocation and the Self' theorizes contemporary self-making as constituted through feedback from constant connection on social media. Using the metaphor of echolocation, Markham shows how young people's sense of self relies on getting a response to one's performance of self in everyday life and, increasingly, on social media. Echolocation is communicative, locative, and requires constant connection. Drawing from an eight-year ethnographically grounded study of young people's everyday online experiences, Markham argues that when identity relies on the echolocational response from social media, disconnecting can cause inchoate feelings of existential vulnerability. Theorizing social media through echolocation demonstrates how connection is fundamental to social existence: continuous interaction demarcates the ontological boundaries of the Self and modulates relational positionalities with other people. By attending to micro-processes of sensemaking, the theory of echolocation helps us to understand disconnection, not in terms of binary states, but as modulations of modes, degrees, and moments of connection and disconnection that are entangled in multiple sociotechnical and ideological forces.

DESIRING DISCONNECTION

In 'Desiring Disconnection,' chapters combine interviews, surveys, and thematic analysis to generate critical insights from the interpretive meanings of disconnection's circuits of desire: its commodification through logics of networked visibility such as influencer culture, its tensions between authenticity and anxiety, and its epistemology of choice as consumer citizens within (neo) liberal democracies. Approaching disconnection through the problematics of commodification, ambivalence, and agency, these chapters demonstrate how individuals deal with social media amid a dialectic between individual tactics and macro-structural pressures and norms. They also demonstrate the intersection between affectivity and materiality present in practices of disconnection.

Ana Jorge and Marco Pedroni analyze how influencers from different categories and origins perform authenticity in their visual and textual content about social media detox. '"Hey! I'm Back after a 24h #DigitalDetox!": Influencers Posing Disconnection' reveals how influencers present themselves as hyperconnected subjects under continuous pressure to be accessible to social media audiences and relevant in the attention economy. Influencers use different strategies to disconnect through temporal bounded activities (holidays, weekends) that are narrativized in a variety of ways: oscillating from being the main focus of their content to being a part of their discourses as lifestyle gurus. Some of the social media detox content is sponsored by brands and corporations, which is yet another level of commodification of disconnection. The analysis suggests that influencers accrue symbolic capital for online self-promotion by deploying tropes of mindfulness, mental health, and well-being, while positioning themselves through increased self-control that they inspire other users to adopt.

In their chapter, 'Privacy, Energy, Time, and Moments Stolen: Social Media Experiences Pushing towards Disconnection', Trine Syvertsen and Brita Ytre-Arne interview Norwegian social media users: one set of interviewees were 'ordinary' users, while others self-identified as 'detoxers'. Their analysis maps out gradations of ambivalence between seemingly opposing positions towards social media use between authenticity and performance, euphoria and anxiety. Users from both samples express overlapping discomforts and fascinations with social media, hence the analysis supports the view that connection and disconnection should not be treated as dichotomous positions. The authors propose to look at four non-exclusive dimensions of social media that push towards disconnection, namely systemic, technological, public, and personal aspects. These can, to varying degrees, influence individuals to perceive the need for disconnection. They find that users are ambivalent not just to social media but also to the strategies and solutions they choose to handle social media problems.

In 'Quitting Digital Culture: Rethinking Agency in a Beyond-Choice Ontology', Zeena Feldman probes these feelings of ambivalence through an analysis of 491 responses to an online survey, 12 semi-structured interviews, and 169 'audience statements' from a participatory art installation from the Quitting Social Media project. According to Feldman, discourses of disconnection admonish tech while valourizing and commodifying individual choice and responsibility. At the level of participants, networked practices were framed as existing beyond choice because of its structural necessity for themselves and society. The author then considers these findings in relation to economist Albert Hirschman's (1970) seminal framework about consumer power strategies of 'voice' and 'exit'. In making sense of the ways user participation and resistance operate alongside one another, Feldman proposes how viable user agency can be recovered in sociotechnical contexts where permanent disconnection proves increasingly untenable.

DESIGNING DISCONNECTION

Ideal uses and users are always part of technology design (Grint and Woolgar 1991; Akrich 1992; Docherty 2020). Since the early 2000s, the designs of social media have focused on connections. People, services, products, but also desires, behaviours, and traits, have been brought together by the designs of social media. Through these designs, companies in charge persuade us to believe in their vision that technology unifies us and turns the world into a better place (Vaidhyanathan 2018). This vision has always had its cracks, which the techlash has rendered even more visible: fake news, hate speech, and emotional manipulation are examples that have gained publicity. These cracks are deepened by fears of exploitation, manipulation, marginalization, and discrimination that can erode solidarity and sociality (Yeung 2018). When the utopias of social media turn into dystopias, designs of disconnection come into play.

Simone Natale, Paolo Bory, and Gabriele Balbi (2020) describe the narratives where digital media companies position themselves as agents of social change as 'corporational determinism'. Niall Docherty (2020) has explicitly described how social media sites appropriate the idea of healthy habits and well-being into their ideal user models and nudge them towards better and healthier social media choices. Docherty (2020, 9–10) points out that when social media sites begin to script what is healthy, they do it within the parameters of their business. In this model, reckoning with social media does not mark a point of departure from social media but rather is an intensification of the logic of connectivity; it gives the user a feeling of being in control. The interest in user health and well-being can also be read in the wider context of business ethics, which, in this volume, Aleena Chia and Alex Beattie point out has become an important component for product development and public relations. The two chapters of this section trace the designs of disconnection on two levels: the corporate and the individual.

In the chapter 'Ethics and Experimentation in The Light Phone and Google Digital Wellbeing', Chia and Beattie analyze The Light Phone and Google's Digital Wellbeing Collection to understand how designs of disconnection destabilize dominant ways of seeing, doing, and thinking. Central to their argument is that products of disconnection have the capability to produce disconnection as a sensation: experiences of distance from devices and platforms that do not actually break digital connections. Following Kathleen Stewart (2011), this chapter analyzes disconnective sensations as 'atmospheric attunement'. Important here is that while the designs they examine are part of corporate branding, atmospheric attunement is an affective relation that does not exhaust the potential of disconnection. As such, their argument can be placed in contrast to Simone Natale and Emiliano Treré (2020) who argue that 'the emancipatory potential of disconnection as a form of critique and sociopolitical change is often deactivated and subsumed by the dynamics of digital capitalism under the innocuous facade of escape'. In other words, Chia and Beattie show that while corporations protect themselves with disconnective designs, these designs do not foreclose but engender other ways of living that engage with the politics of the techlash in agnostic ways.

Start-ups are designing 'dumb' phones, fashion designers create clothes that protect from surveillance, even technology companies think of how to design models for healthy use. But what would it mean to drop out of this rat race entirely? Can one design a life that is disconnected and does not agree to the terms and services of these companies? How can we locate this other way of living? In their chapter 'From Digital Detox to 24/365 Disconnection: Between Dependency Tactics and Resistance Strategies in Brazil', Marianna Ferreira Jorge and Julia Salgado address these questions by examining a project by Brazilian artist Ana Rovati who decided to live a life without connective media for one year. For the authors, Rovati's project makes visible that one does not simply choose to disconnect but needs to design their life around that decision—so intertwined are our daily lives with computational networks that Rovati lost contact with 90% of her friends to the extent that, for some, her project was comparable to self-harm. But this self-imposed solitary unhappiness also pushes the artist and the authors alike to ask how we mix happiness with the endless rhythms and flows of stimuli that the commodified forms of social networks throw towards us at accelerated paces. The story of Rovati illustrates that the script for a happy life that is disconnected is not in instant reliefs defined by isolated moments and events. Rather, it exists in longer durations where real changes can take place and become visible.

DELAYING DISCONNECTION

Disconnections are practices of temporal modulation that operate through the earmarking, extending, and abbreviating of time on sites, in apps, and with devices. In 'Overcoming Forced Disconnection: Disentangling the Professional and the Personal in Pandemic Times', Christoffer Bagger and Stine Lomborg interviewed knowledge workers about their pandemic lockdown, asking how communication media structured and shaped a new normal of everyday working life. Bagger and Lomborg report that the domain of the professional was often experienced as all-encompassing: eclipsing spatial boundaries, temporal divisions, and social contexts. Covid-19 restrictions meant that knowledge workers had to renegotiate boundaries between the professional and the personal, by holding the fort of home against the assimilative tide of work demands. Left to their own devices—literally and figuratively—knowledge workers had to demarcate the use of videoconferencing apps for social activities and social media apps for work activities. Bagger and Lomborg conclude that, more than rejection, disconnection can be understood as practices of selecting the optimal mode from a range of alternative modes of communication.

In their chapter 'Disconnecting on Two Wheels: Bike Touring, Leisure, and Reimagining Networks', Pedro Ferreira and Airi Lampinen use interviews with enthusiasts to investigate bike touring as a disconnective activity. While both are interested in the boundary play between work and leisure, Bagger and Lomborg investigate the everyday rhythms of domestic space, while Ferreira and Lampinen investigate temporary liberties outside of ordinary life on the open road, thereby positing an analytic of disconnection as inspiration for the design of the self. The analysis suggests that digital technologies hold some promise in addressing the loss of self-control. Like the other chapters in this volume, the authors eschew easy dichotomizations of connection and disconnection, and its associations with authenticity and artifice in communication. Instead, this chapter uses niche leisure activities to question the normativity of the techlash by reframing problematic smartphone use on the level of individuals and communities of practice.

Clara Wieghorst concludes the volume with the chapter 'Analogue Nostalgia: Examining Critiques of Social Media', which analyzes the conservatism of the techlash veiled in semantic networks of nostalgia that connect public desire and popular critique. Combining etymological analysis with close readings of prominent social media scholarship, Wieghorst shows how the 'analogue' is actively produced through the moralizing of connection as the original sin. Based on a fallacy of presentism, the analogue fans desire for disconnection through fantasies about a media-free state associated with conversation and connectedness. By historicizing nostalgia,

Wieghorst shows how the analogue is framed in opposition to a state of connectivity associated with technology and standardization. Instead of mapping disconnective desire onto an arrow of time, this analysis recommends denaturalizing humanities approaches to disconnection to go beyond regressive imaginaries of sociality before media. This will involve reckoning with social media through its socio-technological materialities and alternative temporalities.

Alexander Means and Graham Slater (2021, 517) predict that the pandemic conjecture demands political articulation towards 'common horizons, collective agency, and livable futures.' Sean Cubitt (2021) states that, in order to stamp the future with the demands of the present, the work of planning for post-pandemic futures must be undertaken in crisis. As we reckon with the pandemic denouement on platforms, policies, and psyches, this book presents a preliminary plan to reconstitute and reconfigure the techlash.

REFERENCES

Akrich, Madeleine. 1997. "The de-scription of technical objects." In Bijker, Wiebe E. and John Law (eds.), *Shaping Technology/Building Society*, pp. 205–224. Cambridge, MA: MIT Press.

Amer, Karim and Jehane Noujaim, dir. 2019. *The Great Hack*. Netflix, Video on Demand.

Banet-Weiser, Sarah. 2018. *Empowered: Popular Feminism and Popular Misogyny*. Durham: Duke University Press.

Brennen, Bonnie. 2019. *Opting Out of Digital Media*. Routledge.

Cubitt, Sean. 2021. "Against the new normal." *Cultural Politics* 1(7): 48–54.

Docherty, Niall. 2020. "Facebook's ideal user: Healthy habits, social capital, and the politics of well-being online." *Social Media + Society*, 6(2). doi:10.1177/2056305120915606.

Grint, Keith and Steve Woolgar. 1997. *The Machine at Work. Technology, Work and Organization*. Cambridge, UK: Polity.

Hirschman, Albert O. 1970. *Exit, Voice, and Loyalty: Responses to Decline in Firms, Organizations, and States*. Cambridge, MA: Harvard University Press.

John, Nicholas, A., and Shira Dvir-Gvirsman. 2015. "I don't like you any more": Facebook unfriending by Israelis during the Israel–Gaza conflict of 2014. *Journal of Communication* 65(6): 953–974. doi:10.1111/jcom.12188

Karppi, Tero. 2018. *Disconnect. Facebook's Affective Bonds*. Minneapolis, MN: University of Minnesota Press.

Light, Ben. 2014. *Disconnecting with Social Networking Sites*. London: Palgrave Macmillan.

Lingel, Jessica. 2020. "Dazzle Camouflage as Queer counter conduct." *European Journal of Cultural Studies*, 1–18. doi:10.1177/1367549420902805

Masco, Joseph. 2017. "The crisis in crisis." *Current Anthropology* 58(S15): S65–S76.

Means, Alexander J., and Graham B. Slater. 2021. "Collective disorientation in the pandemic conjuncture." *Cultural Studies* 35(2–3): 514–522.

Natale, Simone, Paolo Bory, and Gabriele Balbi. 2020. "The rise of corporational determinism: Digital media corporations and narratives of media change." *Critical Studies in Media Communication* 36(4): 323–338. doi:10.1080/15295036.2019.1 632469.

Natale, Simone, and Emiliano Treré. 2020. "Vinyl won't save us: Reframing disconnection as engagement." *Media, Culture & Society* 42(4): 626–633.

Neves, Joshua, and Marc Steinberg. 2020. "Pandemic platforms: How convenience shapes the inequality of crisis." In *Pandemic Media*, edited by Philipp Dominik Keidl, Laliv Melamed, Vinzenz Hediger, and Antonio Somaini, pp. 105–114. Lüneburg: Meson Press.

Orlowski, Jeff, dir. 2020. *The Social Dilemma.* Netflix, Video on Demand.

Portwood-Stacer, Laura. 2013. "Media refusal and conspicuous non-consumption: The performative and political dimensions of Facebook abstention." *New Media & Society* 15(7): 1041–1057.

Selwyn, Neil. 2006. "Digital division or digital decision? A study of non-users and low-users of computers." *Poetics* 34: 273–292.

Stäheli, Urs. 2021a, *Soziologie der Entnetzung.* Berlin: Suhrkamp.

Stäheli, Urs. 2021b. "Undoing networks". In Karppi, T., Stäheli, U., Wieghorst, C. and Zierott, L.P. (eds.), *Undoing Networks*, pp. 1–30. University of Minnesota Press/Meson Press.

Su, Norman Makoto, Amanda Lazar, and Lilly Irani. 2021. "Critical affects: Tech work emotions amidst the techlash." *Proceedings of the ACM on Human-Computer Interaction* 5(1): 1–27.

Sutton, Theodora. 2017. "Disconnect to reconnect: The food/technology metaphor in digital detoxing." *First Monday* 22(6). doi:10.5210/fm.v22i6.7561

Stewart, Kathleen. 2011. "Atmospheric attunements". *Environment and Planning D: Society and Space* 29(3): 445–453.

Syvertsen, Trine. 2020. *Digital Detox: the Politics of Disconnecting.* Bingley, UK: Emerald Publishing.

Vaidhyanathan, Siva. 2018. *Anti-Social Media: How Facebook Undermines Democracy and Disconnects Us.* New York: Oxford University Press.

Yeung, Karen. 2018. "Five fears about mass predictive personalization in an age of surveillance capitalism." *International Data Privacy Law* 8(3): 258–269. doi:10.1093/idpl/ipy020

Zuboff, Shoshana. 2019. *The Age of Surveillance Capitalism: The Fight for a Human Future at the New Frontier of Power.* New York: PublicAffairs.

Part I

DEFINING DISCONNECTION

Chapter 1

Why Disconnecting Matters

Towards a Critical Research Agenda on Online Disconnection

Magdalena Kania-Lundholm

Like air and drinking water, being digital *will be noticed only by its absence, not its presence.*

—Negroponte, 1999

When in 1999 Nicolas Negroponte suggested that defining the spirit of age can be as simple as one word, he picked, among others, 'digital' to describe the omnipresence of technology. He also, prophetically, argued that when digital technology is taken for granted, only its absence will be noticed. Today, over 20 years later, terms such as networked society (Castells 1996), social acceleration (Rosa 2013), and culture of connectivity (Van Dijck 2013) have been employed to describe the 'new normal' of ubiquitous connectivity and social media that have transformed our lives in a profound way. At the same time, we are moving away towards what some describe as the post-internet or post-digital era (Mosco 2017, 2018). In the context where normative media practices are those of connectivity and where the latter transforms online commodity into real offline value (Van Dijck 2013), there are growing practices and zones of 'disconnectivity' that, often, serve ideological purposes. In such a social media and internet ubiquitous environment, there is a parallel development with proliferation of services, websites, and self-help guides encouraging users to disconnect and to engage in various media detox practices. For instance, practices of temporal digital media refusal or technology non-use such as turn towards meditation, hiking, yoga, and fishing are just a few of the activities offered at digital detox camps (Sutton 2017; Fish 2017). Even scholars who openly declare themselves not to be 'anti-technology' have the tendency to romanticize the authenticity of the offline

13

face-to-face encounter and conversation (cf. Turkle 2008). All this 'unplugging' talk has a clear purpose to challenge the impact and consequences of the
connectivity culture and social acceleration. At the same time, in recent years,
we have witnessed a rapidly growing, multidisciplinary academic interest
in online disconnection with a focus on, among others, the *anti*social and
disconnective character of social media (Karppi 2018; Vaidhyanathan 2018)
as well as the politics of disconnection as response to the intrusive nature
of social media in the context of neoliberal self-regulation (Syvertsen 2019;
Syvertsen and Enli 2020). Although it still remains unclear to what extent
disconnecting from digital devices and social networking platforms can serve
as an antidotum or a remedy to the problems of digital neoliberal capitalism,
scholars have begun to raise critical voices to demystify disconnection and
develop critiques against the ambivalences and paradoxes of digital societies
(Treré et al. 2020).

    The aim of this chapter is to engage with the existing body of research on
online disconnection studies, also often referred to as technology non-use or
media refusal (Portwood-Stacer 2013; Light 2014). The main contribution is
the delimitation and articulation of online disconnection studies by mapping
over this rapidly growing field of research based on scholarly sources across
disciplines. For this chapter 72 academic sources published between 2003
and 2020 were examined. They include scholarly articles, books, and chapters published in English. Sources were located through searches in academic
databases such as Web of Science and Sociological Abstracts, via Google
Scholar alerts, and by following the topic in other academic discussions such
as blogs and social media platforms. The methodological framework for this
chapter is informed by the scoping review approach which is a way to sum-
marize and map relevant literature and to identify the potential research gaps
(Arksey and O'Malley 2005). The following are the main research questions:
What are the main characteristics of research about online disconnection?
How do researchers discuss the topic of online disconnection? In order to
clarify, in the remainder of this chapter I use the term 'disconnection' and/
or 'online disconnection studies' when I place my own argument; however,
when referring to specific studies I employ the terms used by their authors,
such as 'technology non-use', 'non-participation', and/or 'digital detox'.
Based on the synthesis of the existing literature, I suggest we go beyond
the well-established literature on digital divide that research on technology
non-use has been pursuing so far (Selwyn 2006; Sparks 2013). Instead, I
propose that a critical research agenda should move beyond the normative
ideas of connectivity, usage, and participation, and consider disconnection
as both contingent and context embedded. Furthermore, research on online
disconnection emphasizes the materiality and temporality of the digital and,
by doing so, has the potential to address both the politics of social media and

various forms of media resistance, such as digital detox, Slow Media movement, and others. Finally, I argue for an expanded critical research agenda on this topic and discuss some directions for critically oriented and sociologically informed research.

BEYOND THE NARRATIVE OF TECHNOLOGY NON-USE

Technology non-use and subsequent digital and social exclusion became dominant narratives that have shaped the early studies on online disconnection. With the rise of the 'information age' and the network model of society (Castells 1996), the underlying assumption has been that both access and skills to use digital media technologies are necessary aspects of living in the hyperconnected modern societies. Consequently, technology non-use or 'Internet non-adoption' (Galperin and Viecens 2017) has previously been examined as something deviating from the norm, or a problem to be solved. Additionally, in the context of capitalist networked society the discourse of exploitation has been replaced by a non-hierarchical idea of exclusion (Fisher 2010). Non-use of digital technologies and social media was thus considered an act of *involuntary exclusion*, meaning that individuals due to socioeconomic, infrastructural, or demographic reasons are excluded from access to digital technologies (Selwyn 2006; Van Dijk 2006). This approach has been rather common in the research on digital divide approaching issues of inequality of access and use on both micro and macro levels (Pick and Sarkar 2016). The implicit assumptions which often inform this type of research include, for example, the idea that once access barriers are overcome people will enthusiastically embrace technology with all its promises. Such assumptions are also normative in the sense of emphasizing the primacy of usage and connectivity as the preferred option among technology adopters. The basis of this logic forms an inherent belief that access, technology adoption, and use are routes to social inclusion and progress. What these approaches often have in common is the assumption that lack of resources—economic, social, or discursive—constitutes a major obstacle for people to engage with digital technologies and that usage and connectivity are often desirable options for all individuals and organizations. They are also often based on an implicit notion that 'a single internet can or does exist' (Srinivasan and Fish 2017, 27).

Scholars use a plethora of terms to describe different forms of online disconnection. One of the ways is to provide taxonomies of non-users. These include 'resisters' and 'rejecters' to describe the voluntary non-users. The notions of the 'excluded' and the 'expelled' are employed to describe the involuntary non-users, but also 'net dropouts', 'Internots', 'evaders', and 'dropouts' (Wyatt 2003; Cushman and Klecun 2006; Satchell and Dourish 2009; Verdegem and Verhoest 2009; Reisdorf 2011; van Deursen and Helsper 2015). These studies suggest that tech non-use, either voluntary or not, is a complex activity, rather than a state of inaction and disinterest (Fernández-Ardèvol, Sawchuk, and Grenier 2017). They also suggest that the distinction between use and non-use is rather ambivalent and fluid, since decisions about disconnection are not always a matter of agency and active choice. Scholars emphasize that issues such as institutional expectations, sociocultural practices, and sociotechnical contexts need to be considered a background in which decisions about online disconnection are made (Waycott et al. 2016). In recent years, scholars have begun to question the usefulness of the dichotomies such as 'use/non-use', 'access/non-access', 'consumption/ non-consumption', and 'participation/non-participation' (Light 2014; Neves et al. 2015; Lutz and Hoffman 2017). The idea is to strive towards a more nuanced understanding of technology adoption which not only includes temporal forms of disconnection but also addresses issues that go beyond technology use and users. For instance, one of the arguments is that the traditional binary logic does not hold not only because people have different reasons and motivations behind technology non-use and disconnection but also because the latter also needs to be considered a form of media engagement and not solely a marker of social and digital exclusion (Selwyn, Gorard, and Furlong 2005; Cushman and Klecun 2006). Consequently, understanding of the acts of online disconnection requires also examining motivations and meanings which evolve around such practices.

BEYOND THE NARRATIVES OF CONNECTIVITY AND PARTICIPATION

Narratives of connectivity and participation are central to experiences of digitally mediated social life on a variety of levels. They are often perceived as means of empowerment, social inclusion, and democracy. Focusing on disconnection can potentially challenge the assumptions that connectivity and online participation are highly desirable and necessary aspects of living in modern Western societies. One could even argue that disconnection makes connection possible (cf. Light 2014; Karppi 2018) and that such an approach helps to revisit the binary notion of technology use versus non-use. It points to the fact that 'leaving technology', albeit at times only for a short while, can be a meaningful act (Sutton 2017). Thus, instead of focusing solely on policy, infrastructure, and access to technology (or lack of thereof), some research on technology non-use also examines the role of corporations, governments, and other organizations that make connectivity (im)possible (cf. Baumer et al. 2015). It also means addressing non-use as a subcategory of use rather than its opposite (Kellner, Massou, and Morelli 2010).

Recent scholarly focus on non-participation allows us to revisit the widely shared affirmative framing of online participation. For example, the practice of *lurking* as described by Kushner (2016) implies consuming social media content without generating any. Kushner suggests that this type of 'passive participation' causes threat to the logic of constant connectivity and participation of the corporate social networking platforms. It also challenges the 'sharing is caring' logic which assumes users' active production and consumption of online content in the form of 'prosumption' (Ritzer 2010). Non-participation can also be an active, deliberate choice. For example, Casemajor et al. (2015) argue that when it comes to political activism, there is a dynamic relationship between active non-participation and active participation. Consequently, one of the paradoxes of non-participation is that it can be empowering individuals who actively seek to disrupt, slow down, and resist certain platforms, policies, or regimes of surveillance (ibid., 9). Online non-participation is also an activist strategy observed in milieux associated with radical left and related to political claims to autonomy (Anderson 2016). Driven by the ambition to provide a nuanced understanding of online participation, Lutz and Hoffmann (2017) offer an empirically derived typology of online participation along axes of activity, agency, and valence. They differentiate participation and non-participation, active and passive, positive and negative. In this way, non-participation ranges from practices of abstention and lack of motivation to silencing and exclusion. Each of these types delineates a form of non-participation from a user perspective and provides a broader understanding of this phenomenon. For example, non-participation is not synonymous with lack of engagement and the reasons for it are diverse, ranging from lack of awareness to disinterest, abstention, and exclusion (ibid., 889).

Sometimes decisions whether to disconnect are not necessarily a matter of active, deliberate choice. Disconnecting from a particular device, such as a smartphone, can be a temporary choice and an expression of ambivalence rather than a well-motivated political or lifestyle decision (Ribak and Rosenthal 2015). Similarly, decisions to leave a particular social media platform or an app do not necessarily have to be definite, but can involve temporary leaving. As the study of leaving the online dating app Grindr by Brubaker, Ananny, and Crawford (2016) illustrates, leaving and disconnecting from the app can depend on time, physical situation, and other contextual factors. In other words, the varieties of forms of online disconnection are context embedded and situational and can change over time (Leavitt 2014). Burrell (2012) shows how assessments of technology's efficacy by users are culturally shaped and prone to change over time. While technology non-use can be perceived as rather non-mainstream and sometimes a subversive move in the Western context of nearly ubiquitous access and use, it is the norm in other contexts. For instance, in Ghana non-use of networked technology is widespread, despite the country being one of the most connected in Africa with about 34% of internet users in 2017 (Internet world stats). The dropout behavior of some of early and enthusiastic social media users in Ghana calls into question the foothold the technology once seemed to be gaining and casts the internet's mainstreaming in Ghana into doubt (ibid.).

People not only appropriate technologies differently in terms of assigning meanings to their disconnective practices. They also have different understandings of such practices. As Sutton suggests (2017), 'Leaving digital technology is contextual, can hold different meanings for each person, and is difficult to enact in a strictly binary way.' For instance, when it comes to devices and applications, users might initially be interested in using them, but their interest can fade gradually as they find certain features distracting or annoying. Consequently, disconnecting is as much a 'technical' as a *social act* and users make sense of disconnection in relation to their understanding of the self (Birnholtz 2010; Brubaker, Ananny, and Crawford 2016). This means online disconnection is a dynamic and contested practice and process. Instead of addressing connectivity and disconnectivity as binary opposites, they need to be approached as flexible processes that heavily depend on social contexts and circumstances in which they are enacted (cf. Kaun and Schwarzenegger 2014; Ems 2015). For instance, the ambition to resist corporate social media and their business models can be one of such circumstances.

WHAT DOES ONLINE DISCONNECTION MEAN AND WHY PEOPLE DO IT?

Much research on technology non-use is conducted across different disciplines that are not necessarily in conversation with one another and include media studies, human-computer interaction, journalism studies, sociology, social anthropology, social gerontology, and others (cf. Baumer et al. 2014; Bossio and Holton 2019). In this chapter, I understand disconnection along what Light (2014) defines as temporal 'removal or breaking the connection' which 'can also exist in its own right in relation to connection as a possibility' (ibid.). Instead of referring to a single practice or performance, Light also talks about the 'disconnective power' ranging from dislike buttons, rejecting a friend or a follower, passivity in the form of lurking or *not* liking, sharing, and tagging to moderating use, censorship, and resistance. Hesselberth (2018), on the other hand, refers to 'the gesture to disconnect' but also acknowledges discourses of the 'right to disconnect' proliferating on social media and in academic circles. Different forms of online disconnection include, for instance, reactions against the overload of information, such as digital suicide (Karppi 2011); non-use as performance in practices of digital non-consumption and internet resistance (Portwood-Stacer 2013; Woodstock 2011); and connectivity pushback (Morrison and Gomez 2014). Also, online non-participation can be understood as a communicative strategy in online activism and mediated political action rather than passivity and withdrawal (Andersson 2016; Casemajor et al. 2015). Concepts such as 'media turnoff', 'media disappointment', and 'media resistance' (Woodstock 2014; Syvertsen 2017) are also employed to express reactions to life in the media ubiquitous environment.

The spectrum of different forms of online disconnection also reflects numerous reasons and motivations ranging from morality (due to pornography, violence) to health (net addiction), privacy (violation, hacking), democracy, and culture (fake news, verbal violence, online hate). Motivations and reasons to disconnect include, for instance, too many interruptions, difficulty to use particular devices, social and technical difficulties of leaving social networking sites (Birnholtz 2010; Brubaker et al. 2016), privacy concerns and 'fear of addiction' (Stieger et al. 2013), an attempt to avoid certain people (ibid.), and difficulties and dilemmas pertaining to no longer contributing because being present and absent in the virtual sphere are mixed and unclear (Kushner 2011; Karppi 2011). On the one hand, disconnection can relate to performative identity practices in the form of *individual* acts of self-improvement, well-being, self-control, conspicuous non-consumption, or even 'hipster' lifestyle and social status (Portwood-Stacer 2013; Baumer et al. 2013; Thorén and Kitzman 2015). On the other hand, disconnection can also mean manifestation of a *collective* political stance and points to online (non)-participation as an activist strategy (Casemajor et al. 2015; Gomez et al. 2015; Andersson 2016, see also Kaun and Treré, 2020). Apart from reasons and motivations on why people decide to disconnect, scholars examine, for instance, *the impact of non-use* (Greger 2010);[1] social media 'non-participation' in terms of activity, agency, and social value (Lutz and Hoffman 2017); different *forms of disconnection* (Kaun and Schwarzenegger 2014) such as structural non-use (digital divide), media refusal (communication hermits), strategic non-usage (handling information), media repertoires of abstention (reasons for and against specific media platforms, that is, Facebook, Grindr), and displacement, when users temporarily go online through other users and their social networks (Satchell and Dourish 2009; Portwood-Stacer 2013).

---

[1] See, for example, the special issue on non-use of technology published in the journal *First Monday*, 2015.

Since social problems and concerns often are informed by the cultural and ideological understandings of media technologies at a given socio-historical moment, there have been discussions about the negative impact of digital technologies, particularly social media in terms of health and well-being. Along this trend there is growing body of self-help literature presenting advice and personal accounts of temporal disconnection (cf. Maushart 2011). Some employ food metaphors to describe various forms of digital (ab)use, where effects of digital consumption compare with obesity and addiction (Sutton 2017). In many cases dealing with these issues requires digital detox and considerable amount of self-discipline to overcome the problem (Fish 2017). One of the dominant research narratives of temporal online disconnection assumes that an individual *disconnects from* online media in order *to reconnect* with others, nature or themself. In this case, the practice of disconnection is normative since going offline can possibly reconnect us back with 'true togetherness', something that lies at the core of human sociality (Turkle 2008). However, regardless of individual intentions and motivations to disconnect, living in the media ubiquitous culture requires at least some forms of disconnection.

To put it simply, everyone who is even temporarily engaging and *connecting* with digital and social media on some level *disconnects* at some point as well. Syvertsen (2017) argues that nowadays media resistance is 'part of everyone's toolbox' and to prevent that media become too invasive we need *some* forms of resistance as part of the acceptance continuum. This of course implies a broad understanding of media resistance since clearly not every type of disconnection is synonymous with resistance. Also, disconnection and media resistance are not characteristics of either 'us' or 'them', but rather inherent elements of life and living in the networked society (ibid.). Syvertsen also argues that 'with online and social media, some forms of resistance are becoming more acceptable and widespread' (ibid., 124). Online disconnection acts take place in different contexts, are grounded in broadly shared values, and are often interlinked with each other. For instance, online disconnection can relate to narratives of hope and decline, including hope for better life, better society, social change, decline of humanities, science, language, and history. The existing research on online disconnection points to constantly shifting and blurring boundaries between use/non-use and connection/disconnection. In other words, it challenges the dichotomy, often reproduced by the research and dominant understandings of the digital divide. It has to be noted that the phenomenon of 'blurring' or 'shifting' of boundaries and the altered nature between, for instance, the public and the private are often associated with the emergence of the new technologies and social media in particular (Thompson 2011). Regardless of the terms used and perspectives applied, disconnection is here to stay. What we need at this point, as I will argue later, is to explore and understand the contexts, meanings, motivations, and conditions under which disconnection becomes *relevant*. Because, to put it simply, even if we assume everyone is disconnecting at some point, it does not always need to be a performative act. On the one hand, if we apply Markham's (1998) distinction of internet as a *tool*, *place*, and *way of being*, we can see that in spite of the widely acknowledged ubiquity of internet today, the terms such as 'non-use', 'media refusal', 'rejection', and 'resistance' mostly pertain to internet and new technologies as *tools* one is choosing (not) to engage with. Disconnection, on the other hand, which as Light (2014) points out can exist in its own right in relation to connection as a possibility, resembles more of a *way of being* in a digital world. In the next section I suggest some reasons why this specific 'way of being' needs more of scholarly attention in the future.

DISCONNECTING TO RESIST AND TO RECONNECT

In the past years, practices of media avoidance and resistance have gained increasing popularity. However, as Light (2014) points out, disconnection is not merely about resistance and rejection of technology, but it can also be part of adding value to our experiences. For instance, the Slow Media movement is a response to the culture of hyperconnectivity and a reflection on people's hectic engagement with mediated communication (Rauch 2011). The idea of *slowness* originated as a philosophy and practice prompting people to live a more balanced life as an antidote to speed-obsessed, time-pressed, and hyperconnected life in the twenty-first century (ibid.). Similarly, the Slow Tech approach to ICT design is inspired by the Slow Food movement and Scandinavian design tradition from the 2000s. What they have in common is a critical approach towards not only the culture of consumption and hyper-connectivity, but also the quality of media production and content. While the Slow Media movement focuses on *users* and tech *use*, the Slow Tech emphasizes the importance of *developers* and *design*. In both cases, however, the focus is on the new possibilities for transformation. It means challenging the dominant corporate platforms and their business models, particularly the norms of efficiency, convenience, and maximizing of the corporate profit (Ess 2018).

Provocation to resist prompts users to consider various ways of media refusal and/or digital (dis)engagement. For instance, users might refuse to enrol in data grabbing architectures, by pursuing data security and privacy measures. To some extent also a degree of isolation in the form of temporal disconnection from the online worlds of social networks plays a role. In the 'algorithmic age', consumers and data users are reformatted into data producers who, often, unknowingly generate data that tech firms can crunch in order to make profit. These users help to create a value that they are also dispossessed from and later targeted by advertisers and political campaigners. The question arises how people can make appropriate and productive use of technology while at the same time preserving their privacy and integrity. For instance, Fraser and Kitchin (2017) introduce 'slow computing' to describe a range of practices to oppose, evade, alter, or navigate living in the 'algorithmic age'. In its ideal, rather utopian form, slow computing combines both refusal of accelerated modernity and avoiding of the data grabbing architectures (ibid.). In practice both refusal and grabbing can sometimes be difficult to achieve simultaneously, especially since users often are exposed to data grabbing without their consent. However, as proponents of the idea of slow computing argue, it urges users to rethink the values that are at stake when it comes to digital media engagement. It provides an opportunity for participation at a slower pace and regaining at least partial control of their own time. It also implies reflection and negotiation on their own terms while accepting some of the inconveniences that might arise along the way. Similarly, reflection on the problems associated with ubiquitous computing are increasingly familiar issues for digital designers and developers.

Particularly important in the context of technology design and design communities have been the role of *virtue ethics* which aims to ensure the beneficent implementations and impacts of technology (Ess 2018). Experiences of contentment, flourishing, and simply good life along the values of environmental sustainability, fairness, justice in work, and labour conditions are among the main principles of virtue ethics. These practices do not only openly challenge the culture of constant connectivity, mindless consumption, and its capitalist underpinnings. They also aspire to offer viable alternatives to corporate owned and managed platforms. In other words, disconnecting does not necessarily imply avoidance or complete non-use of technology but rather implies an opportunity to resist and reconnect on alternative terms. These terms might include, for example, a new design for mediated acts of socializing where users can engage in social interaction, content production, and exchange but without serving marketers and infrastructures depending on targeted advertising. These are features of alternative social media, such as *Diaspora, Quitter,* and *Twister,* prompted by the ambition to allow users control and access to technical infrastructures, but also offering new ways to think about media, social networking, and media infrastructures (Gehl 2015). It can be argued that the emergence of the subcultures and infrastructures of media avoidance and resistance offers not only alternative ideals for media usage and design. What is perhaps even more important, it also diverges from techno-utopianism and techno-determinism of the mainstream culture of connectivity (cf. Rauch 2011). Other important aspects in this process are infrastructures, artefacts, and devices themselves which point towards the fact that the digital is deeply embedded in its own materiality.

ENGAGING WITH THE MATERIALITY AND TEMPORALITY OF THE DIGITAL

Turning attention towards the material aspects of digital networks is at the same time a move towards the critical analysis of the variety of physical, embodied, and engendered aspects of networked technologies. It urges to ask what disconnection really means in terms of disengaging with those technologies in everyday life. More specifically, it calls for acknowledging the material aspects of online disconnection, the materiality of software, and how they are situated within broader contexts of production, distribution, and consumption. The 'material turn' in science and technology studies is by some described as a reaction to the constructivist and radical postmodern thought (Ferrando 2013). It can be traced back to the feminist writers who re-inscribe matter not as something stable or fixed but rather as a process of materialization and social shaping of technology (Wajcman 2004). As Wajcman (2004, 46) suggests, 'Technofeminist research has been at the forefront of moves to deconstruct the designer/user divide and (. . .) between the production and consumption of artefacts.' From this perspective, technological artefacts, including networked technologies and digital devices, are socially shaped when it comes to their design, content, and use. It also means that technological systems always have their technical, economic, political, and cultural elements (ibid., 37). Other theoretical perspectives that account for the dynamic relationship between the social and the material are the assemblage theory and the actor-network theory. The first understands social systems as complex constellations of elements placed on the material and expressive continuum (DeLanda 2016), while the second highlights the complexity of the non-human elements as active participants of the socio-material system (Latour 2005).

The idea supported by the 'new materialism' approach is that technologies evolve in the process of implementation and use allowing users to radically alter both the meanings and deployment of technologies. In other words, material artefacts, resources, and devices make society possible. This is also to say that in the era of the 'post-digital' digital networks are embedded everywhere, to the point that 'the human versus computer divide is becoming an anachronism' (Mosco 2017, 9). In a context where the boundaries between access and non-access, use and non-use, human and the machine are increasingly blurred, the attention can be turned towards contexts, meanings, and practices of *disconnection*. This is the moment where digital technology is 'transformed into a symbol whose semiotic power is reinforced through its temporary rejection' (Fish 2017, 358). In the context where connectivity has become a norm, nearly every form of online disconnection, including especially designed digital devices that make disconnection possible, can be regarded as a *response* to the dominant practices and discourses of connectivity. This is the case of, for example, location-based technologies aiming to facilitate disconnection (Beattie and Cassidy 2020).

The studies which focus on different forms of online disconnection often depart from the assumption that one of the prerequisites of living in the media-saturated culture of constant availability and connectivity are practices of *temporal disconnection* and slowing down in order to regain control over one's time, well-being, relationships, and performance (Turkle 2008; Davis 2013). Technology non-use and temporal disconnection encompass discrete practices of non-use where periods of use and non-use, connection and disconnection alternate and can take many forms. For instance, the objects of non-use and disconnection might be a particular device (smartphone), mode of communication (chatting), content genre (celebrity gossip, news), platform type (SNS), or specific media corporation (Facebook) (Portwood-Stacer 2017). Consequently, the studies which focus on various forms of technology non-use and temporal disconnection and interruption often look at the sociocultural significance of acts of refusal rather than solely on motivations and reasons for non-use. From that perspective, the acts of temporal social media interruption become discursive formations rather than 'natural' facts and the focus is on examining the circumstances in which they are made relevant (Satchell and Dourish 2009). More recently, scholars have also begun to critically assess the initiatives of disconnection and slowing down and the role of social media in reinforcing the dominant neoliberal temporalities (Kaun, Pentzold, and Lohmeier 2020). For example, the proliferation of Instagram discourses of online disconnection and temporary interruption not only assert the self-regulation of social media as a social norm, but also reproduce the logics of information capitalism rather than transform it (Jorge 2019).

One of the most prominent contexts where temporal disconnection is employed as a strategy of managing individuals and their performance is the workplace. In order to limit distraction and enhance efficiency and productivity, companies arrange mobile and email-free work hours for their employees. At the same time, in order to sustain self-control, sustain self-governance, and maintain productivity, employees are encouraged to take advantage of various technologies of avoidance, such as applications like 'Freedom', 'Focus Booster', 'Self-Control', and others (cf. Syvertsen 2017; Gregg 2018). Consequently, the goal is not to transform the work environment and working conditions but rather transforming employees' and professionals' behaviour and attitudes towards those conditions (cf. Bossio and Holton 2019). In a similar vein, technological devices such as the Substitute Phone offer design aimed at helping smartphone self-diagnosed addicts to cope with their problems and limit the (ab)use of digital devices. The design incorporates plastic stone beads embedded in the surface of the phone to help users replicate the familiar actions of scrolling, clicking, or swiping (Liptak 2017). In practice this means that temporal online disconnection leads through actual usage of analogue versions of digital technology. What at first glance might look like a contradiction in terms is in fact part of the dialectic of the post-digital age (cf. Pepperell and Punt 2000; Lindgren 2017).

The post-digital is not a 'purely virtual' reality but rather an assembly of both digital and the analogue (Thorén et al. 2018). It is also an era where the digital is not necessarily something new and exciting but rather, in many places, taken for granted. This is to say that nearly all social practices, including work and leisure, are inscribed in the materiality and temporality of sociotechnical infrastructures. In this way technologies are not exogenous but integrated and mutually shaping social practices. What Mosco (2017) calls 'the post-internet society', implies a new stage in digital development that heavily relies on the convergence between Cloud Computing, Big Data Analytics, and the Internet of Things (ibid.). He defines the latter as a 'system of measuring, monitoring and controlling the activity of objects and living organisms through sensors that gather, process and report data over networks' (Mosco 2017, 39). In such context, the return or even revival of the analogue devices marks an era of blurred boundaries between on- and offline as often the trendy gadgets without internet connection heavily depend on digital aesthetics. An example can be the growing popularity of 'dumb phones', such as 'The Light Phone' without internet access, as a response to the omnipresent 'smart' technology (see Chia and Beattie, in this volume). Consequently, the quest towards the 'authentic', analogue life is also a response to the hectic, hyperconnected, and alienating information overload of the post-digital era. It can take a form of a 'hipster's dilemma' when the turn towards 'authentic', original, and analogue is often a personal, consumer, and lifestyle choice (cf. Thorén et al. 2018). Moreover, the turn towards disconnective technology also sheds light on the fact that communicative encounters are always embedded in material structures. This argument goes further and beyond the convergence between the digital and the analogue. Instead, it addresses the fact that the dominant discourse of immateriality and virtual reality has often obscured the ecological, human, and social impacts and costs of digital technologies. Consequently, some scholars critically point out that 'vinyl won't save us' and we need to inscribe engagement into disconnective practices (Natale and Treré 2020), while others urge to develop the 'moral economy of machines' addressing the ecological imprint of digital media and environmental costs of technology (Murdock 2018).

TOWARDS A CRITICAL RESEARCH AGENDA
ON ONLINE DISCONNECTION

As discussed earlier, online disconnection is a growing topic that touches upon a broad variety of practices and contexts. To some extent, the omnipresence of digital networks, social media, and ubiquity of computers have made them invisible. One can distinguish roughly between two main periods of online disconnection research: the era of escapism and temporal opting out and the current period where the main focus is on the normalization of disconnection towards hyperconnectivity as such. It could be argued that different forms of online disconnection today are both *symptoms* and *responses* to the conditions of life and work in digital capitalism. In a way, temporal opting out from online networks becomes for some not a matter of active resistance to connectivity but rather a normalized practice and part of living in the hyperconnected environment. For example, screen-addicted South Koreans competing with each other in 'Space out' contest by 'focusing on nothing' in a local park in Seoul is a typical example of individual initiatives of temporal retreat as a response to stress and digital overload (Purtill 2016). If some 20 years ago going online was an act of brief opting out, then seeking a refuge in the analogue and offline world today marks the era of hyperconnectivity. I suggest that what we need at this point is to push the research agenda even further, beyond the study of *individual* and often *non-transformative* and *non-political* forms of online disconnection towards more collectively oriented, transformative, and political ones (see figure 1.1). This is because the post-digital era implies a substantial shift from what Lindgren (2017) calls 'digitally enhanced' to 'digitally transformative' outcomes of media use where 'social actions and practices (. . .) rely so much on digitally specific affordances that they would not be possible without them' (2017, 295). When both old and new technologies are layered on top of one another and transform sociality we also need to start asking questions about the *social* impact of various forms of online disconnection and disengagement.

Technology is neither neutral nor inherently progressive and beneficial but has been constructed because of competing social relations. Similarly, disconnection acquires a variety of meanings depending on the sociopolitical, economic, and cultural context in which it occurs. For instance, Saskia Sassen (2017) argues that there is much more at stake than 'connectivity' or access when assessing the 'digital'. User capabilities, socio-material affordances of technologies but also questions of power and structural inequalities need to be considered. Disconnection, like online privacy, is not necessarily a personal but rather a systemic issue. Consequently, practices and research focusing on individual and collective albeit non-political practices of detoxing or opting out of social media are not enough to understand the complexity of those

processes. Research examining these practices needs to move further to analyse and understand the role of social discontent and look for its *causes* rather
than symptoms. As Geert Lovink (2018) suggests, the idea of leaving social
media altogether is beyond imagination, so instead we need to find ways to
politicize the situation and avoid offline romanticism. This is indeed a challenge for the field of online disconnection research: How to address the critical
questions in the context where online disconnection is not only commodified
and appropriated but also normalized? To accomplish this task, we need to
address power asymmetries and identify contradictory, open, and dynamic tendencies in disconnective practice(s). Such perspective needs also to address the
dialectic between what society and industries promise, what they can deliver,
and under which conditions. Finally, such an approach needs to consider an
emancipatory aspect and possibility for social change and development.

Figure 1.1 summarizes how online disconnection has been discussed,
practised, studied, and defined so far, including a suggestion on how to move
forward by expanding the critical research agenda from non-transformative
and non-political towards transformative and political notions of online
disconnection.

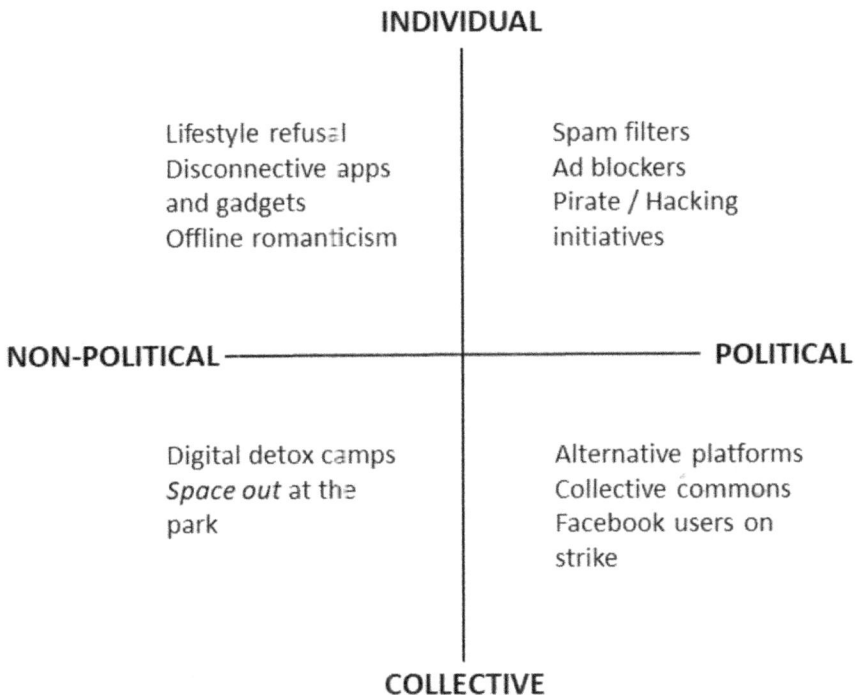

INDIVIDUAL

Lifestyle refusal
Disconnective apps
and gadgets
Offline romanticism

Spam filters
Ad blockers
Pirate / Hacking
initiatives

NON-POLITICAL ———————————————— **POLITICAL**

Digital detox camps
Space out at the
park

Alternative platforms
Collective commons
Facebook users on
strike

COLLECTIVE

Figure 1.1   Conceptualizations of disconnection.

I propose that a critical research agenda on online disconnection should primarily address two aspects that relate to the political economy of digital capitalism. First, it should look at the *conditions of power and labour* in digital capitalism; and second, it needs to address the *ideological underpinnings of capitalism*, particularly the ethos of productivity, efficiency, and profit-making. We need to ask about the conditions that put people in a situation where online disconnection is a necessary step to cope with distraction and emotional distress. It is also about scrutinizing a particular cultural and economic logic of the post-digital era that manifests in platforms such as, for instance, Facebook (cf. Karppi 2018). In the context of the attention economy where the goal is to commodify the audience's attention, disconnection becomes a practice that is incorporated into capitalist mode of production. So, for instance, the questions of dealing with digital addiction and enhancing well-being of users have recently become a high stake on the tech giants' agenda. Ironically, the solution for dealing with technology and information overload is to introduce even more technology (Haig 2018). The goal of the critical research should be to explore and understand how capital appropriates disconnective technologies as sources of control. For example, we need more studies that explore how the notions of 'authenticity', 'self-empowerment', and 'personal growth' are employed to promote disconnective technologies and practices, particularly in the corporate context. Also, recognizing that the dominant discourse often fetishizes non-usage (Baumer et al. 2015) and points towards online disconnection as a matter of individual choice is an important aspect in the critique of information society. More research is needed when it comes to the colonization of user attention, particularly in the context of dealing with 'digital well-being' and the variety of ways tech companies have an ambition to deal with problems such as digital addiction by offering more products and services. Additionally, in order to address disconnection as more of a systemic rather than personal issue or problem, one needs to recognize the power structures and social relations that mutually constitute the process of production, distribution, and commodification of resources, including disconnective technologies. One of the ways could be, for instance, to examine disconnection in the context of struggles over the regulation and structure of social time. This particularly refers to the construction of work time, where temporal online disconnection is sometimes promoted as a solution to work overload and social acceleration. We also need to remember that studying different forms of online disconnection and disconnective practices is like looking at the other, less acknowledged, yet persistent side of the connectivity coin. Namely, if we accept the notion of hyperconnectivity as dominant in the modern, networked societies, we also must accept the ontological shift towards the post-digital era. In other words, studying online disconnection is important because we have reached the situation when digital and social media are so ubiquitous to the point of being 'technologically boring and *socially* interesting' (Lindgren 2017, 298, my emphasis). Therefore, I suggest, understanding online disconnection as an ongoing *social* process and practice closely related to connectivity allows to challenge dominant, normative ideas and narratives about connectivity, (non-)usage, and participation. It also allows us to reflect upon the nature of decisions to disconnect as a broader commentary and critique of the hyperconnected and accelerated living. In the context where the digital and analogue are not necessarily opposites but rather exist in a relation with one another, disconnection urges a reflection about the materiality and temporality of the digital and practices that surround it. It also urges to see online connectivity as a political issue.

To politicize the question of disconnectivity means to acknowledge that connectivity and 'being online' has historically been linked to the position of economic and political power. In the context of hyperconnected culture having the option to opt out is a privilege (cf. Portwood-Stacer 2013). This holds particularly true when it comes to dominant Western perceptions of advanced technology and mainstream media reporting on refugees carrying smartphones as bogus asylum seekers (Leurs and Smets 2018). Such perceptions often depart from an idea that network connection and ownership of smart technology are a luxury that only few can afford, which further reinforces the notions of high-tech orientalism. Consequently, rather than questioning who is connected and who remains excluded we should be asking about the power and privilege to 'switch off' (Noonan 2011). That power goes beyond single acts of media refusal and technology non-use but pertains to more sophisticated strategies including pirate initiatives, ad blockers, and developing counter-protocols. In other words, these are, as Hesselberth (2018) poignantly argues, strategies of civil disobedience that are available to few. We need to remember that media resisters and disconnectors generally belong to the media-savvy crowd, so temporal disconnection can be as much a marker of identity as a practice of self-discipline and self-regulation. This particularly refers to those elite disrupters. Addressing the political aspects of disconnection means also that the focus shifts from technology non-use towards society, social relations of power, and inequalities. In this way disconnection is more than a 'first-world problem' of some few individuals. In fact, with new technologies and innovations some old questions of power, identity, and social change remain more important than ever (cf. Golding 2018). We also need to consider the concerns which scholars raise in relation to the challenges posed by the post-digital era, including security and privacy threats as well as questions of environmental protection and sustainability (Mosco 2018). In particular, the issues can be relevant in relation to practices of resistance against centralized, commodified, strictly controlled, and corporate owned digital empires represented by the 'Big Five' of tech (ibid.). In this way disconnection goes far beyond temporary opting out and touches instead upon critique of the current status quo and possibly envisaging viable alternatives to it. The research agenda on online disconnection should address the politics of online withdrawal that understands disconnection as an inherent element of connectivity. In this way, we can come to realize that online disconnection is not necessarily an 'anti-technology' approach but rather an imperative that bears the potential of an incorporated critique of capitalism and potential for social change.

REFERENCES

Andersson, Linus. 2016. "No digital 'castles in the air': Online non-participation and the radical left." *Media and Communication* 4 (4): 53–62.

Arksey, Hilary and Lisa O'Malley. 2005. "Scoping studies: Towards a methodological framework." *International Journal of Social Research Methodology* 8 (1): 19–32.

Baumer, Eric, Morgan G. Ames, Jed Brubaker, Jenna Burrell, and Paul Dourish. 2015. "Refusing, limiting, departing: Why we should study technology non-use." CHI Workshop, Toronto, Canada.

Beattie, Alex, and Elija Cassidy. 2020. "Locative disconnection: The use of location-based technologies to make disconnection easier, enforceable and exclusive." *Convergence*. doi:10.1177/1354856520956854

Birnholtz, Jeremy. 2010. "Adopt, adapt, abandon: Understanding why some young adults start, and then stop, using instant messaging." *Computers in Human Behavior* 26: 1427–33.

Bossio, Diana, and Avery E. Holton. 2019. "Burning out and turning off: Journalists' disconnection strategies on social media." *Journalism*. doi:10.1177/1464884919872076

Brubaker, Jed R., Mike Ananny, and Kate Crawford. 2016. "Departing glances: A sociotechnical account of 'leaving' Grindr." *New Media & Society* 18 (3): 373–390. doi:10.1177/1461444814542311

Burrell, Jenna. 2012. "Technology hype versus enduring uses: A longitudinal study of internet use among early adopters in an African city." *First Monday* 17 (6). http://firstmonday.org/article/view/3964/3263

Casemajor, Nathalie, Stéphane Couture, Mauricio Delfin, Matthew Goerzen, and Alessandro Delfanti. 2015. "Non-participation in digital media: Toward a framework of mediated political action." *Media, Culture & Society* 6: 850–866. doi:10.1177/0163443715584098

Castells, Manuel. 1996. *The Rise of the Network Society: The Information Age: Economy, Society, and Culture*, vol. 1. Oxford: Blackwell Publishers.

Cushman, Mike, and Ela Klecun. 2006. "How (can) non-users engage with technology: bringing in the digitally excluded." In *Social Inclusion: Societal and Organizational Implications for Information Systems*, edited by Eileen Trauth,

Debra Howcroft, Tom Butler, Brian Fitzgerald, and Janice DeGross, 347–364. Boston, MA: Springer.

Davis, Mark. 2013. "Hurried lives: Dialectics of time and technology in liquid modernity." *Thesis Eleven* 118 (1): 7–18.

DeLanda, Manuel. 2016. *Assemblage Theory*. Edinburg: Edinburg University Press.

Ems, Lindsay. 2015. "Exploring ethnographic techniques for ICT non-use research: An Amish case study" *First Monday* 20 (11). doi:10.5210/fm.v20i11.6312

Ess, Charles. 2018. "Democracy and the Internet: A retrospective." *Javnost—The Public* 25 (1–2): 93–101.

Fernández-Ardèvol, Mireia, Kim Sawchuk, and Line Grenier. 2017. "Maintaining connections. Octo and nonagenarians on digital 'use and non-use'." *Nordicom Review* 38 (1): 39–51.

Ferrando, Francesca. 2013. "Posthumanism, transhumanism, antihumanism, metahumanism, and new materialisms. Differences and Relations." *Existenz* 8 (2): 26–32.

Fish, Adam. 2017. "Technology retreats and the politics of social media." *TripleC* 15 (1): 355–369.

Fisher, Eran. 2010. *Media and Capitalism in the Digital Age: The Spirit of Networks*. London: Palgrave MacMillan.

Fraser, Alistair, and Rob Kitchin. 2017. *Slow computing*. Prepared as a position paper for 'Slow computing: A workshop on resistance in the algorithmic age' (2017), Maynooth, December 14th 2017. https://osf.io/preprints/socarxiv/rmxfk

Galperin, Hernan and M. Fernanda Viecens. 2017. "Connected for development? Theory and evidence about the impact of internet technologies on poverty alleviation." *Development Policy Review* 35 (1): 315–336.

Gehl, Robert W. 2015. "The case for alternative social media." *Social Media + Society* 1 (2). doi:10.1177/2056305115604338

Golding, Peter. 2018. "New technologies, old questions: The enduring issues of communication research." *Javnost—The Public* 25 (1–2): 202–209.

Gomez, Ricardo, Kirsten Foot, Meg Young, Rose Paquet-Kinsley, and Stacey Morrison. 2015. "Pulling the plug visually: Images of resistance to ICTs and connectivity." *First Monday* 20 (11). http://firstmonday.org/ojs/index.php/fm/article/view/6286

Greger, Sebastian. 2010. "The Absent Peer. Non-Users in Social Interaction Design." MA thesis, School of Art and Design, Aalto University.

Gregg, Melissa. 2018. *Counterproductive. Time Management in the Knowledge Economy*, Durham and London: Duke University Press.

Haig, Matt. 2018. 'Google wants to cure our phone addiction. How about that for irony?.' *The Guardian*, May 10, 2018.

Hesselberth, Pepita. 2018. "Discourses on disconnectivity and the right to disconnect." *New Media & Society* 20 (5): 1994–2010.

Jorge, Ana. 2019. "Social media, interrupted: Users recounting temporary disconnection on Instagram." *Social Media + Society* 5 (4). doi:10.1177/2056305119881691

Karppi, Tero. 2011. "Digital Suicide and the Biopolitics of Leaving Facebook." *Transformations* 20. http://www.transformationsjournal.org/wp content/uploads/2016/12/Karppi_Trans20.pdf

————. 2018. *Disconnect. Facebook's Affective Bonds*. Minneapolis, MN: Minnesota University Press.

Kaun, Anne, and Christian Schwarzenegger. 2014. "'No media, less life?' Online disconnection in mediatized worlds." *First Monday* 19 (11). https://firstmonday.org/ojs/index.php/fm/article/view/5497/4158

Kaun, Anne, Pentzold, Christian and Lohmeier, Christine (eds.). 2020. *Making Time for Digital Lives: Beyond Chronotopia*, London: Rowman & Littlefield.

Kaun, Anne and Emiliano Treré. 2020. "Repression, resistance and lifestyle: Charting (dis)connection and activism in times of accelerated capitalism." *Social Movement Studies* 19 (5–6): 697–715.

Kellner, Catherine, Luc Massou and Pierre Morelli. 2010. "(Re)Examining the non-use of ICT." *Questions de communication* 18: 1–10.

Kushner, Scott. 2016. "Read only: The persistence of Lurking in Web 2.0." *First Monday* 21 (6). doi:10.5210/fm.v21i6.6789

Kushner, Scott. 2011. "Virtually dead: Blogospheric absence and the ethics of networked reading." *Communication Review* 44 (1): 24–45.

Latour, Bruno. 2005. *Reassembling the Social: An Introduction to Actor Network Theory*, Oxford: Oxford University Press.

Leavitt, Alex. 2014. "When the user disappears: Situational non-use of social technologies." CHI 2014 Workshop: Considering Why We Should Study Technology Non-use (Toronto).

Leurs, Koen, and Kevin Smets. 2018. "Five questions for digital migration studies: Learning from digital connectivity and forced migration in(to) Europe." *Social Media + Society* 4 (1). doi:10.1177/2056305118764425

Light, Ben. 2014. *Disconnecting with Social Networking Sites*, London: Palgrave Macmillan.

Lindgren, Simon. 2017. *Digital Media & Society*. London: SAGE.

Liptak, Andrew. 2017. 'The Substitute Phone is designed to help smartphone addicts cope with their absence'. *The Verge*, November 26, 2017. https://www.theverge.com/2017/11/26/16701950/substitute-phoneklemens-schillinger smartphone-addiction

Lovink, Geert. 2018. 'Distraction and its discontents'. *Eurozine*, March 28, 2018.

Lutz, Christoph, and Christian Pieter Hoffman. 2017. "The dark side of online participation: exploring non-, passive and negative participation." *Information, Communication & Society* 20 (6): 876–897.

Markham, Annette. 1998. *Life Online: Researching Real Experiences in Virtual Space*. Walnut Creek, CA: AltaMira Press.

Maushart, Susan. 2011. *The Winter of Our Disconnect: How Three Totally Wired Teenagers (and a mother who slept with her iPhone) Pulled the Plug on Their Technology and Lived to Tell the Tale*; 1st American edition. New York: Jeremy P. Tarcher/Penguin.

Morrison, Stacey, and Ricardo Gomez. 2014. "Pushback: Expressions of resistance to the "evertime" of constant online connectivity." *First Monday* 19 (8). doi:10.5210/fm.v19i8.4902

Mosco, Vincent. 2018. "A critical perspective on the post-internet World." *Javnost— The Public*, 25 (1–2): 210–217.

———. 2017. *Becoming Digital. Toward a Post-Internet Society*, London: Emerald Publishing Limited.

Murdock, Graham. 2018. "Media materialities: For a moral economy of machines." *Journal of Communication* 63 (2): 359–368.

Natale, Simone, and Emiliano Treré. 2020. "Vinyl won't save us: Reframing disconnection as engagement". *Media, Culture & Society* 42 (4): 626–633.

Negroponte, Nicholas. 1999. *Being Digital*. New York: Knopf.

Neves, Barbara Barbosa, João Monteiro de Matos, Rita Rente, and Sara Lopes Martins. 2015. "The 'non-aligned': Young people's narratives of rejection of social networking sites." *YOUNG* 23 (2): 116–135.

Noonan, Katrine, 2011. 'The power to switch off.' *Courier Mail*, August 23.

Pepperell, Robert, and Michael Punt. 2000. *The Postdigital Membrane. Imagination, Technology and Desire*. Bristol, Portland: Intellect.

Pick, James, and Sarkar, Avijit. 2016. "Theories of the Digital Divide: Critical Comparison." 49th Hawaii International Conference on System Sciences (HICSS).

Portwood-Stacer, Laura. 2017. "Media refusal". In *Wiley Blackwell Encyclopedia of Sociology*, 2nd edition. London: Wiley Blackwell.

Portwood-Stacer, Laura. 2013. "Media refusal and conspicuous non-consumption: The performative and political dimensions of Facebook abstention." *New Media & Society* 15 (7): 1041–1057.

Purtill, Corinne. 2016. 'In South Korea "pacing out" is now a championship sport.' *Quartz*, June 17. https://qz.com/709389/in-south-korea-spacing-out-is-now-a-championship-sport/

Rauch, Jennifer. 2011. "The origin of slow media: Early diffusion of a cultural innovation through popular and press discourse, 2002-2010" *Transformations*, 20.

Reisdorf, Bianca. 2011. "Non-adoption of the internet in Great Britain and Sweden." *Information, Communication & Society* 14 (3): 400–420.

Ribak, Rivka, and Michele Rosenthal. 2015. "Smartphone resistance as media ambivalence." *First Monday* 20 (11). doi:10.5210/fm.v20i11.6307

Ritzer, George. 2010. "Prosumption: Evolution, revolution, or eternal return of the same?." *Journal of Consumer Culture* 14 (1): 3–24.

Rosa, Hartmut. 2013. *Social Acceleration. The New Theory of Modernity*. New York: Columbia University Press.

Sassen, Saskia. 2017. "Digital cultures of use and their infrastructures." In *The Sociology of Speed. Digital, Organizational and Social Temporalities*, edited by Judy Wajcman and Nigel Dodd, 72–85. Oxford: Oxford University Press.

Satchell, Christine, and Paul Dourish. 2016. "Beyond the user: use and non-use of HCI." Proceedings OZCHI 9-16, *49th Hawaii International Conference on System Sciences (HICSS)*, Koloa, HI: 3888–3897.

Selwyn, Neil, Stephen Gorard, and John Furlong. 2005. "Whose internet is it anyway? Exploring adults' (non)use of the internet in the everyday life." *European Journal of Communication* 20 (1): 5–26.

Selwyn, Neil. 2006. "Digital division or digital decision? A study of non-users and low-users of computers." *Poetics* 34: 273–292.

Sparks, Colin. 2013. "What is the 'digital divide' and why is it important?." *Javnost— The Public* 20 (2): 27–46.

Srinivasan, Ramesh and Adam Fish. 2017. *After the Internet*. New York: Polity Press.

Stieger, Stefan, Christoph Burger, Martin Voracek, and Manuel Bohn. 2013. "Who commits virtual identity suicide? Differences in privacy concerns, Internet addiction, and personality between Facebook users and quitters." *Cyberpsychology, Behavior, and Social Networking* 16 (9): 629–634.

Sutton, Theodora. 2017. "Disconnect to reconnect: The food/technology metaphor in digital detoxing." *First Monday* 22 (6). doi:10.5210/fm.v22i6.7561

Syvertsen, Trine. 2017. *Media Resistance. Protest, Dislike, Abstention*. London: Palgrave Macmillan.

———. 2019. *Digital Detox: The Politics of Disconnecting*. Bingley: Emerald Publishing.

Syvertsen, Trine, and Gunn Enli. 2020. "Digital detox: Media resistance and the promise of authenticity." *Convergence* 26 (5–6): 1269–1283.

Thompson, John B. 2011. "Shifting boundaries of public and private life." *Theory, Culture & Society* 28 (4): 49–70.

Thorén, Claes and Andreas Kitzman. 2015. "Replicants, imposters and the real deal. Issues of non-use and technology resistance in vintage and software instruments." *First Monday* 20 (11). doi:10.5210/fm.v20i11.6302

Thorén, Claes and Mats Edenius. 2018. "Digital disconnect and assemblages of power: Exploring technology non-use in the age of the post-digital." *Comunicazioni Sociali* 68: 68–79.

Treré, Emiliano, Simone Natale, Emily Keightley, and Aswin Punathambekar. 2020. "The limits and boundaries of digital disconnection." *Media, Culture & Society* 42 (4): 605–609.

Turkle, Sherry. 2008. "Always-on/always-on-you: The tethered self." In *Handbook of Mobile Communication Studies*, edited by James E. Katz, 121–137. Cambridge: MIT Press.

Vaidhyanathan, Siva. 2018. *Anti-Social Media: How Facebook Disconnects Us and Undermines Democracy*. Oxford: Oxford University Press.

Van Deursen, Alexander and Ellen J. Helsper. 2015. "A nuanced understanding of Internet use and non-use among the elderly." *European Journal of Communication* 30 (1): 171–187.

Van Dijck, José. 2013. *The Culture of Connectivity. A Critical History of Social Media*. Oxford: Oxford University Press.

Van Dijk, Johannes. 2006. "Digital divide research, achievements and shortcomings." *Poetics* 34 (4–5): 221–235.

Verdegem, Pieter and Pascal Verhoest. 2009. "Profiling the non-user: Rethinking policy initiatives stimulating ICT acceptance." *Telecommunications Policy* 33 (10–11): 642–652.

Wajcman, Judy. 2004. *Technofeminism*. London: Polity.

Waycott, Jenny, Frank Vetere, Sonja Pedell, Amee Morgans, Elizabeth Ozanne, and Lars Kulik. 2016. "Not For Me: Older Adults Choosing Not to Participate in a Social Isolation Intervention." Paper presented at CHI2016, San Jose, USA.

Wyatt, Sally. 2003. "Non-users also matter: The construction of users and non-users of the Internet." In *How Users Matter: The Co-Construction of Users and Technology*, edited by Nelly Oudshoorn and Trevor Pinch, 67–79. Cambridge: MIT Press.

Woodstock, Louise. 2011. "Performing Internet resistance: Attempting to opt out of online participation." Paper presented at the Association of Internet Researchers conference (Seattle), October 13.

———. 2014. "Media resistance: Opportunities for practice theory and new media research." *International Journal of Communication* 8 (19): 1983–2001.

Chapter 2

The Ontological Insecurity of Disconnecting*

A Theory of Echolocation and the Self

Annette N. Markham

I run my fingers across my phone before I touch my partner every morning. My day begins with me and my phone. It ends with me and my phone. Not just my phone obviously, but all the things it connects me to. I didn't plan it this way, but my life is entirely wrapped up in this device. I don't know what I would do without it.

—(Participant N, 2018)

This statement, offered by a participant in a long series of ethnographic studies I conducted on youth making sense of their digital media, is not an unusual comment about our relationships with mobile devices. In 2010, Booz and Co (now part of Strategy&) designated a new label for millennials: Generation C, for Connected (Friedrich et al. 2010). Between 2010 and 2013, this label evolved from a demographic to psychographic label to include 'individuals, irrespective of age, who use an abundance of technology during their daily routine' (Jenblat 2018, np). It includes people who are, or feel, constantly connected, carrying out everyday life in digitally saturated ways. While the category 'Generation C' never really caught on outside corporate marketing spheres (e.g. Solis 2011), the state of being constantly connected has grown globally; even before Covid-19 prompted most of the world to 'stay at home', citizens around the globe were becoming more and more 'tethered', as Sherry Turkle would say (2011). No longer limited to social, leisure, learning, and work activities, the use of digital platforms is required even to receive essential governmental services (Estonia's 'e-Estonia' program was an early adopter and exemplar of this practice).

---

* This chapter has been previously published in abbreviated form on the author's website annette-markham.com.

Those who are heavily connected are likely also recipients of competing and opposing discourses (Tiidenberg et al. 2017) about what they should do about being tethered: even as marketers, governments, and platform providers continue to nudge, if not require, people to be more (and more and more) connected, regular 'moral panics' counter this discourse in waves, citing narcissism, addiction, and other ills as reasons to be less tethered, do some digital detox, and disconnect. The latter set of grand narratives impacts participants in a series of studies I have facilitated since 2012, who voice strong support for the 'need' to disconnect, even temporarily. As one participant remarks in a 2016 autoethnographic fieldnote discussing their feelings about an upcoming experiment to disconnect from all digital media for 24 hours, 'I know I should be happy I'm going to disconnect for 24 hours. It might help with this addiction LOL.' Whether the 'I'm addicted to the internet' or 'I really need to be less connected' sort of statements are internally or externally motivated, their persistence is an acknowledgement—even since the mid-1990s—of the ongoing sensibility that we are 'too connected' and should be doing something about it. This is for good reason, since the contemporary expectation of constant—versus intermittent—co-presence has been associated with stress and anxiety, among other negative effects (see also Birnholz et al. 2012; Pielot and Rello 2018).

When thinking and talking about disconnecting, there is much oversimplification of what this means; young people in a series of ethnographic studies I will describe later, for example, tend to explain connection and disconnection as binary opposites. As if online/offline is a light switch. This oversimplification occurs despite their own recognition, in their self-study of their lived experience, that disconnecting constitutes a range of practices (Dremljuga 2017; Jorge 2019), that the state of disconnection varies (Light 2014), and that the distinction of online/offline is simply untenable and has been since the advent of the internet, something I and many other scholars have written about since the mid-1990s (Markham 1998).

People can experience deep existential vulnerability after disconnecting, whether for a few moments or much longer (Markham 2017). Why is this? What is so meaningful about being connected that makes it difficult to disconnect? Looking at the micro-level processes of contemporary digital media use, as well as our message and email histories, we can witness a dizzying quantity of continuous back and forth interactions across multiple conversations and networks. This in itself is not surprising. People who enact daily life in digitally saturated societies simply take for granted and perhaps don't even notice the resonant buzz of these swift, numerous, overlapping, and entangled interactions. In the era of interfaces with predictive capabilities, and interactions with algorithmic underpinnings, how does this continuous call and response, ping and echo feature of interaction influence one's Self?[1] In an era where fame and wealth are associated with digital social influence (Jorge and Pedroni, this volume), how might this continuous call and response have such value that if disrupted, can create existential anxiety? The interactions are not simply between people, but also between people and the features of interfaces, which means the elements of platform design become interlocutors, intimate partners in the ongoing dynamic of locating and stabilizing a sense of Self, or more specific to the concept I develop in this chapter, a sense of ontological security.

Echolocation is a compelling metaphor for thinking about how anyone in a digitally saturated society is in constant orientation and reorientation in relation to others, continually building a sense of Self by moving in and through various social worlds as a part of everyday life. This navigational model of echolocating the Self is mostly invisible. It is not until a person feels a sudden feeling akin to what has been called 'ontological insecurity' that they can recognize the degree to which their sense of stability or ontological security was reliant on a continuous stream of interactions with other elements in their ecosystem. This focus highlights how a person's being in the world, in a phenomenological sense, relies on *getting a response to* one's performance of self in everyday life. Echolocation as a social theory is conceptually intended to augment or adjust the classical foci of social theorists, especially those in symbolic interactionism focusing on the performance or negotiation of Self in everyday life through habitual and routine communication processes. Within a discussion of digital disconnection, the concept of echolocation is a heuristic that gives close attention to the features and importance of the responses in a world of ongoing digital connectivity, to a person's sense of Self.

Echolocation is not only interactive and communicative, but locative. Consider a bat's shrieks, a dolphin's clicks, or the ping of a submarine's radar in the old school game of *Battleship*: After being emitted, uttered, or sent out, these signals bounce off objects in space, returning an echo that the bat, dolphin, or ship interprets to determine the relative size and location of these objects. Likewise, a theory of social echolocation posits that people send out continuous pings in their social environments and, as the Self receives responses from Others and objects in social space, they are able to not only construct a map of where things and others are in these spaces but locate, or position, themselves in relation.

In this chapter, I first describe how the theory emerged from fieldwork with youth and their social media use. Second, I explain more about how

---

[1] Self and Other are capitalized in some parts of this chapter to depict when these are considered proper nouns. This is tricky nomenclature practised by interpersonal communication scholars, existential philosophers, and between the two, symbolic interactionist theorists.

echolocation works, by detailing the core concept of the echo in relation to its counterpart, the ping. Third, I sketch two conceptual aspects of Selfhood that connect closely to connection and disconnection, which I also connect to the processes of continuous interaction between Self and Other: ontological security and ontological insecurity. Finally, I turn to a discussion of the reverberation qualities of echolocation when it is occurring in multiple everyday interactions, which is linked to the importance of being constantly connected. This conceptual discussion contributes specificity to what is happening and what is at stake when we are abruptly disconnected, by focusing on the existential relevance and importance of continuity of interaction. For many of us studying self-identity in deeply digitized and algorithmically mediated times, the contemporary condition goes far beyond simple notions of connected or disconnected. This theoretical clarification adds another layer to help scholars and practitioners understand why and how it remains so difficult to disconnect from digital and social media in this epoch.

ECHOLOCATION: BACKGROUND OF THE THEORY

The theory emerged from an eight-year and ongoing ethnographically grounded study of young people (18 to 30 years old) and their everyday uses and lived experiences of social media (Markham 2019). As part of their participation, groups of international students situated in classrooms in the United States and, later, Denmark would disconnect from all (or most) digital media for 24 hours. Focused on building their own skills for studying how people use and frame social media through an ethnographic lens, participants would generate elaborate self-reflexive fieldnotes as part of autoethnographic explorations of their own digital experience. To clarify, this study is part of a larger project of critical pedagogy whereby the research is designed to prompt critical reflections and build students' abilities to be skilled ethnographic researchers of their own lived experience (Markham 2019). After their participation in the experience, students would be invited to add their multimedia fieldnotes, analyses, and narratives to a growing collection of materials. Some of these materials, given with permission to use, inform this analysis. All snippets presented are slightly revised composites from more than one participant to represent but not replicate the actual materials. This practice follows my 'fabrication as ethical practice' approach (Markham 2012), to help maintain contextual integrity and engender a sense of privacy for participants who might read this chapter.

In addition to self-reflexive fieldnotes, participants would produce multiple video narratives as part of their interpretive analysis, in response to particular sequences of experimental prompts over a period of several weeks. This often included a sequence of cultural prompts like 'What am I doing here?', 'Why do I do this versus something else?', 'How was I feeling at that moment?', and 'How do I feel about this person (myself) as a part of society?'

A common phenomenon emerged time after time: disconnecting for even short periods of time generated a surprisingly deep vulnerability that participants could not rationalize or adequately explain to themselves (Markham 2020). This sentiment was not expressed as fear of missing out (FOMO) on events or news about the world or updates on the lives of friends and families, as both they and I would have expected before the 'digital media fast' experiment began. Rather, it felt like they didn't know where they were in the world. To be clear, this was an affective response not focused on the idea that they didn't know where *others* were, but focused on *where they, themselves, were, in their larger social networks.*

Even though this feeling would subside quickly, it represents a momentary fracture in the ontological security of the lifeworld. Diving into the granularity of the interaction, I began to see how it also seemed to have a pattern that reminded me of how whales, dolphins, or bats navigate through space using sonar. I turn now to a discussion of how the fundamental qualities of echolocation, the 'ping' and 'echo', are inherent parts of the human communication process.

THE INHERENCY OF THE PING AND ECHO IN EVERYDAY LIFE

Sonar is a term we often associate with echolocation, the method by which bats, dolphins, whales, and certain other creatures navigate. The core process is 'call and response' whereby signals are first sent out and then interpreted on their return. A bat shrieks in the dark. A dolphin clicks. A radar system sends out an audible p i i i i i i n n n n n g. (Markham 2021)

The word 'ping' comes from the terminology of sonar. It is a short or sharp sound signal emitted by an echolocation system (like a bat), which begins the process of sonifying the acoustic environment in order to locate objects in space. Among social media users, it might be used to suggest a short message to 'ping me' to see if I am around, or available. It is also a term for the software or network utility used to test the speed of a network. One can use this utility to 'ping the system', measuring how long it takes for a message to get sent to and returned.

An information-transfer oriented model of human interaction emerged in the 1940s that in many was built on the practice of sonar or radar. What later became well known as the 'SMCR model of communication' (Sender

Annette N. Markham

→ Message → Channel → Receiver) depicts communication as a process whereby a sender encodes a message that is then transmitted through a channel to a receiver, who will decode the message. Messages will carry information insofar as the signal is clear. The originators of this model (Shannon 1948; Weaver 1949) were thinking about how information encoded as electrical signals flows through telephone lines. Shannon's 1948 model (figure 2.1) highlights how information could pass effectively from sender to receiver, barring disrupting factors such as noise caused by birds pecking or scratching on the copper wires.

This SMCR model of communication (Sender → Message → Channel → Receiver) has persisted as a starting point to think about how humans communicate with each other (see figure 2.2), despite the deeply flawed presumptions and focus on a linear, one-way process. Communication studies

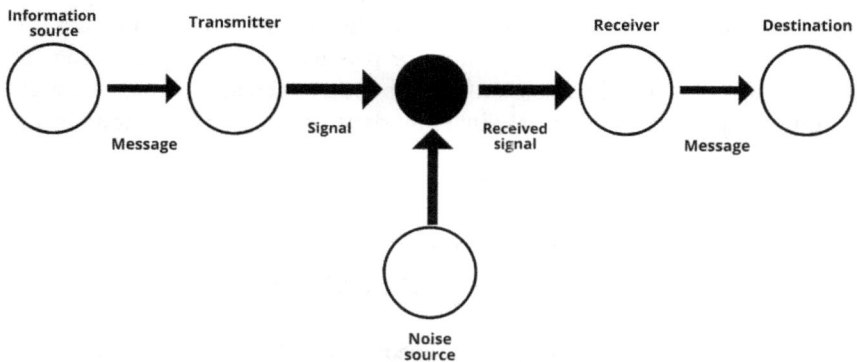

Figure 2.1   Original Information Transmission Model by Claude Shannon, which Became the SMCR Model of Human Communication. *Source*: Adapted from Shannon, 1948.

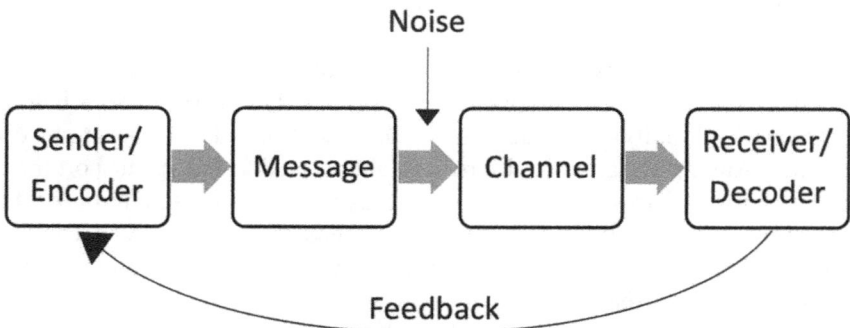

Figure 2.2   Common Simplification of the SMCR Model for Entry-Level Textbook Discussions of Human Communication Interactions. *Source*: Image by Author.

scholars have sensibly added countless clarifications over the decades in basic textbooks, such as: that the receiver is also simultaneously a sender; that the process is interactive, an ongoing process of exchange; that many social, psychological, cultural, personal, and technological filters will function in more complex ways than simply adding 'noise'; and that many elements of a media ecology influence how and whether anything resembling 'shared understanding' occurs as a temporary or consistent outcome of this process. In other words, 'communication as transmission' was long ago replaced by communication as exchange, transaction, social construction, or communication as co-constitutive, dialectical, dialogical, and relational.

The focal point for most corrective revisions to SMCR tended to add relationality and meaning. But if we step back from this line of thought and return to the micro-processes of information theory, we can add the other central feature to any model involving transmission of a signal: it will always involve an echo of some sort.

Centrally, a communication theory based on echolocation pays particular and detailed attention to what is happening in the *feedback* part of a continuous interaction cycle, and what happens afterwards, which is the part of the SMCR model that most interests cyberneticists or systems theorists. Although difficult to visualize in a static image since the processes are active/continuous and physical, figures 2.3 and 2.4 provide basic illustrations of how sound and light signals/pings yield echoes that will have information value for the sender.

The characteristic of the echo is everything that matters in this process. If measured as sound, the pitch and loudness of the responding echoes help

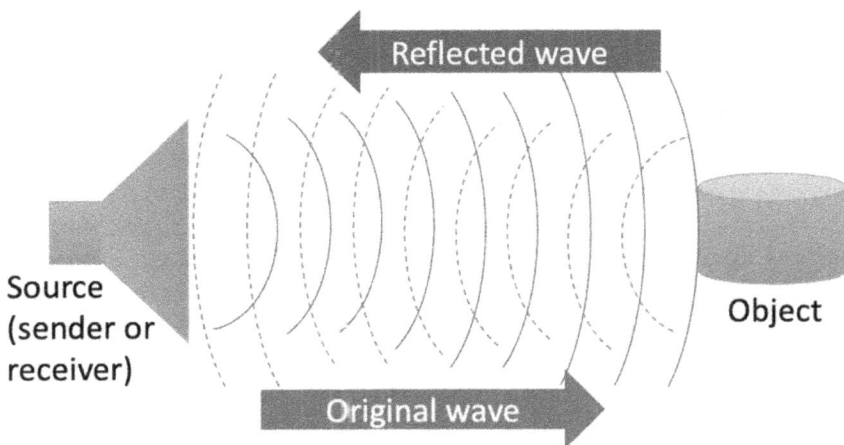

Figure 2.3   Common Visualization of Sonar. *Source*: Image by Author.

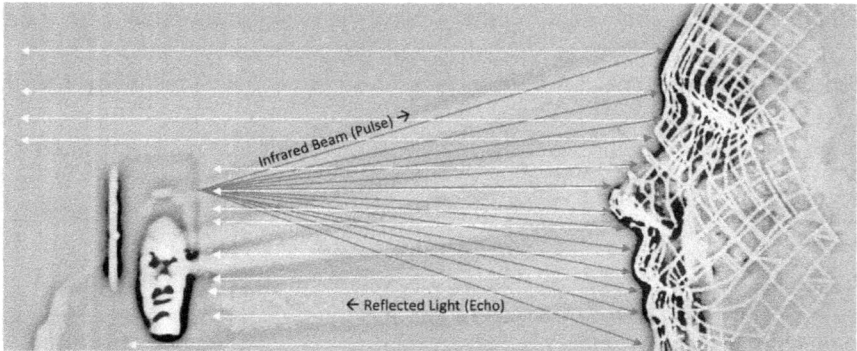

Figure 2.4   Visualization of One Type of Pattern of Lidar Used in Facial Recognition.
Source: Image by Author.

determine where you are in relation to the object against which your original ping/signal bounced. The speed at which the echo returns yields information about distance. The repetition of signaling generates multiple echoes that can be compared to determine movement, changes in position, and relative differences. Any of these measurements are complicated by the fact that the angle at which the echo hits your ear is rarely 'straight on'. Living creatures like dogs, humans, and bats have particularly adapted ears to distinguish angles of echoes and make sense of where the returning sound is coming from, but 'echosorting' must be built into mechanical systems like submarines. The recent work of Boutin and Kember (2020) to build drones that can echolocate focuses on how this echo sorting is accomplished both mechanically and algorithmically.

Applied in a non-acoustic framework to explore how people communicate interpersonally, the ping and echo are inherent qualities, occurring swiftly and subtly. This is seen most obviously in the turn-taking in face-to-face conversations, where people are in a constant flow of utterance and reply, or, drawing on Karl Weick's concept of the 'double interact' (1969), continuous three-part cycles of interaction that form the basic building blocks of culture: the act, the response (the interact), and the response to the response (the double interact). It is relatively easy to identify a similar cycle when we start paying attention to non-verbal and paralinguistic behaviours like smiles, raised eyebrows, second glances, and other sensorial features of interaction. We can notice this as I sit in a coffee shop with a friend, telling them a story about a terrible situation that happened to me. As I speak, I look across the table, watching their reactions. They nod. They frown occasionally. They roll their eyes at the appropriate moments. These are constant forms of feedback that reassure me my friend is listening. When their eyebrows raise at a particular detail, I extend my explanation. At another moment I pause in my story, look down. I notice I am spinning my coffee cup in its saucer, around and around. They ask, 'What's wrong? What happened?' I look up, notice the care in their eyes, and continue with a particularly painful part of the story. Importantly, in a typical communication interaction between people, this is never a singular process but a continuous series that functions at multiple levels simultaneously.

When mediated by the digital, the call and response features of communication are made more visible because they are deliberate technical accomplishments by persons—such as typing LOL versus just laughing aloud in response to something another person said or did. When using social media platforms and apps, or messaging on smartphones, the pings or echoes are mediated by other elements of the interface. I send out a message to my friend on SMS, and my phone soon shows a small message next to my text to say 'Delivered'. This tells me my friend has received the message on their device. My phone then alerts me again, showing me three animated ellipses. This tells me my friend is typing, likely composing a response. In echolocation terms, I can say my ping has reached the object in space and sent back at least two echoes to me. Another echo will occur when I receive the message itself, or no message at all. Various pings or echoes are built into interface design. I see them as red notification dots on smart devices; or the hearts and thumbs and other emojis that I have received on my posts; or in the checkmarks and double checkmarks in instant messaging apps, indicating my message was sent, received, seen, or read.

What is typically called 'feedback' takes on more of the properties of echolocation when we consider what is done in response to the ping. How do we make micro-adjustments based on information we receive? How is the ping and echo occurring in moments when we may not even notice we are 'interacting' at all? Take the example of how facial recognition is used to unlock the iPhone: I tap on my smartphone to wake it up. It lights up. I click it again and a message pops up to read 'face not recognized'. I shift my position, adjusting my neck and head slightly. The lock screen disappears. Or take an everyday Google search. Google sends multiple, seemingly instantaneous echoes throughout a single search. As I type into the search bar, I send a signal that doesn't bounce off a clean surface like lidar bouncing off a perfectly smooth mirror. Rather, my signal sinks into the interface enough for the interface to interpret the ping as incoming information, compute plausible outcomes of my continued typing. It then generates an informational ping that offers different possible completions to my search phrase. This functions as a series of echoes to what it thinks I am signaling. This process is swift; each time I add another letter, the response from Google search changes. As another example, advertisements appear in the middle of various platform-based newsfeeds, representing an echo to some signal we previously and most likely unwittingly sent out. I am often bewildered by what my actions must have signalled to receive odd or misfitting responses. I am even more bewildered when the ads fit me so well they must have magically read my thoughts, mirroring my perception of my identity without a single ripple of distortion.

While these are intriguing examples of interpersonal interactions, my goal here is not to pursue the extraordinary infrastructural elements of these pro-cesses but to consider the connection between what we might conceptualize as echoes and the construction of the Self. Focusing on the echo side of the ping/echo interaction exchange, so to speak, we can speculate about what is happening in and just following the moment of the checkmark, push notifi-cation, or other form of informational echo. In the next section, I elaborate on the way these are moments of locating and positioning. We immediately identify the relative position of the Self in relation to the object(ive) relations in (social) space. This positioning of Self in the social lifeworld is continu-ous, repetitive, and for the most part unnoticed since it is highly trained and routinized. Less obdurate and more existential, we can see the dynamic of maintaining a sense of *ontological security*, visibilized only in moments of *ontological insecurity*. I explore these three ideas more closely in the next section.

LOCATING, MAPPING, POSITIONING

Engineers focused on self-driving cars, drones, or commercial fishing boats, which all rely on radar, sonar, and lidar, face the 'complementary problems of localization (determining where you are in an environment) and mapping (determining the shape of your environment)' (Schnieders Lefever 2020, np). In an oddly parallel way, Giddens was interested in these same issues when discussing 'positioning' as a key element of how consciousness and Self are constituted through the dialectical dynamics of structure and agency, or what he called 'structuration' (1984).

Giddens drew on the earlier studies of Goffman, Laing, and Garfinkel, among other popular sociological theorists, to discuss how identity is constructed through the ongoing enactment of everyday habitual routines. These are not enacted in a vacuum of isolation but with others, in public or semi-public social moments. Giddens argues this is less about social roles, which is the popular anchor for identity based on Goffman's early works (1959, 84), and more about 'social positions', or as he amends his own use of the term 'positioning'. Positioning can be physical-sensory, in that it often involves bodily and gestural movement in relation to materiality outside the body. Positioning is also cognitive, as one engages in sense-making about the Self's place in the world, through discursive and communicative interactions, in relation to larger structures of meaning or what Giddens calls 'societal totalities', generalized notions of society that guide and help us make sense of our everyday lives in the context of larger social formations, a phrase akin to Taylor's later notion of the 'social imaginary' (2002, 106).

Locating the Self in digital spaces relies on not only being connected, but being responded to, as many authors including myself have argued over the past 25 years (Markham 1998; Sunden 2003; MacKinnon 1995). The spatial, relational, and temporal qualities of 'positioning' help specify how connectivity is not optional. In a physical sense, we can easily understand how we are bodies in constant motion. We spend our entire waking life comparing what is immediately around us at close range (I see the curb and need to step off it into the street) with what is more distant (I see the other side of the street, en route to the office building I see in my mind, the place I am trying to reach, and I notice the traffic patterns are typical, representative of my hundreds of thousands of prior experiences with this moment). For me, like for most people, I enact multiple sensory and cognitive instances of 'constant comparison' in a relatively seamless way together to help me situate and navigate. Applied to the social rather than physical lifeworld, this becomes a matter of understanding what and where the Self is, in relation to the Other. And of course, the agency that goes along with this is fraught, as one is not just positioning but being positioned and repositioned, continually, which can constrain one's positionality directly, or, as Judith Butler (1991) elaborates, influence what one eventually believes is possible.

It is not until we are disconnected abruptly that we become aware that we have been in this constant mode of positioning the Self through various, and more or less non-stop, flows of interaction or information exchange through digital and social media. Paul Frosh describes this elegantly in his work on digital poetics (2019) and my own work extends Garfinkel's 'breaching experiments' from the mid-twentieth century, which so clearly illustrated the degree to which we experience everyday norms, relations, and rituals as seamless and natural, when in actuality they are an outcome of continuous accomplishments. A sudden disruption reveals and highlights that, if not how, these taken-for-granted states must be achieved, over and over again. In these moments of abrupt disconnection, one's lifeworld, the Other, and the relative position of the Self all become remarkable in different ways. Participant E notes, 'It's a feeling of invisibility, I guess, more than anything. I thought I would have more FOMO, but it's more like I'm ghosting myself. Where am I even?' This is a particularly interesting snippet from a participant's longer autoethnographic narrative about the angst that follows disconnection. The Self is (or seems to be) absent from the lifeworld, which is a common feeling expressed by participants. The feeling of absence is perhaps less about being completely gone than not knowing one's position.

Notably, Participant E adds the idea that they have ghosted themselves. This adds a curious phenomenon; ghosting is considered a particularly cruel behaviour in relationships in digitally saturated societies. It occurs when someone stops communicating abruptly, ignoring or blocking attempts to contact them. Although at first glance one would think that the response to being ghosted is to think that the person who stopped communicating disappeared, it is common to also feel the opposite. As Denitsa Kisamova (2020) writes in her blog, for example, 'I was ghosted to the extent where I wondered if we had ever met in the first place. Go figure. He stopped returning my calls. He walked pass through me [*sic*] in the hallway. He started dating some other girl without telling me.'

Kisamova describes the situation as one where she has disappeared or at least become transparent enough that 'he walked pass through me'. This describes a sensation whereby Kisamova herself has disappeared, from her own world. Even if one doesn't have this sensation of disappearing from their own lifeworld, 'you're left in a state of limbo', as blogger Brenna Holman writes (2016, np). There follows an immediate inability to know what to do next. It is not just that there is nothing out there, but that one's own agency is called into question. Participant E ends their videolog with a particularly poignant demonstration of this affective register, asking the question, 'Where am I even?'

A sensation of dislocation accompanies the act of disconnecting from social media. This feeling might last five minutes or a day and then seems to dissipate. As Participant G asks, 'Why am I so nervous to be gone from the world? It's not like I will be disappeared forever.' This statement illustrates a common sensation that when G disconnects, they feel they are gone from the world, not that they feel the world is gone.

More could be analysed in these statements, but here, I use them to demonstrate that in addition to the typical absent/present and FOMO discourse of disconnecting/connecting, there is for many a radical sensation of the Self disappearing when disconnecting, which highlights not only that connecting is deeply rooted to one's sense of being, but that this connection is a form of locating, mapping, and positioning the Self.

I include this somewhat extensive section on the ping because, for me, shifting for a moment away from interpersonal communication to consider how pings matter in navigation helps me see how relationality so commonly used in symbolic interactionist and social constructionist discourse is being achieved in the micro-moments of interactions.

EXPLICATING THE CONCEPT OF
ONTOLOGICAL SECURITY

The concept of 'ontological security' is a useful tool for discussing how we understand the Self as an autonomous subject in the world. Jennifer Mitzen (2006, 342), drawing on Giddens's earlier elaborations of the concept (1984, 1991), summarizes ontological security as a sense of stability that emerges in response to 'the need to experience oneself as a whole, continuous person in time—as being rather than constantly changing—in order to realize a sense of agency'. Although people might, at times, understand theoretically that their self-identity is a temporary outcome of a constant, dialogical negotiation of Self and Other—thus agreeing with the contemporary philosophical conceptualization of Self as relational—a person's sense of security in the world relies on a belief that the Self is an individual with meaning, a being that has somewhat stable boundaries. That this is taken as a tacit matter of fact is made clear when we consider that people who experience the Self otherwise often earn an official disorder label, such as split personality, borderline personality disorder, or schizophrenia.

This sensation of wholeness is delineated in part by our body, which provides constant evidence that we exist as an entity. Since many decades, if not centuries, of thought have been devoted to this topic, I sketch only a few relevant concepts of ontological security later. Judith Butler's work nearing the end of the twentieth century extends classic symbolic interactionist theories, giving new depth to the idea of a relational Self. As she notes, any sense of a 'stable contour', 'bodily ego', or 'spatial boundary' relies on 'identificatory practices' (1991, 14) which are processes of relation, in interaction. Gender is constructed iteratively as it is performed, over and over, its characteristics reinforced repeatedly in response to the mirror of the Other, or how an individual perceives it ought to be performed based on how others respond to their various performances. This resonates with Cooley's (1902) interactionist concept of the 'looking-glass theory of self', though Butler draws more on Lacanian psychoanalytic thought for her analysis. Notably, Butler's work emphasizes the hegemonic, regulatory, and decidedly non-neutral ways that the dynamics of structure and agency impose a particular starting point for these iterative cycles, which is not fully presented in my depiction.

The position I take here, aligning with Garfinkel (1963), Laing (1959), Goffman (1967), and Giddens (1984), is that despite the differences in perspectives on how the Self (or one's social role or social position) is stabilized, a key moment is that at some points, the oscillating dynamics of interaction slip beneath our notice because they have become learned, habitual, routine, and tacit. The 'negotiation' of self-identity is less salient and we simply *are* in the world. This is not to say the Self remains obdurate or unchanging.

Indeed, as Butler (1993, 104) notes, the Self is 'incessantly reconstituted . . . constantly marshaled, consolidated, retrenched, contested, and, on occasion, compelled to give way'. But our sense of ontological security is strongest when these processes are transformed into infrastructures for being.

Like many invisible infrastructures or frames of *being in the world*, we notice ontological security when it is disrupted. The capacities of digital social contexts of the 1990s helped disrupt the myth that the Self is a stable and singular entity (Gergen 1991). The internet augmented and actualized the ideas of multiple, fragmented, protean, distributed, or flexible Selves. To be physically distant yet intimately connected in synchronous or asynchronous ways with others meant one could play with one's performance of identity, which became a common practice for those with means and leisure time. It was possible to build multiple concrete identities in various digital places and be with others beyond simply building an imaginary of multiplicity. Thus, people experienced and then shared their experiences of radically moving beyond the Self as a singular entity. Globally distributed networks of connection highlighted in the 1990s what sociologists or philosophers like Martin Buber had long known, that whatever we describe as Self requires and emerges in continuous interaction with whatever we understand to be Other. And if we have multiple relations, we are essentially multiple beings in contexts. Sociologist and psychologist Sherry Turkle provides exemplary discussions of these dynamics and practices in her 1995 work *Life on the Screen*.

THE DISORIENTATION OF DISCONNECTION: ONTOLOGICAL INSECURITY

Most basically, if our sense of ontological security in the world relies on our belief that we know ourselves, and this recognition of the Self is stabilized through a constant differentiation or positioning in relation to other elements of our immediate ecosystems (as part of the 'not Self'), it follows that ontological insecurity occurs when our recognition of ourselves falters, or when a part of the constant comparison framework of Self-Other breaks down, or when the system of interaction between Self and the world is disrupted. Arguably, all of this happens to varying degrees when people who rely on the internet for their social networks are disconnected.

Ontological insecurity is associated with deep anxieties. But these need not be long-lived. A sensation of not knowing, or a loss of cohesion and stability, can be momentary, like when you feel dizzy because you are off balance. Once you stabilize, the feeling passes. Or it can occur with age, as the image in the mirror no longer resembles what we expect to see. It can occur when we are misrecognized, or when we disassociate, a common outcome following trauma whereby we feel foreign to ourselves and for various reasons and in various different ways, disconnect from our feelings, memories, perceptions, or identity. For most people untroubled by severe psychosis, as Laing would say (1959), ontological breaks like these are temporal and ad hoc.

Whether long-lived or momentary, ontological insecurity is associated with intense existential disorientation. To explore how this is connected to echolocation, it is useful to go back to a core question such as 'How do we recognize ourselves?' This basic question of the Self has received centuries of coverage in philosophy, and in the twentieth century, phenomenology, psychology, and sociology. For example, John Paul Sartre and Simone de Beauvoir explored the concept of ontological security through existentialist philosophy and phenomenology. The existentialists were particularly fascinated by the 'pervasive anxiety' that comes with building selfhood through the challenge of innumerable 'either/or' choices at every step of one's life, an idea Sartre borrowed from Kierkegaard, as Sarah Bakewell (2019, 18) notes. Sartre's existentialism focuses on the dizziness that accompanies this continual making of the Self. This dizziness is akin to vertigo, except that

> it is not the fear of falling so much as the fear that you can't trust yourself not to throw yourself off. Your head spins; you want to cling to something, to tie yourself down—but you can't secure yourself so easily against the dangers that come with being free. (Bakewell 2016, 19)

This sensation of vertigo and dizziness as an outcome of excessive freedom of will is a typically delightful overstatement of the existentialists. But the anxiousness arising from a sensation of vertigo can also come from being unable to orient yourself. There is a grounding stability in knowing where one is positioned in relation to other entities or elements of the environment. The feeling of being rooted or stable is not necessarily one of being entirely still or unmoving, however, since that does not describe the human, physically or mentally. We are in constant action and reaction, moving through the life-world. Tia DeNora (2000, 84), in describing the interaction between people and music as a form of attunement and orienting, suggests the following:

> that the creaturely ability to locate and anticipate environmental features engenders a kind of corporeal or embodied security, by which I mean the 'fitting in' or attunement with environmental patterns, fostered by a being's embodied awareness of the materials and properties that characterize his or her environment.

DeNora also suggests that we can become unstable when we lose this attunement to the rhythms of environments. Using the example of someone skipping rope when there is no comprehensible timing of the rope hitting the pavement, DeNora describes the process of searching for and failing to 'locate and appropriate . . . resources with or against which to "gather oneself" into some kind of organized and stable state' (84). This 'embodied insecurity' is in contrast to 'embodied security', which comes from 'one's ability to fit in, or situate oneself, bodily' (ibid.).

The anxiety of ontological insecurity manifests in different ways. In my studies, participants used the word 'disorientation' frequently. Participant B, for example, remarks in a 2014 autoethnographic videolog at the outset of the 24-hour media fast:

> It has not been fun. It is only 10 am and I don't know how I will make it through an entire day. I literally don't know what to do. And I don't mean because I don't have things to do. But because I am disoriented. I just don't know why I feel this way.

Participant C writes in 2015, 'I feel disoriented, apart from everyone and everywhere. How could I be so addicted that I can't be offline even for a day?' Orienting, if you think about navigating or wayfinding, is generally accomplished through a process of oscillating from near to far, inward-out and then outward-in orientations, or looking out towards the horizon and back at one's feet to see where one is placed, physically. For my participants, this sensation of disorientation references more than simply being absent from the digital social context, it indicates not knowing they are, or being nowhere, unable to place or position the Self on a map anywhere, or perhaps even find the map.

Slightly different than the sensation of disorientation, my participants also felt general nervousness, anxiety, and self-doubt about the existence of the 'Self for Others' (a concept that Laing and other symbolic interactionists would use to emphasize that the Self is relational, social, and often far more other-referential than self-referential). Participant A says the following in a 2019 videolog:

> I feel nervous. It's so quiet in here and I keep turning over my phone to see if I have any notifications. Then I remember that I'm supposed to be on a media fast and I turned off notifications. Why do I care so much whether I get a notification? I think it is because it assures me that people are out there or that I'm still in here [points at their own chest in video].

Drawing on the work of existential philosopher Rollo May, Gustafsson and Krickel-Choi note that anxiety is different from fear: 'Anxiety is internal. Because anxiety *strikes at the foundation of the personality*, it is not possible to "stand outside" of it and treat it as an object to run away from' (2020, 886;

my emphasis). This is useful to help us understand at least one reason that the anxiety people feel from disconnecting from social media seems so deep. Participant A's anxiety is a fairly common case in point. Loss of connection with others seems to remind A that they require Other for assurance that they, themselves, exist. More precisely, as with many participants in my studies, this is not so much a loss of connection as a loss of the continuous responses from others. As I have noted elsewhere (Markham 2020), this absence is felt as a loss of multiple, rather than single, feedback loops, which suggests the importance of the continuous stream of calls and responses. The visual image is not so much an individual having a controlled interaction with a single other person, but a person in a naturalized, tacit, ongoing process of continuously marking the sociality of Self by bouncing signals off multiple objects in immediate or ongoing contexts. Until it is absent, this phenomenon of being constantly unstable is not apparent.

Here, I shift away from the more philosophical considerations of the stability of the Self, to return to how disconnection can be discussed through the lens of echolocation. Disconnection has been associated with angst, disruption, and other uncomfortable, visceral feelings, as many scholars have described in depth (Karppi 2011, 2018; Light 2014; Paasonen 2015, 2016). While DeNora (2000) focuses on physical embodiment, we can take their idea of attunement to certain rhythmic features of the environment and connect this to how the seeming ambient materialities of digital media function at another level of echolocation, which moves beyond the single ping and echo. The absence of a response may be felt as the sudden loss of a comforting reverberation of continuous echoes, a characteristic chorus of everyday affective and social reverberations that are central in digital communication.

REVERBERATION AS A SENSE OF RELEVANCE IN THE SOCIAL WORLD

Many of my participants have talked about their practice of deleting Instagram posts that don't get adequate likes in a short period of time. This response was common especially in the years when the selfie was novel (*c.* 2013–2018). As participant K put it:

> I will post and then wait for the likes. If I don't get enough likes in a few minutes, I'll probably delete the post.

I asked, 'Why would you delete the post?'
They replied, 'It means it's not a good picture!' They paused, looking at me as if I should already know the answer. I shrugged and didn't reply, so

they continued, 'and if it's a picture of me, I'd be embarrassed to keep it up there. You know, without so very many hearts.'

I waited a moment and then asked, 'How many is enough? How long will you wait before you take it down?'

'Oh, it depends on what time it is. If I know my friends are online or it's evening, I'll only wait about five minutes. But if I post something really early in the morning, or when we're in class, I'll wait longer. It depends.'

They added, 'I don't know. I'm sure I won't get as many likes as Kim Kardashian just got on her post. But I should get a few. It depends on how many people are likely to see the post.' Chuckling, knowing they couldn't really answer the question, they added, 'I don't know. Enough. You know.'

This nervousness about not knowing whether or not one's message was good enough to receive a reply makes sense to me. I can relate this with my own hesitations to press the send button, my self-doubts in swiping right on dating apps, or my constant glancing at the phone after I have made what I think is a particularly funny joke to a friend and I am waiting for the phone to light up, letting me know they laughed.

But there is something different in this participant's situation than my own. The echo, for me, is a singular indicator of a response to my call. For them, it is relevant in terms of speed and quantity. This means it is not relevant as a singular indicator. When echoes come more and more swiftly to a bat winging its way through the darkness of night, both the bat and the object grow larger, in relation to each other. A bat will send out between 160 and 190 chirps per second. The returning echoes give precise information about the contours of the object. As objects grow closer, the number of chirps increases. Because the bat does not want to miss the mosquito, it marks the outlines of the object with these sonic reverberations.

Transposing this example of a bat mapping their relative position to objects in space to the example of posting an Instagram image mentioned earlier, we can say that when the responses come swiftly in the form of likes and hearts, part of what is being mapped is the relevance of the person who posted. Many likes (whatever 'many' means) in a certain number of minutes is akin to being closer to, and therefore larger in, the surrounding social space.

What if nobody responds at all? The absence of an echo would suggest that the ping never hit anything; nothing is out there. But in all likelihood, the participant knows that others are out there scrolling through Instagram posts—after all, they just watched Kim Kardashian's heart count climb on her latest post while they were waiting to see how many posts they received on their own post. This raises the question, 'What is not out there? The others? Or the Self?' My participants would suggest the Self is every bit as absent as the Other. More to the point here about relative size, the absence of a response could indicate that the Self is so far distant from the object they are seeking, the pings are taking too long to return to the origin. Rather than being non-existent, the Self is irrelevant.

While one could explore many alternate interpretations to what is happening in the above example of the Instagram post, the heuristic value of echolocation is to consider how the characteristics of the echo function when we look at the interaction as one of continuous locative and positional call and response. In societies privileged by 'always-on' access to the internet, being connected is the primary way that one can build and sustain social relevance. For many people, swift and substantial echoes to their pings provide quantifiable evidence of this relevance. One can imagine the stress of maintaining likeability in this way. No wonder this young person said they would only wait five minutes for the adequate threshold of responses before deciding to remove the post. Indeed, numeric indicators on Instagram were causing so much pressure and distress among youth that Instagram removed this feature in 2019, citing well-being as the reason.

The interaction between Self and Other has always been more about the response than the performance or utterance. In information theory, this might be called feedback, which could be as simple as some sort of response by the system signaling that some data, information, or message has or has not been received. In communication theory, this response has been generally considered as a reply, in the form of a speech act, an utterance, or other gesture or signal that conveys symbolic meaning. Mead (1934), focusing on the importance of interactions between humans, theorized that the response of Other is centrally important to the construction of Self. He would say that 'humans are talked into humanity'. What he meant is not just that a person talks, but that through talking with others, they interact in a continuous exchange of symbols that build meaning, not just in the immediacy of the context, but over time. This notion is foundational to the by now well-accepted understanding that the Self is at its core (whatever that is taken to mean) *relational*.

How can we effectively characterize the constant and incalculably swift back and forth of interaction that generates this relationality? How do we get at these granular, microscopic processes of sensemaking? Echolocation helps us focus on how these processes function less like speech acts and more like an underlying hum to everyday life. This hum is the combined reverberation of multitudes of vibratory replies to embedded, embodied, and habitual signals we have sent out. As pings bounce off numerous other elements in the ecosystem, wave after wave of responding signals are sent back towards the source. Each returning echo carries information, of course, but the oscillation of countless signals creates a reverberation effect, a repeated assurance of 'I am responded to, therefore I am'. When disrupted, we begin to notice that there was a deeply meaningful rhythm to begin with, through which we were keeping our ontological balance. These *social and affective reverberations* are central features in the ongoing positioning of a sense of Self in relation to Other, whether or not we notice these.

To conclude this chapter, it is worth considering what is at stake in this conceptual development. Self-identity is an ongoing dynamic of interdependencies within larger ecosystems of continuous inter/intra-activities. These are neither value-neutral nor formed solely through human conversation. This means the technologies through which the Self can send out signals and use their interpretation of the echoes to position themselves in social relations are built and controlled by corporate entities, which have specific ambitions to maximize people's time online. They do so by, among other strategies, fine-tuning the algorithmic logics and predictive analytics that filter, or, more precisely, mediate interactions. By controlling how interactions play out in heavily connected environments, companies foster dependence on their platforms and digital technologies in general. The importance of these dynamics is that they most powerfully function at a level beneath our awareness to modulate not only what we pay attention to in competing networks all clambering for our attention (Paasonen 2016), but also how the Self is valued in a relational sense.

In an influencer era, marked by individuals gaining fame and wealth through their influence, they are notable because they are relevant. And relevance is centrally about followers through social media. The currency of choice, if not necessity, is amplification through engagement. This is fostered through speed and quantity of responses to one's messages, whether in the form of likes, comments, or shares. All of these function as echoes with information value for the Self.

Even in typical, rather than micro-celebrity scales of interactions, a single person's day is occupied by thousands of interactions with dense and distributed networks of close and loose ties. These may be direct or indirect, as mentioned at the outset of the chapter, as one interacts with close friends, followers or imagined audiences of posts, and various automated agents in the form of platform features or interface design. An echolocative theory of communication gives us a frame through which we can see how ontological security is deeply linked to the quality and characteristics of responses, which in turn relies on constant connection.

Returning to the point that began and undergirds this chapter, any discussion of disconnection is at some level a discussion about the interaction of Self and Other, but this is not often acknowledged, at least in popular media discourse around digital detox. To get away from the 'always-on' feature of contemporary life, the urge or pressure to disconnect seems an easy answer. And the proselytizing about the greater virtue or authenticity of experience that happens face to face or in physical form versus digitally comes not only from news outlets decrying addiction or narcissism, but from everyday users, as Ana Jorge (2019) notes in her analytical work in this area. Disconnection scholars push back against these oversimplifications by adding nuanced accounts of how users manage connection and disconnection at different moments or levels, in varying ways and degrees, or by explicating the sociotechnical and neoliberal entanglements of multiple agential forces that complicate this process. This chapter adds another layer to this discussion by both acknowledging and focusing on the powerful and central relevance of the interaction process through which the Self is continuously modulating an ontological position in relation to and with other people, as well as various non-human elements of situations. A theory of social echolocation insists that connection is fundamental to existence and continuous interaction demarcates the ontological boundaries of the Self. Whether using digital media or not, people engage in a tacit, habitual frenzy of back and forth, call and response, constant comparative process to make sense of the Self. Exploring these tacit interactive and echolocative properties of interaction can add depth to how we understand what constitutes 'connection' or 'disconnection', which can further break down these concepts as too-easy binaries of much more complicated processes.

REFERENCES

Barad, Karen. 2007. *Meeting the Universe Halfway: Quantum Physics and the Entanglement of Matter and Meaning.* Durham, NC: Duke University Press.

Boutin, Mireille, and Gregor Kemper. 2020. "A Drone Can Hear the Shape of a Room." *SIAM Journal on Applied Algebra and Geometry* 4 (1): 123–40. https://doi.org/10.1137/19M1248534

Bruton, Louise. 2019. "So You've Been Ghosted: What Now?" *Image.* Accessed March 1, 2021. https://www.image.ie/life/so-youve-been-ghosted-what-now-158180

Butler, Judith. 1993. *Bodies that Matter: On the Discursive Limits of Sex.* London, UK: Routledge.

———. 1991. *Gender Trouble: Feminism and the Subversion of Identity.* London, UK: Routledge.

Cooley, Charles. H. 1902. *Human Nature and the Social Order.* New York, NY: C. Scribner's Sons.

DeNora, Tia. 2000. *Music in Everyday Life.* Cambridge, UK: Cambridge University Press.

Dremljuga, Ramona-Riin. 2017. "The Disconnected that Remain Connected: Practising Partial Disconnection in the Digital Age." *Selected Papers of Internet Research: Proceedings of the Association of Internet Researchers 18th Annual Conference,* Tartu, Estonia (October 17–21). Accessed April 1, 2021.

Friedrich, Roman, Michael Peterson, Alex Koster, and Sebastian Blum. 2010. "The Rise of Generation C: Implications for the world of 2020." Strategy&.pwc.com. March 26. Accessed March 1, 2021. https://www.strategyand.pwc.com/gx/en/in sights/2002-2013/rise-generation-c/strategyand-rise-of-generation-c.pdf

Frosh, Paul. 2019. *The Poetics of Digital Media*. Cambridge, UK: Polity.

Garfinkel, Harold. 1963. "A Conception of, and Experiments with, "Trust" as a Condition of Stable Concerted Actions." In *Motivation and Social Interaction*, edited by O. J. Harvey, 187–238. New York: Ronald Press.

Gergen, Kenneth. 1991. *The Saturated Self*. New York, NY: Basic Books.

Giddens, Anthony. 1984. *Constitution of Society*. Berkeley, CA: University of California Press.

———. 1991. *Modernity and Self-Identity: Self and Society in the Late Modern Age*. Cambridge, UK: Polity.

Goffman, Erving. 1959. *The Presentation of Self in Everyday Life*. New York, NY: Doubleday Publishers.

Gustafsson, Karl, and Nina C. Krickel-Choi. "Returning to the Roots of Ontological Security: Insights from the Existentialist Anxiety Literature." *European Journal of International Relations* 26 (3), 875–895. doi:10.1177/1354066120927073

Holeman, Brenna. 2016. "On Ghosting (and What to do if it Happens to You). *This Battered Suitcase* (August 8): np. Accessed April 12, 2021. https://www.thisbatt eredsuitcase.com/on-ghosting-and-what-to-do-if-it-happens-to-you/

Jenblat, Omar. 2018. "Is Your Business Prepared For Generation C?" *Forbes* (January 29): np. Accessed January 20, 2019. https://www.forbes.com/sites/forbesagenc ycouncil/2018/01/29/is-your-business-prepared-for-generation-c/#5afc6d30a4be

Jorge, Ana. "Social media, interrupted: Users Recounting Temporary Disconnection on Instagram." *Social Media + Society* 5 (4). doi:10.1177/2056305119881691

Jorge, Ana, and Marco Pedroni. "'Hey! I'm back after a 24h #DigitalDetox!': Influencers posing disconnection." In *Reckoning with Social Media*, edited by Aleena Chia, Ana Jorge, and Tero Karppi. London: Rowman & Littlefield.

Karppi, Tero. 2011. "Digital Suicide and the Biopolitics of Leaving Facebook." *Transformations Journal of Media and Culture*, no 20. Accessed April 1, 2021: http://www.transformationsjournal.org/issue-20/

Karppi, Tero. 2018. *Disconnect: Facebook's Affective Bonds*. Minneapolis, MN: University of Minnesota Press.

Kisamova, Denitsa. 2020. "How Ghosting Affects Your Mental Health." *Invisible Illness* (April 4): np. Accessed April 12, 2021. https://medium.com/invisible-illnes s/how-ghosting-affects-your-mental-health-c46f2cdb4635

Laing, Ronald D. 1959. *The Divided Self*. London, UK: Tavistock.

Light, Ben. 2014. *Disconnecting with Social Networking Sites*. Cham, Switzerland: Palgrave.

MacKinnon, Richard C. 1995. "Searching for the Leviathan in usenet." In *Cybersociety: Computer-Mediated Communication and Community*, edited by Steve Jones, 112–137. London, UK: Sage.

Markham, Annette N. 1998. *Life Online: Researching Real Experience in Virtual Space*. Walnut Creek, CA: Alta Mira.

————. 2012. "Fabrication as ethical practice". In *Information, Communication, and Society* edited by Charles Edgley, 279–294. Farnham, UK: Ashgate Press.

————. 2017. *Echo-Locating the Digital Self.* Accessed March 1, 2021. https://annettemarkham.com/2017/09/25844/

————. 2019. "Critical Pedagogy as a Response to Datafication." *Qualitative Inquiry* 25 (8), 754–760. doi:10.1177/1077800418809470

————. 2020. "Echolocating the Digital Self: A Conceptual Framework." AoIR Selected Papers of Internet Research 2020 (October). doi:10.5210/spir.v2020i0.11272

————. "Echolocation as Theory of Digital Sociality." Unpublished manuscript. Last modified April 1, 2021. PDF.

Mead, George. H. (1934)1967. *Mind, Self and Society from the Standpoint of a Social Behaviorist.* Chicago, IL: University of Chicago Press.

Mitzen, Jennifer. 2006. "Ontological Security in World Politics: State Identity and the Security Dilemma." *European Journal of International Relations* 12 (3), 341–370.

Paasonen, Susanna. 2015. "As Networks Fail: Affect, Technology, and the Notion of the User." *Television and New Media* 16 (8), 701–716. doi:10.1177/1527476414552906

————. 2016. "Fickle Focus: Distraction, Affect and the Production of Value in Social Media." *First Monday* 21 (10). doi:10.5210/fm.v21i10.6949

Pielot, Martin and L. Luz Rello. 2017. "Productive, Anxious, Lonely: 24 Hours without Push Notifications." *Proceedings of the MobileHCI Conference.* Vienna, Austria.

Schnieders Lefever, Kelsey. 2020. "With a Speaker and Four Microphones, Drones can Echolocate like Bats." *Techexplore.* Accessed March 1, 2021. https://techxplore.com/news/2020-03-speaker-microphones-drones-echolocate.html

Shannon, Claude. 1948. "A Mathematical Theory of Communication." *The Bell System Technical Journal* 27 (July, October), 379–423, 623–656.

Solis, Brian. 2011. *The End of Business as Usual: Rewire the Way You Work to Succeed in the Consumer Revolution.* Hoboken, NJ: Wiley.

Sunden, Jenny. 2003. *Material Virtualities: Approaching Online Textual Embodiment.* New York, NY: Peter Lang.

Taylor, Charles. 2002. "Modern Social Imaginaries." *Public Culture* 14 (1), 91–124. https://muse.jhu.edu/article/26276

Tiidenberg, Katrin, Annette Markham, Gabriel O. Pereira, Mads Rehder, Jannek Sommer, Ramona-Riin Dremljuga, and Meghan Dougherty. 2017. "'I'm an Addict' and Other Sensemaking Devices: A Discourse Analysis of Self-Reflections of Lived Experience on Social Media." *Proceedings of the 8th International Conference on Social Media and Society.* Article No. 21. http://dl.acm.org/citation.cfm?doid=3097286.3097307

Turkle, Sherry. 1995. *Life on The Screen: Identity in the Age of the Internet.* New York, NY: Simon and Schuster.

————. 2011. *Alone Together: Why We Expect More from Technology and Less from Each Other.* New York, NY: Basic Books.

Weaver, Warren. 1949. "The Mathematics of Communication." *Scientific American* 181 (1), 11–15.

Weick, Karl. 1969. *Social Psychology of Organizing.* Boston, MA: Addison-Wesley.

Part II

DESIRING DISCONNECTION

Chapter 3

'Hey! I'm Back after a 24h #DigitalDetox!'

Influencers Posing Disconnection

Ana Jorge and Marco Pedroni

According to the 2020 Global Digital yearbook report by social media managing sites Hootsuite and WeAreSocial (2020), the number of internet users keeps growing, with 59% of the world's population now connected to the web and the average internet user spending more than 6.5 hours online each day. Most importantly, social media use (especially through mobile connection) is flourishing more than any other form of web consumption, according to the same sources. At the same time, there are discourses circulating on social media (Jorge 2019) and self-help books (Syvertsen and Enli 2020) about the value of interruptions of using those same platforms. Moreover, there is 'a proliferation of calls to reduce both the range of digital devices and communication platforms, and the time spent using them, issued by those who are already connected and digitally savvy', like bloggers, activists, or 'populist experts' (Kunstman and Miyake 2019, 902). So why do bloggers—or, as they are increasingly known, influencers—who live off social media, disconnect from them? If at all, how do they call their audiences to disconnect? How is social media dis/connectivity constructed through these endeavours as they are presented to audiences?

This chapter looks at how influencers are reckoning with social media. By focusing on different discourses from social media posts to coverage in popular media we explore these apparently contradictory gestures where influencers position themselves against the very platforms that have helped them to gain attention in the first place and on which they depend. Hesselberth (2018, 2002) argues that studies on *discourses* of disconnectivity do not capture the *gesture towards disconnectivity*, which should be looked at without the 'primacy of logos'. Yet we feel it is urgent to study the meanings of disconnection among visible figures *inside* social media as an important part of the paradox, to unpack how their discourses are articulated with other types of discourse. We analyze the content production by influencers on social media—Instagram, YouTube, blogs, podcasts—and their visibility on media serving as testimonies of those experiences. We selected influencers in the fields of fashion, beauty, lifestyle, travel, fitness, and sports, as we aimed to explore the meaning of the practice across different forms of narrativization of everyday life. In our exploratory, qualitative research, we searched for influencers of all tiers—from nano- and micro- to macro- and mega-influencers, according to current industry categorizations[1] and influencer-ranking platforms, together with social media celebrities—to capture different levels of compromise with platforms. We considered influencers from English-, Italian-, and Portuguese-speaking contexts, for linguistic capacities of the authors. Our search was conducted through titles, tags, or hashtags such as 'social media detox', 'quit media for x days', 'x days off social media' (on the aforementioned languages) on Google, YouTube, and through hashtags on Instagram, considering the period of 2015 to 2020. Given the nature of search engines and social media, nano- or micro-influencers were more difficult to find. Our overall sample was composed of 30 influencers, mostly female. We used some of the news media on the topic to track influencers associated with these practices; in some cases, where campaigns were at place, we sought for additional influencers involved. Our corpus consisted of at least one form of social media or media content by each of the influencers—the cited pieces are included in appendix. For all the selected content, we extracted extensive transcription notes, and did an inductive analysis to identify a limited number of themes (Corbin and Strauss 2008). Our analysis develops in three parts: first, it shows how influencers portray their job as hyperconnected and at the verge of breaching; second, it looks at their practices of disconnecting—and motivations for those practices—as they are narrativized in their social media content or news media; and, last, it examines the ways in which they return to connectivity and advise the audience based on their experience.

---

[1] Categorization is proposed by the global influencer marketing agency Viral Nation, based in Canada. For the purpose of our analysis, we excluded two further categories: celebrity personalities and social publishers. The number of followers, here, works as a criterion for differentiating influencers and for building an influencer marketing vocabulary where each category is sold for their particular advantages to potential advertisers: in this way, for instance, Viral Nation presents nano-influencers as producers of 'great quality and cost effective content' for 'hyper-targeted, loyal and engaged audience segment' and micro-influencers as industry experts who 'focus on a specific niche' and 'tend to have stronger relationships than a typical influencer' (https://www.viralnation. com/services/influencer-marketing-agency/); bigger influencers, such as those that Launchmetrics classify as mega (500K–2M followers), are considered important—despite their high cost—as 'they are guaranteed to reach an extremely high number of social media consumers' (https://www .launchmetrics.com/it/risorse/blog/tipi-di-influencers).

LIVING THE INFLUENCER LIFE—
PERFORMANCE ANXIETY

Influencer has become a buzzword to designate the job or occupation of a YouTuber, blogger, Instagrammer—or, more recently, TikToker—depending on the platform they started at, or on which they are more prominent in. Competing words—like content creator, talent, digital entrepreneur, or celebrity—are also used by some practitioners to distance themselves from the inflated label of influencer. In an early attempt to define influencers, Van Dijck (2013, 40) presents them as internet users 'with a large network of connected followers and friends'. The accumulation of large following takes place 'through the textual and visual narration of their personal lives and lifestyles [and the engagement] with their following in digital and physical spaces' (Abidin 2015). Social media influencers gather audiences around the intimate narration of their lives (Berryman and Kavka 2017), accumulating visibility in a process of celebrification (Jerslev 2016). Often, influencers traverse social media platforms and explore their different affordances, adapting to their continually changing settings and algorithms, to promote an online persona and media brand (Cunningham and Craig 2017, 71). Their audience is manifest in numbers of subscribers, views, likes, and replies to indicate following, engagement, and influence, which can be converted into capital (Hearn and Schoenhoff 2016) through monetization as advertisers pay influencers 'to promote commodities to their audience through their various profiles' (O'Meara 2019, 3). This, in turn, is the condition to sustain professionalization, meaning taking this as a full-time job, or even entrepreneurialism, when they use this visibility to ramp up their own businesses. Van Dijck's definition, based on the size of the network as a defining feature, proves to be problematic today, where the intensity of the ties with followers and strength of connection to the digital are paramount.

Influencers play an ambivalent role in the political economy of social media: while they are self-commodified and revert the visibility they acquire to their own gains, they are also co-opted by platforms, as they are crucial to gather and engage audiences to spend time on the platforms (Stehling et al. 2018). Social media practitioners appear to be both exploited and exploiters: on the one hand, they depend on platforms' affordances and may suffer from forms of non-remuneration like gifting; on the other, they exploit their audiences' attention by transforming their followers into the target of advertising (Pedroni and Pofi 2018). From this perspective, influencers play the role of intermediaries in the economic capital accumulation process (Fuchs and Sevignani 2013, 258) typical of the attention economy (Senft 2013).

In this economy based on the practice of *presencing* via digital platforms (Couldry 2012), influencers continuously compete for visibility, that is, for the attention of the audiences. Successful content creators often portray themselves as busy entrepreneurs, using every bit of their time to expand and value their digital exposure. The ephemeral functions of social media such as Snapchat and Instagram Stories, later also Facebook Stories, tend to accentuate this pressure to be connected and continually creating content. An example is how influencers create content for Instagram Stories while driving (Lungeanu and Parisi 2018) or to fill dead moments during travels, opening Questions & Answers to the audience via Instagram Stories, for instance.

Brubaker (2020, 788) defines hyperconnectivity as a state in which 'the pervasive quantification of visibility and popularity, the sheer superabundance of consumable content, and the intensified competition for attention compel us all, in some measure, to individualize the digital self'. Influencers are, to this author, an extreme case in point against the background of hyperconnectivity. Social media influencers narrate their everyday lives while continually monitoring their performance through quantification.

As professionals working through social media, influencers do show signs of performance anxiety, when they refer to the continuous monitoring of metrics of their content creation. Performance anxiety can be seen as a product of the neoliberal logic of visibility that applies to digital platforms practitioners, who act as entrepreneurs of the self: they are required to manage their online identity and networks as both assets to be cultivated and fed, and investments aimed at reaching relational and symbolic advantages (e.g. popularity) through self-promotion (Gershon 2011). Neoliberalism stands here as a principle of socialization (McGuigan 2014)—derived from the homonymous economic doctrine—and a discursive-ideological frame (Harvey 2005) that transforms market values into forms of personal self-management. Influencers turned into brands act as responsible for their brand (Duffy and Hund 2019; Gershon 2017). Self-branding, a form of labour typical of post-Fordist economy (Hearn 2008) based on reputation as a currency (Hearn 2010, 425), is defined by Marwick as 'a series of marketing strategies applied to the individual, [. . .] a way of thinking about the self as a saleable commodity that can tempt a potential employer' (2013, 166). Accordingly, failure in measurable performance is perceived by influencers as a failure of their entrepreneurial project.

Ellie Cleary, the author of travel blog SoulTravel, says her six months off Instagram started because 'there seems to be a desperation—that has got worse in recent months—to do anything for followers,' due to algorithms in Facebook and Instagram; and she wanted to escape constant comparison: 'I quickly got into a habit of looking at what others were doing and comparing myself and my results to them. The quality of my photos, my captions, my number of likes and followers.' Also the UK-based, and at the time fitness influencer, Molly Teshuva (@Progress Pure) talks about the feelings that led her to take a social media break 'for a while':

> It [Instagram] was becoming so incessant with me to the point where it was all about likes and followers and numbers. It made me feel kind of worthless . . . so instead of looking at accounts which were growing a lot thinking that they were doing the right thing and that I had to create content that looked like that because I was doing the wrong thing. I had been going on this path for such a long time without realizing it that I was no source of creativity for myself.

Several of them mention that they start to scroll through social media as soon as they wake up. While picking up phones first thing in the morning was found also among ordinary users of smartphones (Ytre-Arne et al. 2020), influencers associate this habit with checking the interactions they receive from audiences, and keeping an eye for the other content producers. Los Angeles Sports & Health content creator Lavendaire self-diagnoses as follows: 'I tend to check YouTube or Instagram when I'm awake, just because reading comments and things like that will wake me up. But I realize that that's a very distracting way to start my day.' Alayna Joy says, 'It's the first thing I do when I wake up, I lay in bed and check my phone.'

In a series of interviews conducted by Kelley (2020) on social media burnout, several influencers admit the danger of an overuse of digital devices, which is solicited by the need of managing one's followers. As Instagrammer Lauren Talulah Smeets, also known as @curvy_roamer, puts it, 'Feeling particularly stressed about not doing enough in terms of content or audience interaction is a frequent thing. I can get overwhelmed by unopened messages in my DMs or in feed post comments' (in Kelley 2020). Neda Varbanova (@healthywithnedi) confesses that 'as much as I love to interact with my community, it can be a lot, and sometimes it gives me anxiety'. To manage that, she highlights the importance of 'scheduling time blocks' and unplugging to get digital anxiety under control (ibid.).

This pressure that influencers feel to not only be connected but also grab the attention of the audience is also the result of increasing competition among a growing number of creators. 'The saturated market of lifestyle blogging accentuates these pressures as users compete to become visible and heard among the noise of lifestyle advice' (Baker and Rojek 2020, 77). At the same time, influencers must deal with the injunction of the attention economy while negotiating availability and distance from the audiences (Baym 2015). Marwick (2015) talks of strategic intimacy to capture the exposure of the influencers' behind-the-scenes as a tool to grow metrics and reputation. Abidin (2013) found that the interaction between lifestyle influencers and their followers aimed to give the impression of intimacy and an 'illusion of "reciprocity and rapport" between a sincere persona and a loyal audience'. This perceived interconnectedness was sustained in tenets such as immediacy (the need to quickly respond to readers), constancy (the expectation from readers that bloggers are always online), and exclusivity (the expectation from the audience to have their question personally and directly answered). These demands on the relationship bear special implications for a pressure on influencers to be constantly connected.

The risk hovers over influencers that social media may undermine the creativity that their labour of content creation entails. Lalah Delia, the author of wellness site *Vibrate Higher Daily*, identifies the symptoms that lead her to undertake a social media detox:

> Sometimes, I have nothing new, relevant, or creative to add. Sometimes, my mind and passion aren't in it as usual. [It is not uncommon that burnout can cause others to feel] complete exhaustion and even physical and psychological symptoms: such as headaches, eye-strains, fatigue, irritability, energetic heaviness, insomnia, and, in extreme cases, even depression and a sense of low self-worth. (Kelley 2020)

On their blog, TwinsThatTravel also state, 'Inspired by Brooke Saward's recent video—"Instagram Is Not Real Life"—we chat through our recent adventures, but also discuss what was going on for us at this time: anxiety, anti-depressants [*sic*] and feeling ever so slightly exhausted.'

On the contrary, food influencer Nathalie Rhone (@allgoodeats) claims not to have felt burnt out by social media. She links this lack of anxiety to the way she creates content, which is 'very organic, [. . .] just an extension of my private practice and daily life' (in Kelley 2020). Her thesis echoes the narrative, quite common especially during the first wave of lifestyle blogging in the 2000s (Findlay 2015), that influencers genuinely talk about their personal life and taste, contra their representation of economic agents aiming at monetizing their online performance.

As creative workers, influencers' labour is informal, at times messy and casual, at times privileged and aspirational, lacking in routine but with specific pressures relating to the type of emotional labour demanded by the attention economy. Furthermore, when blogging is constructed as an extension of the self, there is little differentiation between labour and leisure in their lives (Duffy 2016). For some, their love for the areas of life that motivated them to create their social media visibility—travel, fashion, beauty, and so on—can become overwhelming when they have to adapt their life too much to creating content in the interest of accumulating visibility. For instance, travel bloggers report how they could use social media and digital detoxes as they often are working to report their travels and do not find the space to actually enjoy the travelling experience. It is not surprising, then, to see a fashion and travel influencer like Sabrina Musco experiencing a week of digital detox in the countryside where she was born: she reports that every summer she spends at least a week in her birthplace, having the phone turned off, as a remedy for the stressful work schedule and the excess of travels during the rest of the year. 'In between goals [there] is a thing called life, that has to be lived and enjoyed,' she writes.

GETTING AWAY FROM IT ALL . . .

For some influencers, experiences of disconnection appear in the midst of the narration of their ordinary lives. For instance, Hannah Witton recounts her detox during holiday on an island in one of her YouTube videos through a journal she kept. Witton says she put her phone away (in a bag while travelling, and in the drawer when she arrived at the destination), practising what Mannell (2019) calls disentanglement (facing down or putting away the mobile) as well as signal jamming (turning off Wi-Fi or setting the airplane mode). These types of disconnective affordances of mobile services allow users to limit their social availability through social media, as much as to refrain from using them. It seems a severe measure against the will to use it (Plaut 2015). Hannah was reachable through her partner, but says announcing to family and friends that you are going on detox is important since everyone has the expectation that people will be connected all the time—a point she expressed in an interview to Tanya Goodin's podcast (2019). On the video, Witton reflects on what she was missing out without her smartphone: reminders to take pills or apps to get transport, for instance. This sex and relationships YouTuber also embodies the ambivalence that users hold towards connectivity during holidays: on the one hand, phones afford safety to the users (Dickinson et al. 2016), on the other, users deploy 'a range of refrainment practices and tactics for reducing their availability to a necessary minimum' (Rosenberg 2019, 11). Witton still dreamt once 'about YouTube analytics', which speaks of the monitoring creators have to do on their job—but she chose not to expand on it.

Other influencers use detox as content strategy, narrativize disconnection as an ostensive part of their stories. For YouTubers, this means, of course, that they had to have at least a camera with them to produce their vlogs. In her video blog 'I Tried a 48 Hour Digital Detox (Living Without Technology)', Canadian YouTuber Alayna Joy starts with the following decision: 'I am about to embark on a 48-hour digital detox—leaving behind all technology (smiles), all of the digital world for 48 hours. (sighs) That means no phones, no computers, no TVs, no games for 48 hours. No music.' She says she will miss her computer, where she works, plays, and spends most of her free time—more than her phone. She read throughout the day, at home and at a cafe; she cleaned the house, played card games with her partner, and prepared food. As the 48 hours go by, she says she misses digital technology to set time, to guide meditation, for 'those aspects like GPS or Google searches, music!, my address book'. She concludes: 'I've come to realize that I don't use social media and the internet and all these things that we're not allowed to do—I don't think I use them in a way that hinders my life.' Thus, it was just an experimentation that allowed her, the creator, and her audience to know more about herself. In the same manner, she advertises this as part of a 'I tried' series, where she asks suggestions about what to try next—now her channel also includes '30 Days Without Alcohol/I Tried Going Sober', for instance.

Influencers also use these contents on social media detox for self-reflexivity over their performance. In that sense, contents on social media breaks allow the followers to get to know them better as they talk about the self which is always at the centre of their narrative (Genz 2015). In other words, when they talk about disconnecting, they are constructing their persona to their audiences. As we will go on to see, they portray themselves as subjects in control, or doing the labour of self-control, especially over time. Some influencers play with the contradictions embedded in a detox that needs digital devices to be recorded and transformed into content. The beauty Instagrammer and YouTuber Estée Lalonde experiences a 48-hour detox with no phone, no iPad, no internet and jokes about the fact that people in the street seem like zombies with their phones. The video ends with Lalonde saying that in case of an apocalypse with no internet she will be able to survive.

The end point to the experience of digital disconnection of YouTuber Sky Life is slightly different to Alayna's or Lalonde's. In her video 'I Did a DIGITAL DETOX for 72 Hours', she recounts how she spent a weekend on a festival without using social media. To justify the need for such an act, the video shows journal articles' abstracts and news clipping in between the vlogger's narration, to highlight that platforms are addictive and negatively affect mental health. Many of those studies, replicated in news media, stem from behavioural psychology and are part of the backlash against tech companies for manipulating their users. Similar to Witton's break is the fact that Sky Life did this detox on a weekend at a festival out in the desert of California—as if to connect more with the event and place. But at the end, she positions herself as mindful yet vulnerable: 'I like to think that generally I'm very conscious of how I interact with social media and how it affects me, and I still struggle with the addictive nature of these platforms.'

SoulTravel, Lavendaire, or Sorelle Amore allude to a wider lexicon of social media toxicity (Sutton 2017; Syvertsen 2020), including the social comparison that affects every user. This toxicity is perpetuated through a mechanism of technology addiction, which can be detected through symptoms and signs, which the users can—to the influencers, should—seek to find in themselves as well. Ella Mills (n.d.) says that 'because [phone] it's addictive, isn't it?', which seems to accept it as inevitable and unchangeable. The fact that influencers embark in and replicate this discourse of technology as addictive contributes to turning it into an accepted truth that transfers the responsibility on to the user—or to technologies, products, and services the user can search for to help them manage the use (Guyard and Kaun 2018).

The trope of social media toxicity is especially repeated and accentuated among food, health, sports, and wellness influencers. Wellness influencer Lalah Delia's famous tweet reads, 'Detox your timeline, your page, your home, your refrigerator, under your counters, your closet, your ride, your phone, your life & mind.' For food influencers, controlling the use of social media is something to compaginate with alongside control over one's diet and general use of time to seek self-actualization and development. Ella Mills, owner and author of Deliciously Ella and a true 'wellness entrepreneur' (O'Neill 2020), is exemplary in embodying this message. The theme of social media detox is recurrent in her podcast episodes ('Do We Need a Digital Detox'; 'Dealing with Stress'), her Instagram ('Detox Over 2019 Christmas Break'—more below), and interviews. For this group of influencers, talking about the need to control social media in particular appears in combination with self-control over food and other habits, and in association with a healthy lifestyle that has to be continually built through mindfulness, acknowledging the challenges and 'temptations'. This is a typical neoliberal discourse where outside, macro structures are left untouchable and the individual seeks to cope with them at their end.

Ella Mills will often emphasize that technology is 'amazing' because it brought her to this point—a successful business around food, being healthy and happy with her family—but needs to be put into its right place in a good life. 'Luckily I can only ever find one downside, which is that it's hard to go offline and sometimes it's nice to disconnect just to reenergize yourself, but otherwise I love it so much,' she said in an interview (GetTheGloss 2013). Besides doing regular social media detox over weekends or Sundays—'We've had the best kind of family day. Nice to take some time over the weekend to be offline,' she said on an Instagram story in early January 2020—Ella has done social media breaks during the Holidays. On 9 December she and her husband announced on Instagram they had

> decided to take three weeks off over Christmas to switch off, recharge and most importantly enjoy our teeny Santa and her first Christmas. We're off on an adventure tomorrow and cannot wait to soak up some much needed sunshine

and quiet time as a new family. I'll be offline and doing a little digital detox
until the 1st, which I'm so excited about. [. . .] P.S any queries while we're off
social, email us. (Deliciously Ella 2019a)

On 30 December, followers learned they had had an 'amazing trip to
Thailand' (Deliciously Ella 2019b).

To *Women's Health*, she had said about social media break of 2017
Christmas: 'I really felt the benefit and was so much more *productive and
present*, [. . .] and it also gave me a bit of time off from work, which for me
is close to impossible to get unless I turn social media off' (Head 2018, our
emphasis).

. . . OR SOME OF IT

In November 2016, Kendall Jenner deleted her Instagram profile without any
warning. Some days later she declared:

> I just wanted to detox. [. . .] I just wanted a little bit of a break. I would wake
> up in the morning and look at it first thing, I would go to bed and it would be
> the last thing I looked at. I felt a little too dependent on it so I wanted to take a
> minute. (Bakkila 20/11/2016)

In an interview to Ellen DeGeneres, she said she was surprised that this
move got so much attention from the media (CNN, among others, talked
about it) and followers. Genuine or not, detox practices performed by influencers generate online buzz. Alongside a growing market of disconnection,
opting out or interrupting social media use can also work as 'a tool for online
self-promotion' (Kunstman and Miyake 2019, 902).

Among our cases, we found some rather extreme cases of the commercial-
ization of disconnection, through what we may label as *branded digital detox*.
In these cases, social media detoxing is sponsored by brands, thus not initi-
ated by the influencers—thus, getting off social media is, in fact, a job that
seeks to create value for the sponsor, by transference from the influencer. We
found a first case of this among travel and tourism bloggers: Vienna Tourism
promoted Unhashtag Vienna, inviting several medium-sized influencers for
an analogue stay in the imperial city around 2019. The challenge was to 'take
fewer photos and experience more' and to 'refrain from doing what they normally do best: documenting every aspect of their journey and sharing it with
a hashtag'. If some sex and relationships or lifestyle influencers use travelling
to disconnect, for the travel influencers the digital excess and stress is felt
because their work is done in what is for others a leisure activity.

One of the bloggers behind TwinsThatTravel says that seeing the city without digital technologies made it 'the first time I truly experienced *mindful travel*' (our emphasis). In the blog post to recount the experience—as this was most likely imposed by contract—one of the authors states, 'Freed from having to find "Instagrammable Vienna", I instead found myself on a wholly different path—seeking out Wes Anderson's Vienna.' The experience is aestheticized just the same, but through an imaginary filled with analogue. The Tourist office created the scene with analogue cameras and by inviting the influencers to the city's famous cafes. TwinsThatTravel and other influencers from different countries, invited into the city, participated in staging a retro, hipster, and vintage environment. The orchestrated ambient of this campaign proves right the claim made by Natale and Treré (2020, 628): 'The emancipatory potential of disconnection as a form of critique and sociopolitical change is often deactivated and subsumed by the dynamics of digital capitalism under the innocuous facade of escape in connection to issues of authenticity, mindfulness and nostalgia.'

Self-care is also one of the contexts where disconnection is easily commodified, in forms of episodic, surgical disconnection. Sponsored social media detox was also the basis of an Estée Lauder campaign in late 2018. Global (Italian) macro-influencer Chiara Ferragni announced on Instagram Stories that she would be spending a day offline, which is highly unusual as she is permanently posting, especially on Instagram. On a post the next day, she explained that she had been getting time off the blue light of smartphones and wearing the Estée Lauder cream overnight. Similarly, Portuguese lifestyle influencer Anita da Costa also announced her social media detox ('I'll see you in 24h. #DetoxDigital'), and came back the next day, in a Sponsored Partnership with Estée Lauder, to say, 'Hey! I'm Back after a 24h #DigitalDetox! All for the sake of a good skin!', inviting followers to read more on the blog, where she presents highly stylized pictures. She reports she was challenged by the cosmetics brand to completely shut down digital technology, but acknowledges that

> it's not easy for an influencer to turn off completely from the digital world. So instead of making a total blackout, I'm doing a social media detox. [. . .] Besides being OFF social media for 24 hours, I decided to only open the computer to do what's strictly necessary.

In these campaigns, spending time off social media is a way to get more audience attention to uninterrupted, and continuously monetized, content production. In the case of Ferragni, on the one hand, 'the "fake" social media detox clearly worked, generating buzz both during her absence with followers using #chiaradovesei [Chiara, where are you?] on Twitter, and after her return with 500,000 likes and almost 3,000 comments on the Instagram post' (Fumagalli 2020, 3). On the other, the initiative backfired: 'Not all reactions to her advertising move were positive, and some followers explicitly criticized her choice to give such a shallow message about a very important issue' (ibid.).

For some of these influencers, monetization intersects with entrepreneurialism. Venetia Falconer, fashion influencer, and her partner and food influencer Max La Manna created @48HourChallenge (n.d.) account on Instagram. The initiative is described as follows:

> Venetia and Max La Manna are the founders of social media movement #Offline48 (@48HourChallenge). In order to reconnect they disconnect their phones every weekend and encourage their audience to do the same. To enjoy a fuller, more purposeful life, the couple believe in the power of mindful consumption in every aspect of their lifestyles, and this extends to how we consume digital media.

Their inaugural #Offline48 retreat, consisting of a weekend with no devices 'but plenty of yoga, meditation, sound healing, transformation breath-work, reading, learning, picturesque country walks, delicious plant based food and quality rest', is sold at prices from £195.00. In a promotional video on YouTube, the couple also claim: 'Social media is a brilliant tool, if used correctly. But now, more than ever, we need to create boundaries with how much time we spend online.' They provide followers with tips to 'feel better' through digital disconnection, converting their reputation as sustainability activists and influencers into an asset to monetize.

Leah Itsines, Australian food blogger, partners with a digital detox camp, where she gives a cooking workshop. In these retreats, people are encouraged: 'Ban yourself from social media, emails and TV, and replace them with nourishing food, therapies, and activities' (StyleMagazines 2019) in the middle of the mountains (Eden Health Retreat 2019). One participant reports that 'my digital detox allowed me to have the space to think, discover and update my core values, care for my body, my mind and my soul'. Itsines offers some tips in the press publicity of the camp: 'I also suggest creating your own space for a "digital detox" or even "digital reduction". Like the coffee withdrawals, the digital withdrawals were tough, but after the "work" came the "reward"' (Lake 2018). These examples show how influencers are embedded in a disconnection market, which also further amplifies the discourses.

IN THE SEARCH OF A BETTER LIFE, AND BETTER JOB

A radical example of disconnection can be found in Essena O'Neill, an influencer who disappeared from social media despite her huge following.

In October 2015, she deleted 2,000 pictures from her Instagram account followed by over 600,000 people and renamed it 'Social Media Is Not Real Life'. Presented as an act of detachment from the commercial and self-promotional drift of the influencer work, her move caused a rise of followers up to one million (Elgot 2015). Juxtaposing 'real life' to 'social media life' is a narrative we also found in other influencers' words. Kendall Jenner, for example, declares:

> I think social media has taken over for our generation. I hate it sometimes, like, I literally want to throw my phone so I can't look at it. It's all a made-up world if you think about it. Social media, everything, this interview, everything. It's not real. It's pretty crazy. (Warrington 2015)

Similarly, Huda Kattan claims that 'sometimes you just need extra person-to-person contact. [. . .] Try catching up with your friends and family in real life, instead of only through social media' (Longman 2019). Such a narrative, paradoxically, serves the purpose of building a digital persona by highlighting the risks of living online: by distancing themselves from their role, influencers construct their images as 'real' people, subject to stress, overexposure, and abuse of digital devices.

As Brubaker (2020) acknowledges, hyperconnectivity affects every individual user. And influencers in our study tended to accentuate it as a tension and potential problem for the audience as well. For instance, Ella Mills (n.d.) mentions in her 22 January 2019 podcast episode, 'I've talked to friends about it, we get guilty, we go into bed and there's all these memes of modern couples and we're sitting there with our phones. It's really depressing!'

The burden of hyperconnectivity is used by influencers as part of their authentic performances. Authenticity is a problematic term, largely used within the influencer marketing industry, to reconcile the influencers' commercial work with their loyalty to the audiences. Authenticity is fabricated by cultural industries as an output to be sold (Peterson 1997; Jones and Smith 2005). Pooley (2010) points to this authenticity as 'staged', and Abidin as 'calibrated' (2017) or 'contrived' (2016) where realness and organicity are used as labels to conceal at least partially the commercial nature of influencers' branded content.

This authenticity can work to establish relatability, in a reasoning where the influencer is shown to struggle with using smartphones and social media too much, just like any follower and ordinary user. Relatability, in turn, is crucial to build influencers' role as advisers in dealing with those perceived risks, as true 'lifestyle gurus' (Baker and Rojek 2020). They feed on the 'growing distrust of experts and elites', and 'employ a mixture of selective scientific knowledge' and 'narratives of self-transformation, providing anecdotal evidence, folklore and testimonies about how they have healed themselves and others during difficult times' (ibid.).

As we have shown, many influencers concluded after a digital detox that they were already in control and technology is useful and affords them good things, or at least aware of the risks and taking measures to cope with them. In doing so, through narratives about disconnection, influencers did entice the audiences to be more mindful of the use of social media, by raising awareness; offering practical knowledge such as tips and tutorials on 'how to' manage the digital while preserving its benefits, or through more vague and general mandates. Hannah Witton offers practical advice: 'I recommend people to try it. [. . .] Turn the Do Not Disturb mode in the morning and see how much you get done when your phone isn't pinging notifications' (Goodin 2019). Ella Mills states, 'Limit your usage so you're still in the loop and don't feel like you're missing out' (Head 2018). Also Leah Itsines sees the need to control technology as much as she controls food intake. She sets as a rule, 'No phones at the dinner table. We put all the phones on one side of the table and we all stay present with each other' (Giancarli n.d.). The keyword here is *present*, as attentive interaction with the group. And Alayna Joy says on her vlog, mostly about screens:

> Do I recommend that other people try this [48 hours digital detox] challenge? Yes and no. Yes if you think that social media and the television and those things are taking over your life or they're taking an unbalanced portion of your life, then yes, absolutely do the detox! No, I don't think this is necessary for the everyday person. My takeaway would be that the digital world is not bad, it is bad if you abuse it. Like oh so many things.

Lalah Delia's motto that one should be 'mindful that slowing down to rest, reset, and restore is also being productive' (Kelley 2020) resonates with Sharma's argument that contemporary culture sustains that 'to recalibrate is to learn how to deal with time, be on top of one's time, to learn when to be fast and when to be slow' (2015, 18). Ella Mills is exemplary of the logic of digital detox to recalibrate and be more productive: 'I missed the Deliciously Ella community but came back so energized and buzzing with ideas' (Head 2018).

Controlling social media and overall digital media use is done through an individual, micro-management that privileges mindfulness and sees technology ultimately as a tool. Feeling good and productive is thus the sought outcome, and dispenses a critical view of the social media environment of which they are part. Sharma (2015) sees that technologies are portrayed as something that can help the subject to be more productive, also through 'killing time' in airports and commuting. While this has also been found to potentially generate anxiety for 'wasting time' as people cannot control the time of these breaks (Ytre-Arne et al. 2020), influencers do not criticize their role in this economy. They offer content that fills the breaks their audiences take, scrolling through social media. While they argue audiences should be in control to be mindful of the time they spend online, each individual influencer is also battling to position themself as indispensable.

CONCLUSIONS

Our analysis suggests that social media detox experiences serve to recalibrate the social media influencer's disposition as a worker. Different forms of digital purge are presented as variations of a solution to digital 'excess' that are essential to keep them creative and productive. Influencers' content on interruptions identify some key elements in digital media architecture as especially problematic: smartphones, social media, and Instagram. They echo circulating discourses of the techlash, with a first-person experience of dealing with hyperconnectivity. The interruptions of social media, phone, or digital media use are narrativized and thematized through digital channels in ways that help to construct influencers' online personae to their audiences, or are even commodified on and beyond them. In that sense, disconnection constitutes a pose by the influencers. We see that disconnection designed as a spontaneous but controlled reaction to hyperconnection, in a way that does not harm the influencers' ability to monetize their performance, works as a strategy of *manufactured uncalculatedness*. Whereas cognate concepts of 'contrived', 'calculated', or 'staged' authenticity see it as a stable value and a legitimation device, we argue that this builds up from more pragmatic, goal-oriented, and immediate actions.

Influencers play with the tension between being ordinary users and workers, suffering stress because of their digital overexposure, and not being allowed to be themselves without a continuous presence on social media. If ordinary users find it more and more difficult to disconnect, for influencers radical disconnection would have the additional cost of losing their job or partial income. To some extent, their strategies of limited—or even commercialized—forms of disconnection show their awareness of the contradictions embedded in the influencers' role, which depends on social media exposure to exist, but also relies on the myth of the 'next-door' persona.

Influencers of different categories and tiers self-track, narrate, and seek self-optimization (Brubaker 2020) to claim authority and credibility as lifestyle experts. Therefore, constructing disconnectivity as part of influencers' authentic performances is crucial for their visibility regardless of the levels of engagement and tiers they occupy. But in seeking control over their use of digital technology, influencers promote mostly a 'pedagogy for self-discovery and well-being' (Baker and Rojek 2020) where digital media is to be controlled by a self-disciplined user. How ever important their role in social media platforms, influencers do not have a say in the governance of tech companies. We argue that it is because influencers are deprived of power in the platforms that their discourses cannot rise to a form of engagement and critique to digital capitalism through disconnection (Natale and Treré 2020); this would call for greater awareness about surveillance, transparency, independence from influencers, eventually unionization and concerted action.

Rather, through these endeavours, social media disconnectivity is thus constructed to audiences as important and necessary strategies to recalibrate the user and keep them engaged. Social media influencers' labour, including that of disconnecting and conveying such experience to their audiences, is therefore instrumental to ensure the value of connectivity of the users, and ultimately securing that they continue to generate data for the platforms. Ultimately, in the grand scheme of digital capitalism, it also secures that individuals' leisure time is valuable, whether they are scrolling through social media where influencers offer content for self-actualization, or taking breaks from taking breaks on social media.

REFERENCES

Abidin, Crystal. 2013. "Cyber-BFFs*: Assessing Women's "Perceived Interconnectedness" in Singapore's Commercial Lifestyle Blog Industry *Best Friends Forever." *Global Media Journal: Australian Edition* 7 (1). https://research-repository.uwa.edu.au/en/publications/cyber-bffs-assessing-womens-perceived-interconnectedness-in-singa.

———. 2015. "Communicative ♥ Intimacies: Influencers and Perceived Interconnectedness." *Ada New Media*, no. 8. doi:10.7264/N3MW2FFG.

———. 2016. "'Aren't These Just Young, Rich Women Doing Vain Things Online?': Influencer Selfies as Subversive Frivolity." *Social Media + Society* 2 (2): 2056305116641342. doi:10.1177/2056305116641342.

———. 2017. "#familygoals: Family Influencers, Calibrated Amateurism, and Justifying Young Digital Labor." *Social Media + Society* 3 (2): 2056305117707191. doi:10.1177/2056305117707191.

Baker, Stephanie A., and Chris Rojek. 2020. *Lifestyle Gurus: Constructing Authority and Influence Online.* Wiley.

Baym, Nancy K. 2015. "Connect With Your Audience! The Relational Labor of Connection." *The Communication Review* 18 (1): 14–22. doi:10.1080/10714421.2015.996401.

Brubaker, Rogers. 2020. "Digital Hyperconnectivity and the Self." *Theory and Society* 49: 771–801. doi:10.1007/s11186-020-09405-1.

Corbin, Juliet, and Anselm Strauss. 2008. "Strategies for Qualitative Data Analysis."
In *Basics of Qualitative Research. Techniques and Procedures for Developing
Grounded Theory*, 65–86. Thousand Oaks, CA: Sage.

Couldry, Nick. 2012. *Media, Society, World: Social Theory and Digital Media
Practice*. Polity.

Cunningham, Stuart, and David Craig. 2017. "Being 'Really Real' on YouTube:
Authenticity, Community and Brand Culture in Social Media Entertainment."
Media International Australia 164 (1): 71–81. doi:10.1177/1329878X17709098.

Dickinson, Janet E., Julia F. Hibbert, and Viachaslau Filimonau. 2016. "Mobile
Technology and the Tourist Experience: (Dis)Connection at the Campsite."
Tourism Management 57: 193–201.

Duffy, Brooke Erin. 2016. "The Romance of Work: Gender and Aspirational Labour
in the Digital Culture Industries." *International Journal of Cultural Studies* 19 (4):
441–457. doi:10.1177/1367877915572186.

Duffy, Brooke Erin, and Emily Hund. 2019. "Gendered Visibility on Social Media:
Navigating Instagram's Authenticity." *International Journal of Communication*
13: 4983–5002.

Findlay, Rosie. 2015. "The Short, Passionate, and Close-Knit History of
Personal Style Blogs." *Fashion Theory* 19 (2): 157–178. doi:10.2752/1751741
15X14168357992319.

Fuchs, Christian, and Sebastian Sevignani. 2013. "What Is Digital Labour? What Is
Digital Work? What's Their Difference? And Why Do These Questions Matter for
Understanding Social Media?" *TripleC: Communication, Capitalism & Critique.
Open Access Journal for a Global Sustainable Information Society* 11 (2): 237–
293. doi:10.31269/triplec.v11i2.461.

Fumagalli, Elena. 2020. *Tough Love: When Social Media Influencers' Digital
Detox Goes Wrong*. London: Sage Business Cases original. doi: http://dx.doi.
org/10.4135/9781526496638.

Genz, Stéphanie. 2015. "My Job Is Me". *Feminist Media Studies* 15 (4): 545–561. doi:
10.1080/14680777.2014.952758.

Gershon, Ilana. 2011. "Un-friend My Heart: Facebook, Promiscuity, and Heartbreak
in a Neoliberal Age." *Anthropological Quarterly* 84 (8): 865–894.

Giancarlo, D. n.d. "Top Influencers On How To Detox Digitally." *Beauticate*. https://
www.beauticate.com/how-to/health/how-to-detox-digitally/.

Gregg, Melissa. 2018. *Counterproductive: Time Management in the Knowledge
Economy*. Durham: Duke University Press.

Guyard, Carina, and Anne Kaun. 2018. "Workfulness: Governing the Disobedient
Brain." *Journal of Cultural Economy* 11 (6): 535–548. doi:10.1080/17530350.20
18.1481877.

Harvey, David. 2005. *A Brief History of Neoliberalism*. Oxford University Press.

Hearn, Alison. 2008. "Meat, Mask, Burden: Probing the Contours of the Branded 'Self'."
Journal of Consumer Culture 8 (2): 197–217. doi:10.1177/1469540508090086.

———. 2010. "Structuring Feeling: Web 2.0, Online Ranking and Rating, and the
Digital 'Reputation' Economy." *Ephemera* 10 (3–4): 421–438.

Hearn, Alison, and Stephanie Schoenhoff. 2016. "From Celebrity to Influencer." In *A Companion to Celebrity*, edited by P. David Marshall and Sean Redmond, 194–212. London: Wiley.

Hesselberth, Pepita. 2018. "Discourses on Disconnectivity and the Right to Disconnect." *New Media & Society* 20 (5): 1994–2010. doi:10.1177/1461444817711449.

Hootsuite and WeAreSocial. 2020. *Global Digital Report*. https://wearesocial.com/digital-2020

Jerslev, Anne. 2016. "In The Time of the Microcelebrity: Celebrification and the YouTuber Zoella." *International Journal of Communication* 10 (October): 5233–5251.

Jones, Deborah, and Karen Smith. 2005. "Middle-Earth Meets New Zealand: Authenticity and Location in the Making of The Lord of the Rings*." *Journal of Management Studies* 42 (5): 923–945. doi:10.1111/j.1467-6486.2005.00527.x.

Jorge, Ana. 2019. "Social Media, Interrupted: Users Recounting Temporary Disconnection on Instagram." *Social Media & Society* 5 (4): 1–19. doi:10.1177/2056305119881691.

Kuntsman, Adi, and Esperanza Miyake. 2019. "The Paradox and Continuum of Digital Disengagement: Denaturalising Digital Sociality and Technological Connectivity." *Media, Culture & Society* 41 (6): 901–913. doi:10.1177/0163443719853732.

Lungeanu, Monica Ioana, and Lorenza Parisi. 2018. "What Makes a Fashion Blogger on Instagram? The Romanian Case Study." *Observatorio (OBS*)* 12 (speI). doi:10.15847/obsOBS0001384.

Mannell, Kate. 2019. "A Typology of Mobile Messaging's Disconnective Affordances." *Mobile Media & Communication* 7 (1): 76–93. doi:10.1177/2050157918772864.

Marwick, Alice. 2013. *Status Update: Celebrity, Publicity, and Self-Branding in Web 2.0*. New Haven: Yale University Press.

McGuigan, Jim. 2014. "The Neoliberal Self." *Culture Unbound* 6 (1), 223–240. doi:10.3384/cu.2000.1525.146223.

Natale, Simone, and Emiliano Treré. 2020. "Vinyl Won't Save Us: Reframing Disconnection as Engagement." *Media, Culture & Society* 42 (4): 626–633. doi:10.1177/0163443720914027.

O'Meara, Victoria. 2019. "Weapons of the Chic: Instagram Influencer Engagement Pods as Practices of Resistance to Instagram Platform Labor." *Social Media+Society* 5 (4): 2056305119879671. doi:10.1177/2056305119879671.

O'Neill, Rachel. 2020. "'Glow from the inside out': Deliciously Ella and the Politics of 'Healthy Eating'." *European Journal of Cultural Studies*, June, 1367549420921868. doi:10.1177/1367549420921868.

Pedroni, Marco, and Maria Paola Pofi. 2018. "Commodifying the Followers or Challenging the Mainstream?: The Two-Sided Potential of Curvy Fashion Bloggers." *Observatorio (OBS*)* 12 (spe1): 05–27. doi: 10.15847/obsOBS0001383.

Peterson, Richard A. 1999. *Creating Country Music: Fabricating Authenticity*. Chicago: University of Chicago Press.

Plaut, Ethan R. 2015. "Technologies of Avoidance: The Swear Jar and the Cell Phone." *First Monday* 20 (11). doi:10.5210/fm.v20i11.6295.

Pooley, Jefferson. 2010. "The Consuming Self from Flappers to Facebook." In *Blowing Up the Brand: Critical Perspectives on Promotional Culture*, edited by Melissa Aronczyk and Davon Powers, 71–89. New York: Peter Lang.

Portwood-Stacer, Laura. 2013. " Media Refusal and Conspicuous Non-Consumption: The Performative and Political Dimensions of Facebook Abstention." *New Media & Society* 15 (7): 1041–1057. doi:10.1177/1461444812465139.

Rosenberg, Hananel. 2019. "The 'Flashpacker' and the 'Unplugger': Cell Phone (Dis) Connection and the Backpacking Experience." *Mobile Media & Communication* 7 (1): 111–130. doi:10.1177/2050157918777778.

Senft, Theresa M. 2013. "Microcelebrity and the Branded Self." In *A Companion to New Media Dynamics*, edited by John Hartley, Jean Burgess, and Axel Bruns, 346–354. Wiley. doi:10.1002/9781118321607.ch22.

Sharma, Sarah. 2015. *In the Meantime: Temporality and Cultural Politics*. Durham: Duke University Press.

Stehling, Miriam, Lucia Vesnic-Alujevic, Ana Jorge, and Lidia Marôpo. 2018. "The Co-Option of Audience Data and User-Generated Content: The Empowerment and Exploitation of Audiences through Algorithms, Produsage and Crowdsourcing." In *The Future of Audiences: A Foresight Analysis of Interfaces and Engagement*, edited by Ranjana Das and Brita Ytre-Arne, 79–99. Basingstoke: Palgrave McMillan.

Sutton, Theodora. 2017. "Disconnect to Reconnect: The Food/Technology Metaphor in Digital Detoxing." *First Monday* 22 (6). https://uncommonculture.org/ojs/index.php/fm/article/view/7561/6310.

Syvertsen, Trine. 2020. *Digital Detox: The Politics of Disconnecting*. Bingley: Emerald Group Publishing.

Syvertsen, Trine, and Gunn Enli. 2020. "Digital Detox: Media Resistance and the Promise of Authenticity." *Convergence* 26 (5–6): 1269–1283. doi:10.1177/1354856519847325.

Van Dijck, José. 2013. *The Culture of Connectivity: A Critical History of Social Media*. Oxford: Oxford University Press.

Ytre-Arne, Brita, Trine Syvertsen, Hallvard Moe, and Faltin Karlsen. 2020. "Temporal Ambivalences in Smartphone Use: Conflicting Flows, Conflicting Responsibilities." *New Media & Society* 22 (9): 1715–1732. doi:10.1177/1461444820913561.

APPENDIX

48HourChallenge. no date. '@48hourchallenge'. Instagram. no date. https://www.instagram.com/48hourchallenge/.

Alayna Joy. 2017. *I Tried a 48 Hour Digital Detox (Living Without Technology)*. https://www.youtube.com/watch?v=fuQGr-1qglA.

Anita da Costa. 2018a. 'I'll See You in 24h'. Instagram. 25 November 2018. https://www.instagram.com/p/Bqniir-Ai5i/.

———. 2018b. 'Hey! I'm Back after a 24h #DigitalDetox! . . .' Instagram. 26 November 2018. https://www.instagram.com/p/BqqIznDAF5X/.

anitadacosta. 2018. 'Digital Detox'. *Anita & The Blog* (blog). 26 November 2018. https://anitaandtheblog.com/2018/11/26/digital-detox/.

Bakkila, Blake. 2016. 'Kendall Jenner Returns to Instagram After One Week'. *People*, 20 November 2016. https://people.com/celebrity/kendall-jenner-returns-instagram/.

Deliciously Ella. 2019a. 'Merry Christmas Everyone 😋 🎄 . . .' Instagram. 9 December 2019. https://www.instagram.com/p/B52m-WEDjE0/.

———. 2019b. 'A Belated Merry Christmas . . .'. Instagram. 30 December 2019. https://www.instagram.com/p/B6suYznjnzK/.

Eden Health Retreat. 2019. *Digital Detox with Eden Health Retreat and P.E Nation*. https://www.youtube.com/watch?v=8oalS6CO0ec.

Elgot, Jessica. 2015. 'Social Media Star Essena O'Neill Deletes Instagram'. *The Guardian*, 4 November. https://www.theguardian.com/technology/2015/nov/04/essena-oneill-deletes-instagram-account-social-media.

Ella Mills. n.d. 'Podcast · Deliciously Ella'. *Deliciously Ella* (blog). Accessed 29 January 2021. https://deliciouslyella.com/podcast/.

Estée Lalonde. n.d. '48 Hour Digital Detox'. Accessed 25 May 2020. https://www.youtube.com/watch?v=ezhjAMjJzAc[2]

Get The Gloss. 2013. 'Blogger of the Week: Deliciously Ella'. 27 December 2013. https://www.getthegloss.com/article/blogger-of-the-week-deliciously-ella.

Giancarli, Daniella. no date. 'Top Influencers On How To Detox Digitally'. no date. https://www.beauticate.com/how-to/health/how-to-detox-digitally/.

Goodin, Tanya. 2019. 'Hannah Witton on Phones and Sex'. It's Complicated. Accessed 3 November 2020. https://shows.acast.com/5ee78862f1846357d77ad9fa/episodes/5ee7887f0723ab3252163ca1.

Hannah Witton. 2017. *My Week Without A Phone | Hannah Witton*. https://www.youtube.com/watch?v=rU1rZof4EcQ.

Head, Ally. 2018. 'Five Health Influencers on The Reality of a Digital Detox'. *Women's Health*, 2 February. https://www.womenshealthmag.com/uk/health/mental-health/a707929/digital-detox/.

Kelley, James. 2020. 'How To Manage Social Media Burnout Like An Influencer'. *The Good Trade*. https://www.thegoodtrade.com/features/social-media-digital-detox.

Lake, Mia. 2018. 'I Went On A Digital Detox Retreat And It Literally Changed My Life'. *SporteLuxe*, 30 November. https://sporteluxe.com/i-went-on-a-digital-detox-retreat-and-it-literally-changed-my-life/.

Lalah Delia. 2017. 'Detox Your Timeline . . .' Tweet. @*lalahdelia* (blog). 1 January 2017. https://twitter.com/lalahdelia/status/914659573084098560.

Lavendaire. 2018. *Quitting Social Media: Social Media Detox Challenge | Vlog* 📋. https://www.youtube.com/watch?v=-b1PjFiUbHo.

---

[2] The video was no longer available as of October 2020.

Longman, Molly. 2019. 'Huda Kattan's 7 Tips For Unplugging'. *Refinery29*, 19 June. https://www.refinery29.com/en-us/2019/06/235863/should-i-do-a-digital-detox-huda-kattan.

Our Retreat. 2020. 'Retreat', 27 March. https://www.ourretreat.co.uk/retreat/march-27th-30th-2020/³

Progress Pure. 2017. *Why I Left Social Media and What It Did to Me.* https://www.youtube.com/watch?v=8VwnzdNqqR8&t=1s.

Sabrina Musco. 2019. '~ OUT OF OFFICE ~'. Instagram. 17 August 2019. https://www.instagram.com/p/B09MOxDhM26/.

Sky Life. 2018. *I Did a DIGITAL DETOX for 72 Hours!* https://www.youtube.com/watch?v=49huB5OEov4.

soultravelblog. 2019. 'Instagram Detox: What Happened During 1 Month off the 'Gram'. Soul Travel Blog | Responsible Travel Blog. 21 August 2019. https://soultravelblog.com/instagram-detox/.

StyleMagazines. 2019. Eden Health Retreat. https://stylemagazines.com.au/hit-list/eden-health-retreat/⁴

The Ellen Show. 2016. *Kendall Jenner Reveals Why She Quit Instagram.* https://www.ellentube.com/video/kendall-jenner-reveals-why-she-quit-instagram.html.

Twins That Travel. 2018. 'A Guide to Wes Anderson's Vienna'. *Twin Perspectives* (blog). 2 December 2018. https://twinperspectives.co.uk/wes-andersons-vienna/.

———. 2019. 'Where Have We Been For the Last 4 Months?' *Twins That Travel* (blog). 3 January 2019. https://twinperspectives.co.uk/episode-six-season-two-where-have-we-been-for-the-last-4-months/.

Venetia La Manna. 2019. *WHY WE'RE GOING OFFLINE* . . . https://www.youtube.com/watch?v=bTAIxcfxCHY.

Vienna Tourism. no date. 'Influencers on Digital Detox'. Influencers on Digital Detox. no date. https://unhashtag.vienna.info/en-us/article/influencers-on-digital-detox.

Vienna Tourist Board B2B. 2019. *See Vienna. Not #Vienna.* https://www.youtube.com/watch?v=Pgn3Y7kvJXE.

Warrington, Ruby. 2015. 'The Kylie + Kendall Show'. *The Sunday Times*, 31 May. https://www.thetimes.co.uk/article/the-kylie-kendall-show-lwbpzts7ppt.

---

³ The webpage was no longer available as of October 2020.
⁴ The video was no longer available as of October 2020.

Chapter 4

Privacy, Energy, Time, and Moments Stolen

Social Media Experiences Pushing towards Disconnection

Trine Syvertsen and Brita Ytre-Arne

Social media are essentials of digital life, integrated in work, relationships, public life, and daily routines, and soliciting a variety of emotions and experiences. As disconnection from social media has become a research topic and cultural trend, it is worth asking which aspects of social media prompt users to take breaks or stay away. We continue scholarly investigation of users' coping strategies in the face of intrusive media, understood as media that are experienced as pervasive and potentially exploitative (Mollen and Dhaenens 2018), and everyday agency in social media use (Picone et al. 2019; Ytre-Arne and Das 2020). Through an analysis of users' considerations, we seek to identify more precisely how ambivalence towards social media may relate to actions of self-restriction, hence situating disconnection as part of a broader tendency of media ambivalence.

The analysis draws on two qualitative interview studies conducted in Norway: a broad study of media users mirroring the population and a smaller study of participants who have done a digital detox or disconnected from social media. A striking finding is that respondents in both datasets express similar and overlapping sentiments. In other words, both 'ordinary' users and people who have explicitly engaged in disconnection reveal a high degree of ambivalence; in both datasets we find passion for social media as well as scepticism, disgust, and desires to self-restrict. This finding supports the claim that use versus non-use should not be studied as dichotomous positions, but that various forms of connecting and disconnecting are part of users' repertoires (see also Baumer et al. 2013; Baumer et al. 2015; Brubaker, Ananny, and Crawford 2016; Brites and Ponte 2018; Dremljuga 2018; Light 2014;

Tiidenberg et al. 2017; Kuntsman and Miyake 2019). We contribute to this literature with a qualitative analysis of how users navigate between positive and negative evaluations of social media, and discuss factors pushing them towards disconnection under four themes: systemic and infrastructural aspects, media and technological aspects, public life aspects, and personal aspects concerning sociality and self-presentation.

LITERATURE REVIEW: SOCIAL MEDIA, DISCONNECTION, AND AMBIVALENCE

Both use and non-use of social media have been extensively researched, underlining some shared understandings even in studies with different starting points. Key contributions to analyzing social media use underline how these platforms are entwined in complex social relationships between users (boyd 2014; Baym 2015). This corresponds with understanding digital media use, across platforms and technologies, as part of mundane everyday practices and different social domains (Sandvik, Thorhauge, and Valtysson 2016; Lomborg and Mortensen 2017). As digital media platforms are increasingly perceived as intrusive (Mollen and Dhaenens 2018), while remaining integrated in users' lives, opting out is becoming increasingly difficult (as Feldman illustrates in this volume).

The growing field of digital detox and disconnection studies reflect how dissatisfaction with social media proliferates, and how it is not always easy to act on media scepticism (Syvertsen 2020; Brennen 2019). Several studies identify motives for leaving social media platforms, such as Baumer et al. (2013) who point to privacy, data misuse, productivity, banality, addiction, and external pressures as key motives for Facebook leavers. Similarly, Neves et al. (2015) discuss perceived usefulness, social practices (disclosure of personal data and gossip), and self-presentation and identity as the three characteristics dominant in young people's narratives of social media rejection. Analyses of corporate or media discourses identify similar points of contention (see also Jorge 2019; Syvertsen and Enli 2019; Karppi and Nieborg 2020).

A key insight from studies of both use and non-use of social media is the high degree of ambivalence among users. Users constantly navigate between conflicting positions and exhibit ambivalent sentiments towards social media characteristics. Baym, Wagman, and Persaud (2020, 5) note that people abstaining from Facebook described 'conflicted experiences of its value'; while being sceptical to its dominance, respondents also felt that it served the useful function of staying in touch, not least during a crisis. The ambiguity extends to whether disconnection is beneficial, as Schoenebeck (2014, 779) notes in her study of giving up Twitter for Lent: 'Many users hedge about taking breaks, wondering if they could do it, but not expressing intent to do so. Some users also discuss taking a break but say that they will not, or cannot.' With intrusive media, the gap between desires to disconnect and possibilities for doing so will widen. Although the actions available to users may not solve the problem they are trying to address, narratives of ambivalence are informative because they say something about the motives and actions available to users as they navigate a complex media environment.

Connected to ambivalence is the notion that disconnection and connection should be studied from a non-binary perspective. As Baumer et al. (2015, 1) note, 'One important finding emerging from this work is that, in practice, non-use rarely emerges as a clear-cut, binary distinction in opposition to use.' While the early tradition of studying digital gap and non-use separated users and non-users to a larger degree, the emerging trend in disconnection studies is that there are no clear-cut lines. As noted by Kuntsman and Miyake (2019, 902), 'Digital disengagement is not a single phenomenon but a complex continuum of practices, motivations and effects.'

Our study contributes to these insights in several ways: methodologically, we combine interviews with 'detoxers' and 'ordinary users' instead of treating these as separate groups. As a counterpoint to many studies that deal with abstention or disconnection from specific platforms, most notably Facebook (Baym, Wagman, and Persaud 2020; Portwood-Stacer 2013; Baumer et al. 2013), our study draws on evaluations of social media across platforms. As more systematic knowledge is emerging of why users are dissatisfied with digital media, and how they act upon such dissatisfactions, we provide a framework for understanding how various aspects of social media relate to different user reactions, and to varying motivations for disconnection. We ask which aspects of social media users perceive as positive and negative, creating ambiguous sentiments, and investigate how ambivalence pertaining to different aspects may prompt desires to disconnect.

METHODS: QUALITATIVE INTERVIEWS WITH MEDIA USERS

The analysis is based on two sets of qualitative interviews conducted in Norway: a suitable case as the Nordic countries are consistently placed in the top tier of indexes measuring 'digital readiness' (DESI 2020; CISCO 2019). Hence, social media membership, digital competences, and uses of digital tools are widespread among the population. As a 'media welfare state', Norway is furthermore part of a region with strong historical ideals that media should serve public enlightenment and social use (Syvertsen et al. 2014).

The chapter reveals how normative sentiments are used to evaluate social media between users with varying degrees of awareness or motivation for disconnection.

The first set of qualitative interviews is derived from a study of media repertoires and public connection with 50 respondents mirroring the population according to criteria such as gender, age, occupations, minority, and urban-rural residency (see, for instance, Ytre-Arne and Moe 2018). Respondents were asked to participate in two rounds of interviews and a media diary, producing extensive materials on a series of topics. Some segments of the first interview are particularly relevant: respondents were asked to give a day-in-the-life account of their use of any kind of media, with follow-up questions, and those who were Facebook users were asked to scroll through the Facebook feed while talking about what they saw and how they reacted to it. The interviews also included a question on what people considered as positive and negative aspects of social media, and an invitation to reflect upon their own use in light of these considerations.[1] We will particularly focus on this interview segment in our analysis for this chapter.

The second set of interviews is derived from a study of digital detox, involving ten participants who quit social media or limited their use for shorter or longer periods. Respondents were recruited through snowball sampling, personal networks, as well as blogs and media items describing digital detoxing. The sample includes 6 women and 4 men, 5 in their 20s, the rest in their 30s to 50s. Most are middle-class, with occupations within the fields of health, business, and academia, but the sample also includes students and respondents with less defined occupations. These respondents were asked to describe the circumstances leading up to taking a break from digital and social media, reactions and experiences during a digital detox, as well as questions pertaining to potential values threatened by intensified digital media use. In this chapter we focus on motives, experiences, and participants' views of positive and negative aspects of social media.

Participants were given pseudonyms, with minor details edited to protect their identity.[2] Our overall sample includes 60 participants, inclusive of the

---

[1] Except for the question on the Facebook feed, the interview guide preferred the term 'social media' and picked up on examples of use given by individual respondents, so that Instagram was discussed with some users, Twitter with others, as well as other platforms included. However, the predominance of Facebook use in the group was considerable, and this was the example most frequently mentioned.

[2] We further supply information on age, occupations, and family situation or other background information of particular relevance. We do not list education level, as this would in some cases be evident from occupations, and in other cases in no direct relation.

detox sample (10 respondents). The first set of interviews was conducted in 2016, while the second detox-focused set was conducted in 2018 and 2019.[3]

The interviews are analyzed with the following questions in mind: (1) Which dimensions of social media do users consider positive and negative, creating ambivalent reactions, and (2) How are these reactions related to desires to restrict use? We conducted a thematic analysis in which we first focused on outlining positive and negative reactions to social media, before formulating categories to assess which aspects of social media participants referred to when expressing ambivalent sentiments, and when formulating desires for disconnection. Our analysis is primarily focused on how respondents talk about social media, but we also pay attention to examples of acts or experiences of disconnection.

REACTIONS TO SOCIAL MEDIA: POSITIVE, NEGATIVE, AND PREDOMINANTLY AMBIVALENT

Our first research question concerns the dimensions of social media that users consider positive or negative, creating ambivalent reactions. Ambivalence refers to the simultaneous coexistence of contradictory sentiments, often experienced as straining to deal with (Ribak and Rosenthal 2015; Bucher 2020; Ytre-Arne et al. 2020). Social media ambivalence implies that participants praise some features of social media while criticizing others, but also that the same aspects are met with mixed reactions, leaving users in conflicted positions.

When users in the broad interview study talk about social media, conflicting sentiments are prevalent, even in short statements by the same person: 'I guess Facebook is great, there is just so much nonsense, and easy to be misunderstood and exposed to dangerous stuff,' says Gunnar, a janitor in his 60s. The aspects that are highlighted as positive and negative overlap between the two samples (see below), but among the respondents who have done a digital detox, the ambivalence is, if anything, more intense. Anna, a personal trainer and journalist in her 20s, 'loves social media', yet believes that your 'social antennas' deteriorate: 'You get worse at conversing and being present for those around you.' A strong love–hate relationship is typical for this group, as Anna describes how she missed social media when logged off:

---

[3] The datasets are produced in connection with a cluster of research projects: 'When digital media invades life' (Norwegian Council of Applied Media Research), MeCin and DIGITOX (both funded by the Norwegian Research Council). Thanks to collaborators Faltin Karlsen and Jørgen Bolling, and Hallvard Moe and the rest of the MeCIn project group. Translations from Norwegian were done by authors.

Yes, you kind of miss the feeling of being present in social media and having that interaction with people. . . . But at the same time, I felt that it was so necessary that it went just fine, it was delicious!

'It's addictive,' says Barbara, who is self-employed in her 40s. She deactivates her accounts periodically and does a digital detox every summer. However, she too describes ambivalence and restlessness; logging off is 'a mixture of liberation and abstinence'.

Ambivalence is rational given that social media is not 'one thing' and not easily positioned in participants' lives: they relate to various affordances and communicative cultures on different platforms, engage in cross-media user practices interwoven in their everyday routines, and experience advantages as well as discomforts associated with different forms of use. Users in both samples discuss their ambivalence in detail and situate their user practices between contradictory positions. Later we map how these positions relate to different characteristics of social media to identify the dimensions most likely to push towards disconnection.

DIMENSIONS OF SOCIAL MEDIA: SYSTEMIC, TECHNOLOGICAL, PUBLIC, AND PERSONAL ASPECTS

We conducted a thematic analysis to identify which aspects provoke different reactions (see table 4.1), providing an overview of positive and negative

Table 4.1 Positive and Negative Evaluations Differentiated According to Different Dimensions of Social Media

	Positive	Negative
Systemic and infrastructure aspects	Networking opportunities Efficiency in reaching people	Privacy infringement Abuse of user data *Stealing our privacy*
Media and technological aspects	Personalized content Engaging features	Information overload Addictive design *Time-thief*
Public life aspects	Democratization of information and debate Public enlightenment Making a contribution, gaining recognition	Polarized debates Misinformation Public life invades private life, context collapse *Stealing energy*
Personal and social aspects	Practicality, organizing everyday life Sociability, keeping in touch	Oversharing Peer pressure Fake sociality *Stealing our moments*

positions creating ambivalence across the two interview studies. In addition to differentiating between positions, we find that statements differ in how they refer to social media as pertaining to society or to the personal lifeworld of the respondent. We suggest four categories: *systemic or infrastructure* aspects concerning the power and positions of platforms in society; *technological or media-specific* aspects pertaining to affordances and design; *public life* aspects pertaining to the role of social media for informational and inspirational purposes; and *personal and social aspects* pertaining to personal networks, communication, and self-representation. These are not mutually exclusive categories, but signal that participants sometimes approach social media at a societal level, sometimes as citizens or consumers, and sometimes as private individuals with a more personal view.

The combination of positive and negative experiences creates ambivalence along all four dimensions. Systemic and infrastructure ambivalence implies that while users praise social media for facilitating simple networking and communication, they are also concerned about privacy, misinformation, and abuse of user data. Technological and media-specific ambivalence concerns how algorithmically curated newsfeeds help to serve up relevant information, yet lead to information overload and time-wasting, sometimes connected to smartphone ubiquity and addictive design. A range of public life ambivalences are also reported. While social media enables users to follow interests and play a part in public life, users found it difficult to manage boundaries between public and private personas. Although social media were seen to democratize public life, several expressed discomfort at harshness, toxicity, and polarization. Concerning personal and social ambivalences, people praised the practicality of social media for reaching out, organizing, and keeping in touch. However, on a personal level, prominent negative attitudes referred to oversharing, fakery, and whether social media promoted a positive form of sociality.

In both datasets we find concern for all these aspects, but the personal one is most distinctly expressed as particular to social media rather than a feature of the digital media landscape overall. In contrast, systemic critique of social media is to a greater degree blended with broader criticism of the power of algorithms or potential for or abuse of user data. As will be discussed further, a common notion across the four dimensions is that social media adds to life, but also detracts from it. A metaphor often used is that social media is a thief, stealing something valuable from its users: privacy (data), time, energy, and personal moments. Users deliberate how they can minimize the theft or get back what is stolen.

This takes us to the second part of our research question, as we ask how ambivalence and negative characteristics relate to desires to restrict use of social media, through different strategies of disconnection. By disconnection we here refer to a variety of practices seeking to control or restrict use, from drastic choices such as deleting social media accounts, to more widespread options such as managing affordances and notifications, sharing less or more carefully, or deliberately limiting social media use to practical or organizational purposes. We turn now to a more detailed discussion of the four dimensions and how they push towards disconnection.

SYSTEMIC ASPECTS: 'INFORMATION COULD GET INTO THE WRONG HANDS'

Concerns about systemic and infrastructure aspects, including privacy issues, emerge in several studies of disconnection (e.g. Brennen 2019; Baumer et al. 2013). It is not a dominant category in our material, but a group of users raise such issues. A common reaction is resignation, that there is little one can do. The idea that something is illegitimately taken runs through several narratives, whatever aspects are discussed. With regards to systemic aspects, the broad interview study reveals suspicion that powerful digital platforms invade your privacy, leaving you open to various forms of exploitation. Astrid, a secretary in her 40s, was concerned that information 'could get into the wrong hands, reach the wrong people'. Vidar, a bank manager in his late 50s, concluded that 'people are gullible'. In his view, there are 'people who are fooled into thinking they will get something for free, and then they are sucked into a network used to promote all kinds of things'. One respondent who is specifically concerned is Stig, a military officer in his 30s. Security is important in his work, he explains, but with a smartphone 'it is scary how much information you give away by location only'. He continues, 'They will know more about you than you do yourself. [. . .] My own use is affected by being sceptical. I try to manage the settings so that I will not be traced'. However, even with widespread criticism voiced in the material, few present their concerns as particular to social media but rather as problems pertaining to digital technology in general. Further, few indicate that these concerns push towards acts of social media disconnection beyond trying to manage affordances or stay vigilant.

In the sample of 10 users who have in fact deleted platforms or taken social media breaks, stronger concerns are expressed about systemic aspects, and four participants elaborate on their concerns. Among these, David, a writer in his 50s, details several explanations for giving up social media for long periods but sees systemic aspects as the most 'dangerous'. Specifically, he is concerned about 'how we are collectively influenced, how we give things away, how those who control the networks control us'. Julie, a scholar and musician in her 20s, cites data misuse as one reason for leaving Facebook and other services, although she loves the mechanisms that Facebook offers, for example that you can search for people'. However, she is 'very scared' about the fact that people do not take licence agreements seriously, but just sign:

> If you look beyond social media and to the technological gadgets . . . , the equipment has become much more intuitive. You do not have to fully understand why or how it functions, if it works. It removes some critical thinking from what you are doing and what you are taking part in. . . . A culture has developed [that says]: well, just do it because we must have it. A consensus that it's okay not to know what you are getting into. . . . Which people willingly participate in, because everyone else does it

The underlying notion in Julie's, as well as other respondents' concerns about systemic aspects, is not only that something is taken away or stolen, but also that we all are complicit in facilitating the theft.

TECHNOLOGICAL ASPECTS: 'IT STEALS SO MUCH TIME'

Research on social media addresses how users interact with affordances and manage technological and media-specific aspects of platforms (Mollen and Dhaenens 2018; Picone et al. 2019), also pointing towards the centrality of users' time as commodity (Wajcman 2015; Jorge 2019; Ytre-Arne et al. 2020). In their study of smartphone disconnection, Aranda and Baig (2018, 1, 3) describe two so-called negative behaviour cycles: 'an internal experience of habit and excessive use, and an externally reinforced cycle of social obligation', which both drive time use. They note that participants 'felt very guilty when they spent time on unintentional behaviours'. In our study as well, many users describe a mismatch: the content may be of limited interest, yet, it calls for attention through news streams and notifications. Hence, the possibilities for responding with likes and comments may be experienced as a social obligation.

The phrase 'It steals so much time' was expressed by John, a real estate developer in his 30s, but several use almost identical phrases: a constant flow of trivial information in social media, along with affordances that prolong use, causes frustration, causes resignation, and causes weariness. Respondents describe that valuable time is taken from them and spent on wasteful behaviour, and they are not rewarded accordingly. Magne, a sailor in his 40s, recounts that he was an early Facebook adopter but disliked the advertising and the flow of vacation pictures. He keeps an account, but describes how social obligations overwhelmed him:

> I do not really care on a personal level if someone I went to school with had a nice vacation. So, my use declined. . . . Following up on all the comments, liking stuff, responding. . . . It felt like too much work.

A common irritant is the accumulative effects of over-posting. 'I notice how I react to the things that others post. It's just too much,' says Tore, a police officer in his late 30s. 'People have to learn to restrict their use,' notes Åge, a grocery store owner in his late 40s, and continues, 'You get an incredible amount of information you don't care about. Not everyone is interested in watching the same baby eight times a day for four months.'

Time-waste and unproductive time is a cross-cutting theme also in the interviews with users who have taken a break or abstained from social media. Eva's work is dependent on social media, she is in her 30s and did her first detox in 2013, deleting Facebook for a year. Based on her experience with professionals working with social media she observes that 'if you do not take time for yourself you hit the wall. . . . You spend so many hours unconsciously on social media.' Heidi, a student in her 20s who logged off social media for 3 weeks to prepare for exams, also describes a negative behaviour cycle:

> We tend to get very impatient because everything happens so fast on the mobile. You get notifications and you also get answers back, so it is very easy to focus on that rather than on your homework for example. Concentration is also very disturbed because you often sit and multitask on your mobile.

The stories are rich in detail on how the media and technological features of the platforms are experienced. David, the writer, describes a 'digression machine':

> You go to the computer just to check an email for example, but as soon as you open it you are dragged into social media and suddenly you have been sitting there for ten minutes. Why did I go there? It's a kind of digression machine, you just lose it, it has such a strong logic of its own, or what to say, a pattern that draws you in.

These experiences appear to push users towards formulating desires for disconnection. However, their observations about how social media are cleverly designed to steal your time and keep you hooked also explains why disconnecting is difficult. Many users notice the problematic aspects but do not act on them, at least not permanently.

PUBLIC LIFE ASPECTS: 'IT IS TOO
AGGRESSIVE AND STEALS MY ENERGY'

The debate climate in social media has been an object of extensive analysis, contrasting optimistic potentials for democratization with investigations of problems such as hostility, aggression, and flaming (Jane 2015). Users have been found to avoid political discourse in social media due to perceptions of widespread aggression, that further contrasts with the personal and positive experiences they seek in social media (Kruse, Norris, and Flinchum 2017; Andersen 2020). The ability of social media to conflate audiences into a common space leads to context collapse and problems combining public and private personas (Marwick and boyd 2011).

Many respondents in our broad interview study expressed that they struggle with how to carve out a role in social media that is appropriate and energizing rather than reductive. For some, this was a question of managing public and private appearances. Ove, in his 30s and looking to move on from a temporary job, stopped sharing pictures and personal information: 'I tried to remove my online presence because I planned an application and did not want stupid things to hit me in the face.' Sissel, an adviser, also in her 30s, says that Facebook is 'a difficult medium': 'What to post, what not to post?' She works in the public sector and has 'to be concerned about my role'.

For others, the main concern was the tone of voice in social media debate. Sara, a priest in her mid-40s, describes political debates as 'aggressive' and 'stealing energy'. Again, the notion is that something is stolen or taken away; participating in public life leaves you open to unwelcome intrusions. John, the real estate developer with an immigrant background, also describes a diminishing experience:

> When Norwegians have opinions, they post on Facebook. And it is painful if friends say things like all immigrants should go away . . . 20 years ago we did not have Facebook, and you . . . did not hear those voices. They did not disturb you. But now, it affects us, because we are on Facebook all the way, unfortunately.

Another participant talked about how her situation as an unemployed single mother made her use of social media more difficult. Magnhild wanted to voice opinions and express herself creatively, but worried that society would look down on her, and she also feared personal reactions having to do with a recent break-up:

> You don't know who will read it . . . some things are hard to deal with . . . you don't have control. When I am done with this situation I will post more. [. . .]

I tried Twitter, but I did not have enough time, and that is really for a certain kind of people. People in the media, artists and freelancers who are always cutting edge, I am not there at all. I want to use Instagram more for photos when I get a better phone. And I considered starting a blog, but you know there is that threshold.

Among the 10 respondents who took breaks from social media, half described how they navigate social media platforms successfully for inspirational and educational purposes. However, even if you are successful in running a blog or popular account, the boundary-keeping continues to cause problems. Participating in public life as an expert or educator is one thing, but there was a felt obligation to share more private information to retain popularity. Eva detailed how she deleted Facebook because her public role became invasive. Like Sara (mentioned earlier), she also spoke of an energy drain:

I worked a lot with social media and in the end, it felt like I had people inside my living room. I felt like someone was watching me all the time. It was an uncomfortable feeling. . . . It felt like something was draining my energy. Yuck!

Ian, a health professional in his 30s, described similar experiences. He chose to use social media for educational purposes but was ambivalent about the toll on his private life. He made a choice before the summer of 2018 to log off during holidays, and his family closely monitors and restricts their screen time.

The experiences of aggressive debates and spillover from a public persona into private spaces are described by users as 'energy-drains'. For some, these experiences were mixed with broader concern for how aspects of social media impact negatively on our culture, reducing the possibilities for enlightened public debate. Users described how they restrain their participation, withdrawing from certain platforms or taking breaks to restore their energy. Active participation in public debates, as well as taking the role of expert or inspirational figure on social media, require systematic work to balance the energizing and energy-draining effects.

PERSONAL AND SOCIAL ASPECTS: 'OUR MOMENTS ARE STOLEN'

As respondents felt that social media stole their time and energy, they were concerned about not contributing to the problem by stealing from others. Many felt self-conscious about contributing to overflowing social media with trivial information, leading to questions about what forms of sharing and engagement were acceptable forms of self-representation. A dominant theme in both sets of interviews is that social media present a fake sociality, leading to unhealthy ideals of perfection and peer pressure. It is commonplace to link this to a society where we are eager to display our success. Erik, a taxi driver pushing 40, said:

> People are so concerned with presenting themselves. What they do every day, where they go on holiday . . . right down to what they eat for dinner . . . sharing their lives. I am not all that interested in what they ate last weekend, and pictures from the beach or birthday parties.

Sissel agreed that 'everything is so perfect on Facebook. We post the good side of ourselves.' It is not good if you are 'easily influenced', as she can be, yet, it is worse 'for young people to deal with the pressure of being success-ful'. She and others warned that 'you need to be aware that it is superficial'. 'Facebook is for watching,' echoed Stig, the military officer: 'Keeping track of what others are doing, looking at their happy lives and thinking "there is no way they are that happy."'

As participants turned a critical eye towards themselves, they were left with the difficult question of what it is acceptable to post. Since these deci-sions reflect upon your personal judgement and on how you appear to others, questions of identity management become central (Portwood-Stacer 2013). Kari, who is retired, is one of several participants who expressed ambivalence between following norms and being part of the problem: 'We use Facebook to post vacation photos and nice stuff we do, and I guess you could ask if we contribute to a false positive image. We do. We know.' In both samples, food and vacation pictures recur as the kind of trivial content users get tired of and criticize as a fake form of sociality. Yet, this is the type of content that fills social media accounts, and respondents also admitted that it feels safer than opinions and public life expressions, as discussed earlier.

Another strategy for handling such dilemmas was to consider social media as a mere practical utility, for instance, by not posting at all or significantly limit contacts, thereby reducing expressions of self-representation. Jens, a teacher in his 60s, says:

> I have two friends on Facebook. I don't see the need to expose myself all that much . . . . I think that some of the stuff people post is just really stupid . . . talk-ing about what they eat and showing off a birthday cake, come on . . . all those nice trips, it is just so polished.

Loss of authenticity is a central topic in media and self-help discourses on social media (Syvertsen and Enli 2020). This is also one of the most central themes in this material. Social media helps you connect with people, but it also detracts from sociality, something is taken away or stolen in the process. Participants with children contrasted their own upbringings with that of their kids, to identify what has been lost. For example, this new father states:

> It is so easy to connect. When I was a kid, we had house phones, you know. You had to call that number, and if no one answered you had to bike over and check if someone was there. Now kids meet online more than in real life. [. . .] I think that is bad, you don't get the same socialization. Colleagues tell me their kids are stuck on their iPads playing games. It is a problem. You never learn to be bored. (Petter, 27, carpenter)

In addition to expressing annoyance at the behaviour of others, several described how these experiences led them to reconsider their own user practices in terms of what to post, how to respond, or using social media at all. For some, this led to more distinct acts of disconnection:

> I gave up. It wasn't for me. I can't brag about what I had for dinner, taking pictures of what I did all day. And I don't need to know that stuff. Maybe if I am looking for something specific, saying hello to a friend, but then I can pick up the phone. I just thought . . . after six months or so . . . I can't do this, what's the point? I liked it at first but then I realized it was not my thing. (Ali, unemployed)

> When everyone posts their every thought, you notice that people think about a lot of stuff that is not really all that interesting. It takes time before you can translate that into understanding that what you are thinking is not really interesting to other people. And then you limit yourself. You want to be more special if you share something, it must go beyond what you had for breakfast. (Stine, call centre employee)

Here, we see one respondent who deleted Facebook, and one who realized she was 'part of the problem' and limited her sharing accordingly. She describes how it takes time to get a handle on the problem and adjust use, instituting a new norm that is also difficult to follow: to only post what is special.

Among the 10 respondents who have taken breaks or done a digital detox, 8 were concerned with fake sociality and peer pressure. Anna said the problem with social media is that 'you get more hung up on the facade you have on social media than the person you actually are and your personal qualities'. She found it 'very scary' that it is 'on our surface that we get likes and comments and recognition'. In her 20s, Cathrine has taken several long breaks since 2014 and said that 'self-worth becomes difficult to define because it is constantly measured, and you measure yourself'. One reason why Heidi, a student, took a break was that 'I noticed that I started to care about things that I did not really want to care about: [how many] followers, how many likes you get in photos and such'. Heidi also discussed negative self-image: 'How to value yourself when you sit and look at models who pose for pictures and get millions of likes?' Although social media are useful for artists, David, the writer, reflected, 'The bottom line is that you become more self-absorbed.'

People felt pressured to engage in fake sociality, as Julie, the young scholar, was reluctant to 'take part in the social charade' of Facebook. In social media 'you put on a mask', she said, 'despite the fact that you show your full name. When I was anonymous online in the old days, I dared much more to show who I actually was. That's a vulnerable thing.' Ian was concerned about how social media invades his private life, and particularly detested interruptions to share personal moments as they are happening:

> I'm not on Snapchat myself but it irritates me endlessly, I think without a doubt that it is the worst social medium. . . . It is an enormous moment-thief, our moments are stolen by Snapchat and shared with everyone else and then you are no longer in them yourself.

Here, the aforementioned idea of stolen time is combined with loss of owner-ship of one's own experiences, and control of the kind of person one wants to be. Users may discontinue certain practices because they realize that they themselves can be seen as thieves—stealing others' time and attention.

CONCLUSION

In this chapter we discussed aspects of social media that may lead users to disconnect, joining insights from literature on social media ambivalence with analysis of two interview studies. We outlined a framework of understand-ing social media in terms of systemic, media-specific, public, and personal aspects, and found critique and ambivalence prevalent to all of these: partici-pants criticized social media and the underlying infrastructure for invading their privacy, described how design features lead to time-waste and overload, and accounted for emotional discomfort at harsh polarized discourse or ideal-ized representations of complex realities. Particularly, many found social and personal aspects difficult, leading to balancing acts and inhibitions.

Ambiguous sentiments make social media use more difficult, by raising conflicting emotions in seemingly small decisions ('Should I post this pic-ture?') as well as overall behaviours ('Should I use Facebook?'). One way of dealing with ambivalence is to 'stick with the trouble' (Bucher 2020), which, in this case, would be to continue the difficult navigation of social media use even when experiencing discomfort or disregard for aspects of the various platforms. Another alternative would be to seek ways of avoiding the difficult position through forms of disconnection.

A key finding of our analysis is that social media both adds to and detracts from life. In all the four aspects there is the notion among many that something is stolen or taken away: theft of privacy, time, energy, and personal moments. Users constitute themselves as victims but also as perpetrators, stealing time and energy from others. Both experiences may lead to the discontinuation of certain practices. Importantly, people do not feel robbed in every way or at all times, but threats of losing something valuable loom over otherwise pleasurable activities. Uncertainty about what could happen points to how users of digital media are facing intangible communicative conditions where it is difficult to predict outcomes, placing additional strain on their agency (Ytre-Arne and Das 2020).

In the chapter we discussed how limiting social media use may be seen as a way to retrieve what is lost. Given the differentiated aspects of social media critique that are voiced, acts of limiting use or disconnecting do not necessarily respond to every aspect of the perceived problem, or to the aspects felt most strongly by the individual. Retrieving what is lost is therefore difficult, even when acting upon negative social media experiences through disconnection. In sum, users are ambivalent not just to social media, but also to the strategies and solutions they chose to handle social media problems.

REFERENCES

Andersen, Ida. 2020. "Instead of the deliberative debate. How the principle of expression plays out in the Facebook discussion." PhD thesis, University of Bergen.

Aranda, Julie and Safia Baig. 2018. "Toward 'JOMO': The joy of missing out and the freedom of disconnecting." *MobileHCI '18: Proceedings of the 20th International Conference on Human-Computer Interaction with Mobile Devices and Services*, pp. 1–8. doi:10.1145/3229434.3229468.

Baumer, Eric. P. S., Phil Adams, Vera D. Khovanskaya, Tony C. Liao, Madeline E. Smith, Victoria Schwanda Sosik, and Kaiton Williams. 2013. "Limiting, leaving, and (re)lapsing: An exploration of facebook non-use practices and experiences." *Proceedings of the SIGCHI Conference on Human Factors in Computing Systems*, Paris, France.

Baumer, Eric. P. S., Shion Guha, Emily Quan, David Mimno, and Geri K. Gay. 2015. "Missing photos, suffering withdrawal, or finding freedom? How experiences of social media non-use influence the likelihood of reversion." *Social Media + Society* 1 (2): 1–14. doi:10.1177/2056305115614851.

Baym, Nancy K., Kelly B. Wagman, and Christopher J. Persaud. 2020. "Mindfully scrolling: Rethinking Facebook after time deactivated." *Social Media + Society* 6 (2): 1–10. doi:10.1177/2056305120919105.

Brennen, Bonnie. 2019. *Opting Out of Digital Media*. London: Routledge.

Brites, Maria José, and Cristina Ponte. 2018. "Reasons and circumstances that lead to the non-use of media by young people and their families." *Comunicação e Sociedade* 34: 411–429. doi:10.17231/comsoc.34(2018).2956.

Brown, Lorna, and Daria J. Kuss. 2020. "Fear of missing out, mental wellbeing, and social connectedness: A seven-day social media abstinence trial." *International Journal of Environmental Research and Public Health* 17(12): doi:10.3390/ijerph17124566.

Brubaker, Jed R., Mike Ananny, and Kate Crawford. 2016. "Departing glances: A sociotechnical account of 'leaving' Grindr." *New Media & Society* 18 (3): 373–390. doi:10.1177/1461444814542311.

Bucher, Taina. 2019. "Bad guys and bag ladies: On the politics of polemics and the promise of ambivalence." *Social Media + Society* (July–September) 1–4. doi:10.1177/2056305119856705.

CISCO. 2019. "Digital Readiness Index". Accessed January 17, 2021. https://www.cisco.com/c/m/en_us/about/corporate-social-responsibility/research-resources/digital-readiness-index.html#/.

DESI. 2020. Digital Economy and Society Index 2020. European Commission. https://ec.europa.eu/newsroom/dae/document.cfm?doc_id=67086.

Dremljuga, Ramona-Riin. 2018. "The process and affordances of platform-specific social media disconnection'. *Studies of Transition States and Societies* 10 (2): 82–96. http://publications.tlu.ee/index.php/stss/article/view/674.

Hesselberth, Pepita. 2018. "Discourses on disconnectivity and the right to disconnect." *New Media and Society* 20 (5): 1994–2010. doi:10.1177/1461444817711449.

Jane, Emma A. 2015. "Flaming? What flaming? The pitfalls and potentials of researching online hostility." *Ethics and Information Technology* 17: 65–87. doi:10.1007/s10676-015-9362-0.

Jorge, Ana. 2019. "Social media interrupted: Users recounting temporary disconnection on Instagram." *Social Media + Society* 5 (4). doi:10.1177/2056305119881691.

Karppi, Tero, and David B. Nieborg. 2020. "Facebook confessions: Corporate abdication and Silicon Valley dystopianism." *New Media & Society*. doi:10.1177/1461444820933549.

Kruse, Lisa M., Dawn R. Norris, and Jonathan R. Flinchum. 2018. "Social media as a public sphere? Politics on social media." *The Sociological Quarterly* 59 (1): 62–84. doi:10.1080/00380253.2017.1383143.

Kuntsman, Adi, and Esperanza Miyake. 2019. "The paradox and continuum of digital disengagement: Denaturalising digital sociality and technological connectivity." *Media, Culture and Society* 41 (6): 901–913. doi:10.1177/0163443719853732.

Light, Ben. 2014. *Disconnecting with Social Networking Sites*. Basingstoke: Palgrave.

Lomborg, Stina, and Mette Mortensen. 2017. "Users across media: An introduction." *Convergence* 23 (4): 343–351. doi:10.1177/1354856517700555.

Marwick, Alice E., and danah boyd. 2011. "'I tweet honestly, I tweet passionately': Twitter users, context collapse, and the imagined audience." *New Media & Society* 13(1): 114–133. doi:10.1177/1461444810365313.

Mollen, Anne, and Frederik Dhaenens. 2018. "Audiences' coping practices with intrusive interfaces: Researching audiences in algorithmic, datafied, platform societies." In *The Future of Audiences: A Foresight Analysis of Interfaces and Engagement*, edited by Ranjana Das and Brita Ytre-Arne, pp. 43–60. London: Palgrave.

Neves, Barbara Barbosa, João Monteiro de Matos, Rita Rente, and Sara Lopes Martins. 2015. "The 'non-aligned': Young people's narratives of rejection of social networking sites." *YOUNG* 23 (2): 116–135. doi:10.1177/1103308815569393.

Picone, Ike, Jelena Kleut, Tereza Pavlíčková, Bojana Romic, Jannie Møller Hartley, and Sander De Ridder. 2019. "Small acts of engagement: Reconnecting productive audience practices with everyday agency." *New Media & Society* 21 (9): 2010–2028. doi:10.1177/1461444819837569.

Portwood-Stacer, Laura. 2013. "Media refusal and conspicuous non-consumption: The performative and political dimensions of Facebook abstention." *New Media & Society* 15 (7): 1041–1057. doi:10.1177/1461444812465139.

Ribak, Rivka, and Michele Rosenthal. 2015. "Smartphone resistance as media ambivalence." *First Monday* 29 (11). doi:10.5210/fm.v20i11.6307.

Sandvik, Kjetil, Anne Mette Thorhauge, and Bjarki Valtysson. 2016. *The Media and the Mundane: Communication Across Media in Everyday Life*. Gothenburg: Nordicom.

Schoenebeck, Sarita Yardi. 2014. "Giving up Twitter for Lent: how and why we take breaks from social media." *CHI'14 Proceedings of the SIGCHI Conference on Human Factors in Computing Systems*, pp. 773–782. doi:10.1145/2556288.2556983.

Syvertsen, Trine. 2017. *Media Resistance: Protest, Dislike, Abstention*. Cham: Palgrave.

———. 2020. *Digital Detox: The Politics of Disconnecting*. London: Emerald.

Syvertsen, Trine, and Gunn Enli. 2020. "Digital detox: Media resistance and the promise of authenticity." *Convergence* 26 (5–6): 1269–1283. doi:10.1177/1354856519847325.

Syvertsen, Trine, Gunn Enli, Ole J. Mjøs, and Hallvard Moe. 2014. *The Media Welfare State. Nordic Media in the Digital Era*. Michigan: University of Michigan Press.

Tiidenberg, Katrin, Annette Markham, Gabriel Pereira, Mads Rehder, Ramona Dremljuga, Jannek K. Sommer, and Meghan Dougherty. 2017. "'I'm an addict' and other sensemaking devices: A discourse analysis of self-reflections on lived experience of social media." *Proceedings of the 8th International Conference on Social Media and Society*, Toronto, ON, Canada. doi:10.1145/3097286.3097307.

Ytre-Arne, Brita, and Hallvard Moe. 2018. "Approximately informed, occasionally monitorial? Reconsidering normative citizen ideals." *The International Journal of Press/Politics* 23 (2): 227–246. doi:10.1177/1940161218771903.

Ytre-Arne, Brita, and Ranjana Das. 2020. "Audiences' communicative agency in a datafied age: Interpretative, relational and increasingly prospective". *Communication Theory*. doi:10.1093/ct/qtaa018.

Ytre-Arne, Brita, Trine Syvertsen, Hallvard Moe, and Faltin Karlsen. 2020. "Temporal ambivalences in smartphone use: Conflicting flows, conflicting responsibilities." *New Media & Society* 22 (9): 1715–1732. doi:10.1177/1461444820913561.

Chapter 5

Quitting Digital Culture

Rethinking Agency in a Beyond-Choice Ontology

Zeena Feldman

Life in the UK has reached 'peak digital'[1]. Social media and smartphones are everywhere. In 2019, half of the UK's 10-year-olds owned a smartphone and by age 15, the figure skyrockets to 94% (Ofcom 2020a, 7). On average, Brits checks their smartphones every 12 minutes (Ofcom 2018, 59). Meanwhile, 87% of the UK population is online, and of those, 98% use social media (Ofcom 2020b, 7, 16).[2] And in the largely housebound reality of life post-Covid-19 we are spending more time online than ever, averaging just over four hours a day (ibid., 2).

In short, most of us are online, have a smartphone, and use social media. Such pervasive connectivity may have its benefits but it also has no shortage of critics. Sherry Turkle (2015), for example, warns that our (over)reliance on digital devices reduces our capacity for stillness and contemplation. She writes that 'we often find ourselves bored because we have become accustomed to a constant feed of connection, information, and entertainment. We are forever elsewhere' (ibid., 4). But beyond pure condemnation (or celebration), how can we make sense of the mediated, always-on lives many of us increasingly lead? And how can we understand the varied practices of digital *disconnection* that operate within this technosocial moment of hyperconnectivity, what Leisa Reichelt (2007) calls 'ambient intimacy'?

Digital connection matters. But so does disconnection. This chapter explores how these modalities of (dis)engagement act as existential foils of each other and argues that they must be analyzed relationally rather than as

---

[1] The author is immensely grateful to Josephine West and Rosa Appignanesi for their help sourcing literature for this project.
[2] The 13% of UK's internet 'non-users' are primarily adults aged 75+ (Ofcom 2020c, 5).

separate and oppositional. For instance, the entanglement of connection and disconnection helps explain why—just as online connectivity reaches new heights—we see a parallel rise in digital overload discourses and disconnection-themed products (Prasad and Quinones 2020; Syvertsen 2020; Gregg 2018; Okeke et al. 2018). My goal in this chapter, then, is to analyze these phenomena together and in relation in order to more fully understand the paradoxes and ambivalences of today's connectivity culture. Empirically, I do this by examining findings from my Quitting Social Media (QSM) project: a three-year, mixed-methods exploration of how people in the UK and further afield navigated this historical moment of digital culture defined via social media and smartphone hegemony.

What emerges is a practically and affectively complex portrait of life with the digital, which I argue necessitates a radical rethinking of 'choice' and 'agency'. Tech consumers and analysts routinely claim that if users are dissatisfied with a particular digital service, they can simply stop using it. In other words, the solution is to go cold turkey or, in a throwback to the failed war on drugs, to 'just say no'. But here, I will suggest that analyzing user experiences, practices, and motivations through the lens of individual agency misses the point precisely because that approach profoundly misunderstands how choice operates in contemporary digital culture. The fact is data monopolies structure today's digital communications landscape. Consider, for instance, that Facebook is the world's most populated country (Clement 2020) and that Facebook owns both Instagram and WhatsApp (Shead 2019). This makes clear that opting out is not a realistic option for many of us. It also foregrounds the need to consider how user agency can be reimagined and rehabilitated in this context—dubbed here as the *beyond-choice ontology*—where it is increasingly seen as both necessary and impossible to disconnect.

This chapter attends to these tasks and arguments in four parts. First, I assess the current discourse around the negative effects of hyperconnectivity. I show how these concerns feed into a growing 'digital detox' service industry, and suggest that the demonization of tech valorizes and commodifies individual choice and responsibility. Second, I introduce the QSM project and its methodology. In a third section, I synthesize key themes that emerged from the project, foregrounding intersections between digital connection and disconnection practices. The chapter's final section considers these findings in relation to economist Albert Hirschman's (1970) seminal framework for understanding organizational failure and success. Hirschman's work helps make sense of the ways user participation and resistance operate alongside one another. Through his consumer power strategies of 'voice' and 'exit', I consider how we might recover the viability of user agency in a technosocial context where permanent disconnection proves increasingly untenable.

MORALIZING HYPERCONNECTIVITY

Globally, over half the world's population has a smartphone, and the average internet user has eight social media accounts (Statista 2020a; Global Web Index 2020, 15). What does this abundance tell us? For one, that people find these technologies useful. Whether for work, entertainment, conviviality, or convenience, social media and smartphones have broad application and broad appeal. As such, these technologies have increasingly become part of the fabric of contemporary life. For all their purported utilities and benefits, however, academic analysts and journalists increasingly emphasize the negative effects of technosocial connectivity. Non-profit organizations like Common Sense Media (2020), for example, worry about the impact media technology has on children's 'physical, emotional, social, and intellectual development'. Likewise, neuroscientist Susan Greenfield (2015) warns about the long-term cognitive harms that come with excessive screen time. As the 'media effects' panic around social media and smartphones gains currency (Leick 2018; Rao and Lingam 2021), it is important to understand what exactly is being claimed and to what end. This is important because moral panics themselves, as Kirsten Drotner (1999, 618) notes, tell us very little about media technologies themselves; they instead offer insight into broader societal conditions and anxieties.

As indicated earlier, one of these societal conditions is pervasive connectivity through smartphones and social media apps. The ubiquity and apparent inescapability of digital connection helps to explain the prominent role *addiction* narratives and metaphors play in scholarship critical of contemporary connectivity. Addiction is a central concern in studies of social media use in particular (e.g. Ponnusamy et al. 2020; D'Arienzo, Boursier, and Griffiths 2019; Andreassen, Pallesen, and Griffiths 2016; Griffiths, Kuss, and Demetrovics 2014). Social media addiction, per Hawi and Samaha (2017a, 577), 'is the compulsive use of social media sites that manifests itself in behavioral addiction symptoms'—symptoms consisting of 'salience, tolerance, conflict, withdrawal, relapse, and mood modification' (Griffiths in Hawi and Samaha 2017a, 577). Although elsewhere Griffiths (2010) makes clear that excessive use of social media is not synonymous with addiction, studies on the harmful effects of social media use abound (and the distinction between overuse and addiction rarely features).

Hawi and Samaha (2017a, 582), for instance, find a negative correlation between the amount of time university students spend on social media and their self-esteem. In other words, 'people with lower self-esteem tend to depend on social media more. Furthermore, students who use social media with the intention of enhancing their self-image are at risk of not only lowering their self-esteem but also their satisfaction with life' (ibid., 582–83).

Many other studies of social media use have reached similar conclusions (e.g. Blackwell et al. 2017; Berthon, Pitt, and Campbell 2019). So too have studies of smartphone use and users. Haug et al. (2015), for example, document smartphone addiction among young people in Switzerland, and found that those with high levels of stress and low levels of physical activity were more likely to exhibit addictive behaviors around smartphones. Meanwhile, in a survey of university students in mainland China, Bian and Leung (2015) found that participants reporting high levels of shyness and loneliness were those most likely to be addicted to their smartphones.

Such studies aim at identifying predictors of addiction. But that approach assumes the existence of device or platform addiction *a priori* of attempts to situate user behaviors within participants' life contexts. In the dogged search for signs of addiction, it can be easy to forget that our communication technologies can be meaningful to us in many perfectly healthy ways, too. To that end, I find it far more instructive, following Panova and Carbonell (2018), to consider social media and smartphones as 'problematic technologies' which should 'be studied in [their] sociocultural context with an increased focus on [their] compensatory functions, motivations, and gratifications' (252). This operative shift from diagnosing to problematizing is important. It gets us away from pathologizing the technosocial encounter, and moves us instead towards a more complex, polyvalent appreciation of the ways people integrate and deploy social media platforms and smartphones in their lives. Problematizing is also distinct from demonizing or fearmongering, because it allows space for pleasure. To focus strictly on the ills of the technosocial encounter is to ignore the reality that smartphones and social media can (and do) deliver joy. That these technologies might also facilitate cyberbullying (Qudah et al. 2019; Whittaker and Kowalski 2015) and stalking (Woodlock 2017), perpetuate racism (Gantt Shafer 2017; Mason 2016) and other criminality (Jaishankar 2011), have negative effects on our mental health (Berryman, Ferguson, and Negy 2018) and our relationships (Hawi and Samaha 2017b), contribute to the commodification of sociality (Mejias 2013), and reduce our capacity for boredom and creativity (Turkle 2015) certainly matters. But analytically, there is much more to be gained by approaching social media and smartphones as ambivalent (Ribak and Rosenthal 2015; Ytre-Arne et al. 2020). Life is not black and white; neither are the technologies we use while living it (see Ytre-Arne and Syvertsen this volume).

Villainizing social media and smartphones has another consequence. In foregrounding the 'bad', scholars and journalists implicitly (and at times, explicitly) advocate cutting the cord and embracing tech-celibacy (Lanier 2018; Lovink 2016; Harris 2015; Brennen 2019). This helps explain the recent, formidable growth of the digital detox sector. From self-help books to device-free retreats to internet-blocking software to screen time quantification apps (Henry 2017), the marketplace is rife with products and services aimed at helping hyperconnected individuals unplug. With the increasingly hegemonic perception of social media and smartphones as harmful, the not-so-subtle sociocultural subtext seems to be that the only sensible solution is to quit, to disconnect. Overwhelmed? Just log out. Just say no. The anti-tech discourse and the digital detox marketplace both valorize the individual choice to quit. True to our neoliberal times, disconnection becomes an individualized project and responsibility. And with the prevalence of disconnection products, it becomes a commodified project as well. And while opting out might sound appealing, for most of us, it simply is not viable. Indeed, fetishizing individual choice and agency ignores the entrenched ubiquity of contemporary digital technologies.

To that end, the remainder of this chapter aims to show how and why analysis needs to look 'beyond choice' if we wish to fully problematize digital connectivity. Enter my QSM project. This project focused on the experiences of smartphone and social media users who had considered or tried disconnecting, in order to understand how they negotiated tensions between the variable pains, pleasures, and ambivalences of life online. What can their practices of (dis)connection tell us about how we might 'better' live with the affective peaks and troughs of connectivity?

ABOUT THE QSM PROJECT

The QSM project sought to understand people's motivations for participating in the digital social, *and* their decisions to disengage. It also sought to analyze those motivations in relation to the everyday practices, rhythms, and routines that people developed around their connected devices. More tellingly, this project was a structured way for me to unpack my own sense of feeling overburdened by social media and the smartphone—overwhelmed by their mechanisms, their logics, their ubiquity. So I wanted to talk to people who had either tried quitting a social platform, tried giving up their smartphone, or had at least considered doing so. I wanted, ultimately, to hear about personal experiences of digital culture overload.

To get at those experiences, I focused on four areas of inquiry. First, I wanted to know what drove users to withdraw from social media platforms and smartphones. Was there a single breaking point, or was tech disillusionment a more gradual phenomenon? Second, I wanted to understand the consequences of 'quitting' for lapsed users. For instance, how did technological refusal map onto participants' social or economic pursuits? Did participative stoppages impact individuals' sense of connectedness and well-being? Third, I was interested in the temporal dynamics of disconnection. Did those who quit quit for good? And finally, I was interested in the 'who' of disconnection. What sort of person decides to opt out of digital culture?

As I considered a methodological way into these concerns, it became clear that it was impossible to talk about disconnection without also evoking connectivity. Disconnection—as theory and practice—was possible only through its 'constitutive outside' (Derrida 1997). As such, I came to regard the QSM project as an examination of the discursive and material landscape of digital (dis)connection. It is precisely through the dialectic of connectivity that the affective registers of logging on and logging off emerge, and it is by considering those registers *in relation* that insight can be gained into how users negotiate tensions between the pains and pleasures of participation.

Empirically, the QSM project deployed a mixed-methods approach consisting of 491 responses to an online survey, 12 semi-structured interviews, and 169 'audience statements' from a participatory art installation. This combination of research instruments leveraged the qualitative and quantitative strengths of each tool, and offset their corresponding deficits (Poth 2018).

The online survey, built with Google Forms, asked open- and closed-ended questions. In addition to respondent demographics, these questions captured functional and affective details of social media and smartphone engagements, including identifying platforms and device brands used, app installation and deletion behaviors, positive and negative user experiences, experiences of disconnection, and respondents' broader media consumption habits. The survey also included an optional text field inviting participants to reflect further on their experiences using and/or quitting social media. This optional question was taken up by over 27% of participants.

Most survey responses were received between June and December 2017. UK residents represented 53% of respondents, although in total, residents of 34 countries across 5 continents took part. Those aged 20 to 39 submitted 60% of all surveys. Interestingly, over 68% of respondents identified as female, and only 28% as male. The remainder selected the 'prefer not to say' option. Although the binaried framing of this question is problematic, it is nonetheless striking that female-identifying respondents were so overrepresented in the survey findings. Alongside the survey, I conducted in-depth, semi-structured interviews with five women and seven men. These were done face to face in London between July 2017 and December 2019, and post-Covid-19 in November and December 2020, over Skype with participants in New York and San Francisco. The interviews averaged 37 minutes in length.

My participant recruitment strategy, via academic listservs and a biweekly 'seeking research volunteers' email distributed by my university, privileged those in higher education. To address the intersectional exclusions and biases (Reay et al. 2005) embedded in this sample, I introduced a public artmaking component to this project and set up a participatory art installation titled

'Pleasures and Pressures of Smartphones' at the Science Gallery London's HOOKED exhibition. This gallery and its exhibitions are free to access, and the two evenings in October and November 2018 when I was in residence, programming consisted of 'performances and workshops shaped by [the] Gallery's Young Leaders—15–25 year olds who live, work or study at King's or in the neighbouring boroughs of Southwark and Lambeth' (Science Gallery London 2019). These boroughs are marked by substantial ethnic and economic diversity (ONS 2019; Domman 2019). The installation presented gallery attendees with two prompts—'The worst thing about having a smartphone is' and 'The best thing about having a smartphone is'—and asked them to write their responses on two smartphone-shaped cards. Using an instant-print camera, I then photographed each respondent holding their smartphone and asked them to attach that photograph and their two response cards to the installation's hardware: two metal poles connected by rows of wires.

The combined dataset of survey responses, interview transcripts, and audience statements revealed a number of themes, which I take up below. Together, these themes cohere around Melvin Kranzberg's (1986) observation that 'technology is neither good nor bad; nor is it neutral'. Indeed, my dataset shows that smartphones and social media platforms can inhabit all of these moral registers at once.

THEMES OF (DIS)CONNECTION

The QSM project offers insight into how our digital habits intersect with the conditions of everyday life. As social media and smartphones become the tools by which we engage in projects of meaning-making, it is crucial to ascertain what this pervasive connectivity and digital overload does to our ways of knowing and doing. To that end, three main themes emerged from the QSM dataset. First, participants expressed a sophisticated ambivalence about their digital practices. Second, participants routinely questioned the availability of choice vis-à-vis those practices. Third, digital connection and disconnection were habitually regarded as linked rather than oppositional. I discuss each theme in turn in the following sections.

USER AMBIVALENCE

Studies focused on the harms of digital connectivity routinely, if inadvertently, cast social media and smartphone users as dupes—victims of a techno-industrial complex hell-bent on colonizing life's every crevice (Couldry and Mejias 2019). As noted earlier, this demonization evacuates the possibility of pleasure from the technosocial encounter. It also implies tech users are unaware of the potential ills of logging on. QSM participants powerfully rejected these characterizations.

The project dataset gestured instead to a sophisticated ambivalence that accompanied social media and smartphone use. Participants were fully cognizant of the paradoxes and dilemmas occasioned by their connectivity practices. They discussed positive experiences and affordances alongside negative ones. Nearly all survey respondents (96%) had at some time enjoyed a positive experience on social media but most (74%) also had a negative experience. Yet respondents' narrative accounts revealed their usage was not a zero-sum game. They consistently sought to hold the good with the bad, without discounting the tension this entailed. Pam,[3] for example, explained the trade-offs her Facebook usage involved:

> The amount and nature of distressingly, depressing and negative 'news' [on Facebook] had only depressed me and taking a break from Facebook was part of a strategy to avoid negative influences. [. . .] However, I have drifted back to Facebook because of missing contact and updates with friends.

Additional data points that clearly captured users' nuanced ambivalence towards connectivity have to do with how survey respondents managed social media apps on their phones. Of the 96% (n = 464) of respondents with smartphones, 95% had installed a social media app onto their phone but an almost equivalent number (91%) said they had also considered quitting social media. Indeed, 85% of respondents had at some point deleted a social media app from their smartphone, with 60% of them later reinstalling the deleted app. Here, we see the paradoxes and ambivalences of connectivity on full display. These were also visible in the gallery audience statements. For all the diverse views expressed in the response cards, there was also a fascinating micro-trend: participants writing the same answer on their 'the best thing' and 'the worst thing about having a smartphone' cards. For instance, one participant wrote 'Always being reachable' in response to both prompts. Another wrote 'I am never alone' on each card. This is significant precisely because it challenges normative claims about the deluded or duped user. Indeed, my participants were hyperaware of the contradictions occasioned by their connectivity, and attendant to the ambivalences their usage entailed.

Participants routinely highlighted the utilities and pleasures of their digital entanglements, alongside unwanted features. As one survey respondent explained, 'I would like to quit for good because I find Facebook intrusive

---

[3] Pseudonyms are used for all named participants.

and somewhat Orwellian, but it is useful for staying in touch with people and sharing photos.' Another who disliked 'social media getting too full of energy, too demanding' also said that 'some [social media content] is great . . . and I really love when people scan in . . . old childhood photos and share' them. In short, participants pointed to the coexistence of pain and pleasure, of irritation and salve, within their connectivity practices.

It is perhaps unsurprising that participants' technological dalliances were mired in ambivalence. In the UK (and elsewhere), we are tethered to our devices in a moment of neoliberalism that equates virtue with individualism, self-optimization, and meritocracy (Littler 2017, Davies 2016). This ideology urges us, as subjects, to interrogate how we spend our time, on guard to spot temporal waste. Here, our digital tools can be commandeered by the project of self-improvement. Or they can engender inefficiency. No wonder social media and smartphones are regarded simultaneously as vital *and* as a frivolous waste of time, as necessary but also morally suspect. Indeed, this paradox feeds into the second theme to emerge from the QSM project: the (un)viability of choice.

BEYOND CHOICE

In many ways, today's digital communications ecosystem is a paragon of individual choice. You can choose between myriad smartphone brands and social media platforms. You can choose your TikTok username, Instagram profile photo, LinkedIn connections, and iPhone ringtone. Abundance is everywhere, from unlimited data plans to a veritable avalanche of user-generated content. For example, YouTube alone sees 500 hours of new content uploaded every minute (Statista 2020b), and Google sees 28 billion photos and videos uploaded each week to its Google Photos platform (BBC 2020). This abundance reflects the fact that internet connectivity now intersects with just about every aspect of modern life. It is—particularly post-Covid-19—how we do our work, how we forge and maintain relationships, manage finances, organize leisure activities, and practice self-care (Roose 2020). In the UK, 78% of adults say they could not live without their smartphones (Ofcom 2018, 59). The QSM project findings support and extend this claimed dependency by showing the degree to which smartphones and social media were regarded as essential tools for conducting personal and professional life.

Indeed, the QSM findings suggest that, today, connectivity is not a choice but a necessity. One gallery audience statement indicated that the best thing about having a smartphone is 'it does everything'—its usefulness rendering it indispensable. A survey participant explained that 'social media is something that I use without thinking about it. It's part of life.' The normativity, ubiquity, and ordinariness of social media and smartphones were so consistently assumed by my participants that it threw the very notion of choice into question. How can 'choice' be understood in a landscape where being connected is the default position? How do 'choice' and human agency operate in contexts of deep connectivity? As mentioned earlier, neoliberalism lionizes individual choice. This means if one is not happy with a service or platform, one can simply quit. Advancing this view, one survey respondent said, 'I find it so odd when people complain about social media. It's not compulsory. Be more mindful about it, or just step away.' This is the quintessential expression of individual agency. But the opposition of user to non-user is not particularly helpful in a world where digital participation is regarded as a necessity rather than a choice.

One participant explained, 'I would feel completely comfortable quitting social media and find very limited enjoyment in it, [were it not] the only way of staying in touch with certain friends/family.' Another noted, 'Sometimes I just wish I could skip it . . . [to] have more time or feel better perhaps. But it doesn't feel social to skip Instagram or Facebook for example. It feels like you're not part [of] other people's lives if you quit.' A 15-year-old girl spoke to me at length about the stigma of not being on social media. She said that in her school, 'Only the weirdos aren't on Instagram.' The specter of fear of missing out (FOMO) haunted many of my participants' accounts of why they stayed connected to platforms that didn't always bring them joy. As one of them said, 'I would happily quit if there was another way to stay in touch and not miss out on things.'

On occasion, FOMO morphed into familial commitment. Sam, for instance, explained that 'my spouse deleted their Facebook account. I am now obligated to keep mine active because it is important for someone in my family to have one.' Social media participation here becomes a literal manifestation of what Kylie Jarrett (2016) dubs the *Digital Housewife*, wherein maintaining a Facebook presence serves as a form of familial care. Similarly, another participant explained:

> As an Australian living in Europe, social media (especially Facebook) is the only way to stay in regular contact with family members, especially given the time differences involved and busy lives we lead. Unfortunately, it's so embedded now that it's by far the most convenient way to stay in touch. [. . .] If I lived in a country where my friends/family were all just a phone call away, I'd have quit more than five years ago.

Participants also believed that their economic livelihoods made a social media presence mandatory. As one respondent put it, 'I maintain LinkedIn only because I've found it to be a near-requirement when looking for a new job.' Being searchable and findable online thus becomes—like a degree or previous work experience—another necessary qualification.

My findings make clear that, whether for personal or professional reasons, opting out of digital connectivity is a luxury many of us feel we can't afford. Indeed, digital connection has come to be regarded as essential because we—particularly in the Global North—find ourselves 'in a situation where every waking moment has become the time in which we make our living, and when we submit even our leisure for numerical evaluation via likes on Facebook and Instagram [. . .] time becomes an economic resource that we can no longer justify spending on "nothing"' (Odell 2019, 15). For my participants, this *mise en scène* contributed to a sense of 'reluctant obligation' that accompanied their digital practices. This had a substantial quantitative footprint. While 99% of survey respondents reported having used social media, a whopping 87% also indicated that they had at some point taken a break from that use. The perceived demands of connectivity were so overwhelming, in other words, that they inspired ruptures in use. This 87% figure is a significant increase on Ofcom's (2016) research, which found only 34% of adult internet users in the UK had undertaken some sort of digital detox. While my own research extends beyond the UK, the difference in figures is considerable and suggests that digital disconnection may be a far more common phenomenon than previously thought.

In the context of the 'beyond-choice' ontology that emerged from my findings, this also draws attention to the duration of disconnection. If, as I found, people felt they *must* remain connected, then what did the temporality of digital withdrawal look like? These questions lead to the third theme of my findings: the feedback loop between connection and disconnection.

DISCONNECTING TO RECONNECT

It turned out that the majority of my respondents who pressed 'pause' on their social media participation did so on a temporary basis. Only 15% of survey respondents regarded their social media departure as permanent. With smartphones, I found even less evidence of permanent disengagement. This finding is consistent with Rivka Ribak and Michele Rosenthal's (2015) important work on smartphone resistance, which concluded that digital 'resistances in a neoliberal age of ubiquitous, convergent media are temporary and local'. Instead of an all-or-nothing approach to digital presence, my participants articulated a more complex understanding of their usage practices. Most considered disconnection as a process rather than a fixed state or end goal, wherein periods of disconnection were almost always linked to future connectivity. Disconnection emerged as an integral part of enduring connectivity.

As such, disconnection here can be read as a form of self-care that enables future connection.

Others (Newport 2019; Alter 2017) have looked at how digital disconnection enables (re)connection to the corporeal and material register—to the people, practices, and environments around us. Indeed, it is important to remember that online participation often entails offline disengagement. For instance, an interviewee explained as follows:

> Between phone calls, texts, emails, notifications, my smartphone is always competing for my attention and drawing me away from the room. . . . It takes me away from the people I am with . . . to check whether the most recent buzz of my phone may be more important than what I'm currently doing.

However, my research points to digital disconnection also enabling *digital* reconnection. This hints at a more symbiotic relationship between disconnection and connection predicated not on competition between the two modes but on their coexistence. This helps explain the seemingly contradictory beliefs and practices maintained by the many QSM participants who tried quitting but who ultimately regarded their continued participation as inevitable and necessary.

With social media, the cycle of deleting and then reinstalling apps was a frequently described practice. Hilary, for example, recounted how 'I deleted the Facebook app off my phone so I didn't look at it so often throughout the day. I felt great the first couple of days and didn't even miss it but then it snuck back in.' With smartphones, many participants reported designating specific events or times of day as 'device-free'. For instance, mealtimes were routinely identified as moments to disconnect from the 'electronic elsewhere' (Berry, Kim, and Spigel 2009). While this did not constitute an enduring form of 'quitting,' it was a moment of rupture *within* a broader lifestyle of ubiquitous connectivity. Others regarded weekends and holidays as ideal occasions to disconnect. Helen, for example, said, 'I don't use Facebook from Friday afternoon to Sunday morning every week, plus never on vacation except to say where I am.' Such respites served as opportunities for people to recharge and prepare for the inevitability of reconnection.

My interviewee Gio provided further insight into the coexistence of digital connection and disengagement. For him, the smartphone was essential to his 'work in real estate, where being accessible and responsive is very important. [. . .] [But] being constantly accessible . . . can be exhausting.' Gio understood that his economic livelihood depended on remaining connected, and acknowledged the affective overwhelm of his circumstances. He also noticed that:

> My life is better without my phone when I travel overseas and am less accessible. . . . Not having my phone constantly draw me away lets me forget about

the outside world and enjoy what I am doing at the moment. With that said I can't imagine giving up my smartphone.

Disconnection for Gio was a practice that offered a temporary break from the 'beyond-choice' hyperconnectivity of everyday life.

Many other participants similarly discussed taking short-term breaks. Sarah, for instance, 'found it extremely difficult to quit social media, usually only taking breaks of about a week before getting back on.' Another respondent explained that 'each time I get hooked back into the bleak world of on-line ranting, depressing and scaremongering "news" stories [on Facebook] I have to cut myself off again.' In these cases, quitting was not regarded as a permanent solution or aspiration. Rather, it was understood as a pragmatic form of self-care in the 'beyond-choice' ontology of contemporary digital culture.

Even those participants who took longer breaks from social media bristled at the idea of severing the cord completely. Catriona reported being off Facebook for three months and not missing it, but she insisted that 'deleting my profile would be a lot harder, since I have about 10 years of my life there, and I feel comfortable knowing I can at any point go back and check the memories.' The perceived impossibility of permanent and complete digital disconnection is also reflected in the digital detox marketplace that has gained visibility in recent years. Some products, like digital detox-themed holidays (Sutton 2017; Fish 2017) and self-help books, offer analog ways to temporarily disconnect. Others offer digital solutions to digital overload. The market is full of detox apps, from mindfulness apps to use monitoring apps to app-blocking apps (Gregg 2018), all available for download to your smartphone, tablet, or laptop. Like my respondents' accounts, these products gesture to the limited temporality of disconnection. These apps and detox retreats offer breaks, predicated on the understanding that permanent non-use is a non-option.

Here, the irony of using digital technology to *reduce* use of digital technology, or to cope with excessive use, tells us something significant about the centrality and power of the digital in our everyday lives. The fact that we might regard the very technological artifacts and logics we are trying to escape as means of *achieving* that escape also strikes me as a potent symbol of the technological solutionism that operates in contemporary neoliberalism. Overwhelmed by digital culture? That's your problem! But don't worry, you can fix it if you just find the right app.

Meanwhile, alluding to the data monopolies that dominate this historical moment, a survey respondent considered the practical difficulties of fully opting out:

One complicating factor is that social media are increasingly integrated. [. . .] I would sometimes like to go on a social media diet—manage it better, not quitting but taking it in smaller doses—but it's hard to compartmentalise my usage of it with how connected everything is nowadays.

Disconnection here approximates a reduction in caloric intake, rather than a fast. Similarly, for Annette, disconnection was about decrease rather than total elimination. She 'realised that [social media] can become addictive, [so] I do not use it more than 10 minutes a day—when I use it. Many days I don't.' Others pointed to additional ways of 'digital dieting' (Brabazon 2012). Anya, for example, emphasized the need to be choosy about what one connects to: 'It's easy to let the social pressure to use all these platforms get you. I have learned to be selective. I don't need these things as much as they need me.'

In the next section, I consider where we go from here. Within ubiquitous connectivity that is riddled with user ambivalence, reluctant obligation, and moments of disconnection, can we recover a possibility for agency within the beyond-choice ontology of contemporary digital culture? I attempt to do so by turning to the groundbreaking work of economist Albert Hirschman.

ALBERT HIRSCHMAN AND USER AGENCY IN A BEYOND-CHOICE ONTOLOGY

A key question that emerges from the themes above concerns how we might make sense of people's continued social media and smartphone use in a way that does not reduce it only to a beyond-choice ontology. How, in other words, might we recover the possibility of agency within an all-encompassing technosocial ecosystem where disconnection practices nonetheless abound? This is an important task for two interrelated reasons. First, it honors the contradictions of user attitudes and practices. Second, it offers a pathway for thinking and doing resistance within these paradoxical conditions.

One theoretical framework that helps chart this pathway comes from the economist Albert Hirschman. In his seminal work *Exit, Voice, and Loyalty* (1970), Hirschman considers organizational success and failure, and assesses the role of consumer choice therein. How does consumer action (and inaction) contribute to organizational continuity? Likewise, how can it affect organizational change? Hirschman wrote about large organizations, from governments and nation states to schools, hospitals, and transportation systems. His chief interest was to understand how an organization's stakeholders responded to perceived deteriorations in service quality. What happened, for instance, when parents grew unhappy with the education provision on offer from their local state school? Similarly, how might citizens react to perceived government corruption?

In such situations, Hirschman conceptualized consumer choice as operating along two tracks: voice and exit. With voice, consumers air their grievances and take action aimed at changing an organization's behavior accordingly. To take the state school example, parents exercising voice might launch a petition outlining their complaints and the specific changes they wish the school to make. With exit, however, consumers simply leave the organization. Those dissatisfied parents—provided they had sufficient resources—would simply move their child to a private school. Hirschman (1970) regarded voice and exit as mutually exclusive. One could not deploy both strategies simultaneously. Yet the QSM project found that voice and exit could operate in tandem: participants complained about and took breaks from social platforms and devices, but only temporarily. This challenges the temporality of Hirschman's exit, rendering it a concept that can accommodate stakeholders' disaffection with *and* continued loyalty to a particular service.

Another principle Hirschman proposed is that the easier it is to exit a system, the less likely that voice-based strategies will be deployed. This brings to mind Pippa Norris's (2002, 4) observation about the internet's 'easy-entry, easy-exit' culture, where 'it is simpler to exit than to work through any messy bargaining and conflictual disagreements.' In the context of the QSM project, this poses an existential challenge: Why would one stay and fight when it is far easier to join a different social network or switch to a different smartphone brand? Or, in extremis, where one can completely disconnect? These questions reassert the central paradox of contemporary digital culture, as expressed by my participants: for all its deficits, connectivity is pervasive, necessary, and dominated by data monopolies. In other words, there is nowhere to exit to. And thus, without viable alternatives, voice becomes an impotent strategy.

This is conceptually provocative for a number of reasons. First, it exposes a short-circuiting of neoliberalism in digital culture. Without an alternative elsewhere to escape to, the very viability of individual choice as an animating principle is neutered. Second, the foreclosure of choice, when combined with a corresponding feebleness of voice, diminishes the possibility of resistance and systemic change. As a means of re-inscribing that possibility onto today's (dis)connection practices, it seems to me essential to rehabilitate Hirschman's 'voice' strategy and to reimagine its operations within the beyond-choice ontology that surfaced in my research. Indeed, if giving up smartphones and social media is not on the cards, and permanently leaving Facebook or Instagram feels impossible, then we must urgently consider how voice can be deployed within our digital habitus (n.b. Bourdieu 1977). This requires taking on board the user ambivalences described earlier—the varied pains, pleasures, and paradoxes of (dis)connection. How can these be channelled into meaningful, potentially transformative expressions of voice in an ecosystem reminiscent of Sartre's (1989[1944]) *No Exit*? Let us consider some possibilities.

Conspicuously missing from participant accounts was any reference to formal structures for codifying their grievances. My participants had no shortage of complaints about their social media and smartphone experiences, but regarded the platforms and devices they critiqued as black box mono-liths. These were not considered services that could be held accountable. One respondent, for example, 'saw [Facebook] removing user controls over content & lying to users' without repercussion. Another lamented the unfet-tered 'power and manipulation of the platforms', while a third worried that 'the capacity for algorithms to select content' further undercut user agency. One key to rehabilitating the viability of voice within digital culture, then, is to make social media and smartphone companies accountable to their users. For instance, customer feedback channels could be integrated into platform designs and business models. This would need to exceed giving users a generic email address to send their complaints to. Instead, companies could conduct quarterly user experience focus groups, implement action plans in response, and report on these activities in shareholder reports. They could also give users a proportion of seats on their boards of directors.

Greater transparency could also be required of social media and smart-phone companies. Regulators can mandate companies make annual disclo-sures to account holders about their use metrics, provide reports on how their data has been used and by whom, and disclose how much revenue a user's account has generated. Companies could also make public the demographics of their product development staff. This would draw attention to tech sector monocultures and the resulting biases that get encoded in digital infrastruc-tures. It might even inspire some firms to diversify their staff.

As has been suggested throughout this chapter, platform accountability is also disincentivized by the monopolistic nature of contemporary digital culture. The solution? Break up the data monopolies. To support users' data rights, we could also require companies to make personal data portable, thus enabling users to easily shift between platforms. This would necessitate standardizing various technical protocols, and ending the era of propriety systems. In effect, this means treating connectivity as a public utility. If done effectively, this would enable alternative platforms to meaningfully compete with today's hegemonic brands. If done effectively, no platform could ever again become the world's most populated country. No platform could be rendered indispensable.

Of course, to accomplish any of these reforms requires government regula-tion. Governments must rein in the free market approach that has for decades run rampant in the technology sector (Wladawsky-Berger 2019). We are beginning to see steps in this direction—for instance, with recent antitrust action against Google in Europe and the United States (Whalen 2020; Kang et al. 2020). But more needs to be done. Governments must close tax loopholes that have enabled the biggest players to minimize their tax obligations (Sherman 2019). And corporation tax rates and policies ought to be harmonized around the world, in order to stop giants like Facebook and Apple decamping to low-tax territories (Giles 2019). Fundamentally, government policymaking must respond to the beyond-choice ontology of contemporary digital culture. If properly designed and implemented, these policies would allow users to reclaim individual and collective access to voice and exit within hyperconnectivity. It would also allow people to recover some of the power promised, yet withheld, by neoliberal capitalism.

REFERENCES

Alter, Adam. 2017. *Irresistible: Why You Are Addicted to Technology and How to Set Yourself Free*. New York: Vintage.

Andreassen, Cecilie Schou, Ståle Pallesen, and Mark D. Griffiths. 2017. "The Relationship Between Addictive Use of Social Media, Narcissism, and Self-Esteem: Findings from a Large National Survey." *Addictive Behaviors* 64: 287–293.

BBC News 2020. "Google Photos Abandons Unlimited Uploads Amid Storage Changes." *BBC News*, November 13, 2020. https://www.bbc.co.uk/news/technology-54919165.

Berry, Chris, Soyoung Kim, and Lynn Spigel, eds. 2009. *Electronic Elsewheres: Media, Technology, and the Experience of Social Space*. Minneapolis, MN: University of Minnesota Press.

Berryman, Chloe, Christopher J. Ferguson, and Charles Negy. 2018. "Social Media Use and Mental Health Among Young Adults." *Psychiatric Quarterly* 89: 307–314.

Berthon, Pierre, Leyland Pitt, and Colin Campbell. 2019. "Addictive De-Vices: A Public Policy Analysis of Sources and Solutions to Digital Addiction." *Journal of Public Policy & Marketing* 38 (4): 451–468.

Bian, Mengwei and Louis Leung. 2015. "Linking Loneliness, Shyness, Smartphone Addiction Symptoms, and Patterns of Smartphone Use to Social Capital." *Social Science Computer Review* 33 (1): 61–79.

Blackwell, David, Carrie Leaman, Rose Tramposch, Ciera Osborne, and Miriam Liss. 2017. "Extraversion, Neuroticism, Attachment Style and Fear of Missing Out as Predictors of Social Media Use and Addiction." *Personality and Individual Differences* 116: 69–72.

Bourdieu, Pierre. 1977. *Outline of a Theory of Practice*. Translated by Richard Nice. Cambridge: Cambridge University Press.

Brabazon, Tara. 2012. "Time for a Digital Detox? From Information Obesity to Digital Dieting Fast." *Fast Capitalism* 9 (1): 53–74.

Brennen, Bonnie. 2019. *Opting Out of Digital Media*. New York: Routledge.

Clement, J. 2020. "Number of Monthly Active Facebook Users Worldwide as of 4th Quarter 2019." Statista. https://www.statista.com/statistics/264810/number-of-mo nthly-active-facebook-usersworldwide.

Common Sense Media. 2020. Common Sense Research. https://www.commonse nsemedia.org/research.

Couldry, Nick and Ulises A. Mejias. 2019. *The Costs of Connection: How Data is Colonizing Human Life and Appropriating it for Capitalism*. Stanford, CA: Stanford University Press.

D'Arienzo, Maria Chiara, Valentina Boursier, and Mark D. Griffiths. 2019. "Addiction to Social Media and Attachment Styles: A Systematic Literature Review." *International Journal of Mental Health and Addiction* 17: 1094–1118.

Davies, William. 2016. *The Limits of Neoliberalism: Authority, Sovereignty and the Logic of Competition*. London: SAGE.

Derrida, Jacques. 1997. *Of Grammatology*. Translated by Gayatri Chakravorty Spivak. Baltimore, MD: The Johns Hopkins University Press.

Domman, Mary-Ann. 2019. "Indices of Deprivation 2019." *London Councils*, November 1, 2019. https://www.londoncouncils.gov.uk/members-area/member-b riefings/local-government-finance/indices-deprivation-2019.

Drotner, Kirsten. 1999. "Dangerous Media? Panic Discourses and Dilemmas of Modernity." *Paedagogica Historica* 35 (3): 593–619.

Fish, Adam. 2017. "Technology Retreats and the Politics of Social Media." *Triple C* 15 (1). doi:10.31269/triplec.v15i1.807.

Gantt Shafer, Jessica. 2017. "Donald Trump's 'Political Incorrectness': Neoliberalism as Frontstage Racism on Social Media." *Social Media + Society* 3 (3). doi:10.1177/2056305117733226.

Giles, Chris. 2019. "OECD Takes Aim at Tech Giants with Plan to Shake Up Global Tax." *Financial Times*, October 13, 2019. https://www.ft.com/content/b16fd228 -ea72-11e9-a240-3b065ef5fc55.

Global Web Index. 2020. *Social Flagship Report Q3 2020*. https://www.globalwe bindex.com/reports/social.

Greenfield, Susan. 2015. *Mind Change: How Digital Technologies Are Leaving Their Mark on Our Brains*. New York: Random House.

Gregg, Melissa. 2018. *Counterproductive: Time Management in the Knowledge Economy*. Durham and London: Duke University Press.

Griffiths, Mark D. 2010. "The Role of Context in Online Gaming Excess and Addiction: Some Case Study Evidence." *International Journal of Mental Health and Addiction* 8: 119–125.

Griffiths, Mark D., Daria J. Kuss, and Zsolt Demetrovics. 2014. "Social Networking Addiction: An Overview of Preliminary Findings." In *Behavioral Addictions: Criteria, Evidence, And Treatment*, edited by K. P. Rosenberg and L. C. Feder, 119–141. London: Academic Press.

Harris, Michael. 2015. *The End of Absence: Reclaiming What We've Lost in a World of Constant Connection*. New York: Penguin Group.

Haug, Severin, Raquel Paz Castro, Min Kwon, Andreas Filler, Tobias Kowatsch, and Michael P. Schaub. 2015. "Smartphone Use and Smartphone Addiction Among Young People in Switzerland." *Journal of Behavioral Addictions* 4 (4): 299–307.

Hawi, Nazir S. and Maya Samaha. 2017a. "The Relations Among Social Media Addiction, Self-Esteem, and Life Satisfaction in University Students." *Social Science Computer Review* 35 (5): 576–586.

———. 2017b. "Relationships Among Smartphone Addiction, Anxiety, and Family Relations." *Behaviour & Information Technology* 36 (10): 1046–1105.

Henry, Rachel. 2017. "Digital Detox and the Big Business of Unplugging." *Zendesk Blog*, February 16, 2017. https://www.zendesk.co.uk/blog/digital-detox-big-business-of-unplugging.

Hirschman, Albert O. 1970. *Exit, Voice, and Loyalty: Responses to Decline in Firms, Organizations, and States.* Cambridge, MA: Harvard University Press.

Jaishankar, K. 2011. *Cyber Criminology: Exploring Internet Crimes and Criminal Behavior.* Boca Raton, FL: CRC Press.

Jarrett, Kylie. 2016. *Feminism, Labour and Digital Media: The Digital Housewife.* London and New York: Routledge.

Kang, Cecilia, David McCabe, and Daisuke Wakabayashi. 2020. "U.S. Accuses Google of Illegally Protecting Monopoly." *New York Times*, October 20, 2020. https://www.nytimes.com/2020/10/20/technology/google-antitrust.html.

Kranzberg, Melvin. 1986. "Technology and History: "Kranzberg's Laws"." *Technology and Culture* 27 (3): 544–560.

Lanier, Jaron. 2018. *Ten Arguments for Deleting Your Social Media Accounts Right Now.* London: The Bodley Head.

Leick, Karen. 2018. *Parents, Media and Panic Through the Years: Kids Those Days.* Cham, Switzerland Palgrave Pivot.

Littler, Jo. 2017. *Against Meritocracy: Culture, Power, and Myths of Mobility.* London: Routledge.

Lovink, Geert. 2016. *Social Media Abyss: Critical Internet Cultures and the Force of Negation.* Cambridge: Polity Press.

Mason, Corinne Lysandra. 2016. "Tinder and Humanitarian Hook-Ups: The Erotics of Social Media Racism." *Feminist Media Studies* 16 (5): 822–837.

Mejias, Ulises Ali. 2013. *Off the Network: Disrupting the Digital World.* Minneapolis, MN: University of Minnesota Press.

Newport, Cal. 2019. *Digital Minimalism: Choosing a Focused Life in a Noisy World.* London: Penguin Random House UK.

Norris, Pippa. 2002. "The Bridging and Bonding Role of Online Communities." *The Harvard International Journal of Press-Politics* 7 (3): 3–13.

Odell, Jenny. 2019. *How to Do Nothing: Resisting the Attention Economy.* Brooklyn and London: Melville House.

Ofcom. 2016. *Communications Market Report 2016.* August 4, 2016. https://www.ofcom.org.uk/__data/assets/pdf_file/0024/26826/cmr_uk_2016.pdf.

———. 2018. *Communications Market Report 2018.* August 2, 2018. https://www.ofcom.org.uk/__data/assets/pdf_file/0022/117256/CMR-2018-narrative-report.pdf.

———. 2020a. *Children and Parents: Media Use and Attitudes Report 2019.* February 4, 2020. https://www.ofcom.org.uk/__data/assets/pdf_file/0023/190616/children-media-use-attitudes-2019-report.pdf.

———. 2020b. *Online Nation 2020 Report.* June 24, 2020. https://www.ofcom.org.uk/__data/assets/pdf_file/0027/196407/online-nation-2020-report.pdf.

_____. 2020c. *Communications Market Report 2020*. September 30, 2020. https://www.ofcom.org.uk/__data/assets/pdf_file/0026/203759/cmr-2020.pdf.

Okeke, Fabian, Michael Sobolev, Nicola Lee Dell, and Deborah Estrin. 2018. "Good Vibrations: Can a Digital Nudge Reduce Digital Overload?" In *MobileHCI '18: Proceedings of the 20th International Conference on Human-Computer Interaction with Mobile Devices and Services*, September 2018, 1–12. doi:10.1145/3229434.3229463.

ONS. 2019. Ethnic Groups by Borough. https://data.london.gov.uk/dataset/ethnic-groups-borough.

Panova, Tayana and Xavier Carbonell. 2018. "Is Smartphone Addiction Really an Addiction?" *Journal of Behavioral Addictions* 7 (2): 252–259.

Ponnusamy, Saranya, Mohammad Iranmanesh, Behzad Foroughi, and Sunghyup Sean Hyun. 2020. "Drivers and Outcomes of Instagram Addiction: Psychological Well-Being as Moderator." *Computers in Human Behavior* 107. doi:10.1016/j.chb.2020.106294.

Poth, Cheryl N. 2018. *Innovation in Mixed Methods Research: A Practical Guide to Integrative Thinking with Complexity*. London, Thousand Oaks, New Delhi: SAGE.

Prasad, Aarathi and Asia Quinones. 2020. "Digital Overload Warnings—"The Right Amount of Shame"?" In *HCII 2020: Human-Computer Interaction. Human Values and Quality of Life*, Copenhagen, Denmark, July 19–24, 117–34.

Qudah, Mohammad Farhan Al., Ismael Albursan, Salaheldin Bakhiet, Elsayed Hassan, Ali A. Alfnan, Suliman S. Aljomaa, and Mohammed Al-khadher. 2019. "Smartphone Addiction and Its Relationship with Cyberbullying Among University Students." *International Journal of Mental Health and Addiction* 17: 628–643.

Reay, Diane, Miriam E. David, and Stephen J. Ball, eds. 2005. *Degrees of Choice: Class, Race, Gender and Higher Education*. Sterling, VA: Trentham Books.

Reichelt, Leisa. 2007. "Ambient Intimacy." *Disambiguity Blog*, March 1, 2007. https://www.disambiguity.com/ambient-intimacy.

Ribak, Riva and Michele Rosenthal. 2015. "Smartphone Resistance as Media Ambivalence." *First Monday* 20 (11). doi:10.5210/fm.v20i11.6307.

Rao, Neomi and Lakshmi Lingam. 2021. "Smartphones, Youth and Moral Panics: Exploring Print and Online Media Narratives in India." *Mobile Media & Communication* 9 (1): 128–148.

Roose, Kevin. 2020. "The Coronavirus Crisis Is Showing Us How to Live Online." *New York Times*, March 17, 2020. https://www.nytimes.com/2020/03/17/technology/coronavirus-how-to-live-online.html.

Samaha, Maya and Nazir S. Hawi. 2016. "Relationships Among Smartphone Addiction, Stress, Academic Performance, and Satisfaction with Life." *Computers in Human Behavior* 57: 321–325.

Sartre, Jean-Paul. (1989[1944]). *No Exit, and Three Other Plays*. New York: Vintage International.

Science Gallery London. 2019. "DARK MATTER season coming soon!" April 2, 2019. https://london.sciencegallery.com/news/dark-matter-season-coming-soon.

Shead, S. 2019. 'Facebook Owns the Four Most Downloaded Apps of the Decade.' *BBC News*, December 18, 2019. https://www.bbc.co.uk/news/technology-50838013.

Sherman, Erik. 2019. "A New Report Claims Big Tech Companies Used Legal Loopholes to Avoid Over $100 Billion in Taxes. What Does That Mean for the Industry's Future?" *Fortune*, December 6, 2019. https://fortune.com/2019/12/06/big-tech-taxes-google-facebook-amazon-apple-netflix-microsoft.

Statista. 2020a. "Number of Smartphone Users from 2016 to 2021." https://www.statista.com/statistics/330695/number-of-smartphone-users-worldwide.

_____. 2020b. "Hours of Video Uploaded to YouTube Every Minute as of May 2019." https://www.statista.com/statistics/259477/hours-of-video-uploaded-to-youtube-every-minute.

Sutton, Theodora. 2017. "Disconnect to Reconnect: The Food/Technology Metaphor in Digital Detoxing." *First Monday* 22 (6). doi:10.5210/fm.v22i6.7561.

Syvertsen, Trine. 2020. "The Problem is Personal—and Social: Making Sense of Digital Detox." In *Digital Detox: The Politics of Disconnecting (Society Now)*, pp. 99–124. Emerald Publishing Limited.

Turkle, Sherry. 2015. *Reclaiming Conversation: The Power of Talk in a Digital Age*. New York: Penguin Random House.

Whalen, Jeanne. 2020. "Europe Fined Google Nearly $10 Billion For Antitrust Violations, But Little Has Changed." *Washington Post*, November 10, 2020. https://www.washingtonpost.com/technology/2020/11/10/eu-antitrust-probe-google.

Whittaker, Elizabeth and Robin M. Kowalski. 2015. "Cyberbullying Via Social Media." *Journal of School Violence* 14 (1) 11–29.

Wladawsky-Berger, Irving. 2019. "Digital Technology Drives Free-Market, Free-Trade Capitalism to the Crossroads." *Wall Street Journal Blog*, July 26, 2019. https://blogs.wsj.com/cio/2019/07/26/digital-technology-drives-free-market-free-trade-capitalism-to-the-crossroads

Woodlock, Delanie. 2017. "The Abuse of Technology in Domestic Violence and Stalking." *Violence Against Women* 23 (5): 584–602.

Ytre-Arne, Brita, Trine Syvertsen, Hallvard Moe, and Faltin Karlsen. 2020. "Temporal Ambivalences in Smartphone Use: Conflicting Flows, Conflicting Responsibilities." *New Media & Society* 22 (9): 1715–1732.

Part III

DESIGNING DISCONNECTION

Chapter 6

Ethics and Experimentation in The Light Phone and Google Digital Wellbeing

Aleena Chia and Alex Beattie

'Sorry, one second please.' Joe Hollier interrupts himself in a phone interview as he gives directions to his driver who is navigating the streets of New York, apparently lost. Joe is the creator of The Light Phone, a deliberately designed feature phone that aims to reduce distractions by functioning as a single-purpose device for phone calls only. As he is being interviewed by Alex, one of the authors of this chapter, Joe appears distracted. While extolling the merits of The Light Phone as a single-purpose device for distraction-free activities, Joe is providing directions to his driver. The irony of Joe's multitasking is unacknowledged by either Joe or Alex. After directing the driver for a few minutes, Joe's attention returns to the interview: 'Sorry, confusing roads. . . . Alright, I'm back.'

Claims about a 'distraction epidemic' (Twenge 2017) caused by digital platforms and devices are part of the so-called techlash that journalists, researchers, and policymakers have levelled against the technology industry. Notable Silicon Valley entrepreneurs and developers are coming to terms with their business and design practices and their implications on users (Lewis 2017). Like many tech designers, Joe Hollier is not disillusioned by digital technology per se, but rather by the ideological and socio-economic system underpinning digital technology. This system is the 'attention economy' where media companies, advertisers, and technology platforms treat end-user attention as a finite commodity to compete for (Crogan and Kinsley 2012). Rather than as a fungible resource extracted from individuals, attention has also been conceived in relational terms, as constituted through collective sociotechnical conditions (Citton 2017). In addition to design strategies that challenge the attention economy, individual tactics such as being mindful of time spent on platforms and devices have been adopted by an increasing number of social media users in North America. However, in their study of Facebook users who reported adopting such mindfulness, Baym, Wagman, and Persaud (2020, 9) state that using contemplative practices to restrict social media use cannot aggregate into structural change of the attention economy: 'Disconnective practices may help people find balance in the trap, but it cannot set them free.'

Reckoning with social media means contending with criticisms of constant connectivity from industry, institutions, and individuals as a cultural formation and their proposals to combat it. In this chapter, we analyze how two companies—a tech start-up and a tech giant—deploy experimental practices, to understand the development of technology ethics as a response to the techlash. We examine The Light Phone, contextualizing it within Google's wider innovation ecosystem from which it was ostensibly incubated. In particular, we consider Google Digital Wellbeing Experiments, a collection of mobile applications that 'showcase ideas and tools that help people find a better balance with technology' (Google, n.d.). Drawing from science and technology studies, and media and cultural studies, we analyze entrepreneurial and experimental practices as doing the 'ethical work' of technology workers and platforms. We examine the politics and potentialities of disconnective experiments through the aesthetic and branded registers of digital lightness. We do this by situating textual analysis (Phillipov 2013) of promotional texts about The Light Phone and Google Digital Wellbeing Experiments within the scholarly literature on tech ethics and organizational experimentation. Using a developer interview with Joe Hollier as a jumping off point, we analyze The Light Phone's promotional website. We also analyze two experimental apps from Google's Digital Wellbeing Collection by design and invention consultancy studio Special Projects, within the context of Google Creative Lab.

We argue that the branding of disconnection as a sensation and as a concept aestheticize materiality in varying ways, enchanting disconnection within an imaginary that protects corporations from criticisms about the techlash. The branding of disconnection through sensorially rich imagery—namely, The Light Phone—creates an aperture into an intimate world, channelling public feelings about the techlash into the forms of a life. Stewart (2007) understands these channellings as 'ordinary affects', which are simultaneously abstract and concrete, multiplicitous and fractious, and are less tangible yet more compelling than ideologies or symbolic meanings. The branding of disconnection through stark and stylized imagery—namely, Google Paper Phone—operates like a pinhole camera, flattening the messy vitality of the techlash into a two-dimensional object. This conceptualization of disconnection is informed by conceptual art such as Marcel Duchamp's Readymades, which involves a *relative* devaluing of the sensorial and material qualities and a focus on the ideas conveyed by mundane objects (Cray 2014). Articulating such variations in the aestheticization of disconnection provides a way to draw out their institutional relationalities and critique their translation of public feelings into private fictions.

We begin by reviewing the literature on feature phones, technology ethics, and experimentation. We then discuss how the aesthetics and politics of The Light Phone promotional material position disconnection as a branded sensation that is suspended between memory and fantasy. The Light Phone is a world-building device that projects the textures and sensations of disconnection onto the canvas of one's desire so pleasurably, that its brand affect seems to eclipse the need to disconnect at all. Relatedly, we discuss how Google Digital Wellbeing Experiments frame disconnection as a concept to protect the conglomerate from techlash criticisms about the personal harms of constant connection. We conclude by considering the implications for experimentation in the context of disconnection and discuss the politics of alternative paradigms of disconnection that are not based on mitigating harms or maintaining balance, but on contemplation (Odell 2019) and collectivization (Natale and Treré 2020)

EXPERIMENTS IN TECH ETHICS

We are not the first to analyze the appeal of feature phones like The Light Phone. According to Portwood-Stacer (2013), it has become fashionable in urban parts of the world, such as Brooklyn, New York, to deliberately choose a feature phone over a smartphone device. Choosing an older phone is partly performative, demonstrating an aesthetic taste with regards to phones that signify 'something socially or politically meaningful about the non-user' (Portwood-Stacer 2013, 1042). The performance of wielding a feature phone also constitutes what Monahan (2015) refers to as an 'aestheticization of resistance', where the primary goal is to draw attention to an issue at hand instead of taking specific action to further change. Thorén, Edenius, Eriksson Lundström, and Kitzmann (2017) analyze The Light Phone as producing a different dichotomy between analogue and digital. Utilizing Deleuze and Guattari's (1987) concept of the assemblage, Thorén et al. (2017, 329) argue that The Light Phone allows for a type of digital non-use or analogue connectivity that establishes new boundaries between online and offline spaces: 'The Light Phone-assemblage maintains the ruling order by keeping intact the existing smartphone assemblage through an app that potentially reduces the impulse to disconnect, dissolve and resist.'

Viewing technologized non-use as an assemblage emphasizes how The Light Phone reassembles existing heterogeneous elements (such as communicative availability, physical presence, network access) as well as generates new subjectivities (e.g. mindful technology use). In other words, The Light Phone-assemblage appears to aim to 'fix' the undesirable affordances associated with the smartphone assemblage. Yet Thorén et al. (2017) focus on the nostalgic appeal of The Light Phone, labelling it as a 'predigital' device alongside vinyl records and cassettes, despite The Light Phone operating on the latest mobile networks. In contrast, we view The Light Phone as a progression of Silicon Valley's performance of ethical technology production. We do not believe The Light Phone predates digital production, or is a pushback against digitization per se. We argue, instead, that The Light Phone has been developed as part of tech entrepreneurs' and platforms' experimentation with new ways to politicize the attention of potential customers. In other words, The Light Phone is an experiment in 'ethical' production for users to realize a good or better life with certain types of digital technologies.

Ethics has become a premium component in Silicon Valley's recursive cycles of product development and public relations. Tech companies in Silicon Valley routinely hire tech workers to fill designated roles as the ethical voice of their corporation, pointing out the failings of their industry in the face of public criticisms about disinformation, racial bias, and addiction that are built into digital technologies. In their interviews with such tech workers, Metcalf, Moss, and boyd (2019) state that ethics is framed as a technical problem that can be fixed by designing better systems that will triumph in the marketplace while also serving broader goals of a more just algorithmic and data-driven world. Buffered by tech solutionism and market fundamentalism, this institutionalization of ethics 'operate[s] inside a fraught dynamic: on the one hand, attempting to resolve critical external normative claims about the core logics of the tech industry; on the other hand, doing so while fully embedded within those logics' (Metcalf, Moss, and boyd 2019, 450).

In contrast, The Light Phone creator Joe Hollier identifies as an artist first and a tech entrepreneur second, expressing his company's goal of building better products through the language of artistically-driven ethics. Hollier sees his company's products as distinct from the attention-grabbing designs associated with the advertising business model that undergirds a significant number of apps. When asked about what inspired him to create a product that is designed to be used as little as possible, Hollier stated, 'I've always been a critical artist and I think I've always been interested in how people spend their time, how they create value from experience and gives us meaning and purpose in life.' Hollier expresses discomfort that the major business model in the technology industry is attention retention, where budding entrepreneurs are encouraged to consider 'how many hours or minutes would [your] users spend on your app a day?' The metric of user attention retention is one reason why Hollier considers smartphone technology to occupy an unnecessary presence in people's everyday lives.

Hollier came up with the idea of The Light Phone while attending an entrepreneurial programme for designers called 30 Weeks. 30 Weeks came out of Google Creative Lab, a hybridized marketing, entrepreneurial incubator, and product development division of internet industry conglomerate Alphabet Inc. Based in New York City, Google Creative Lab 'was an early bright spot for quirky thinking inside the company' (Wilson 2019) and launched in 2009 'to find a bridge between technology and traditional creative expression' (Beer 2019). The co-founder of Google Creative Lab, Robert Wong, describes its core mission as experimentation in public relations:

> Our job is to manage and steward the [Google] brand, find new ways to communicate the company's innovations, intentions and ideals, and do work of which we can all be proud. We want people ambitious and crazy enough to think we can actually change the world. (qtd. in Iezzi 2010)

One of the notable graduates of the 30 Weeks program was Hollier. The Light Phone was developed through a partnership between Hollier, an artist, and Kaiwei Tang, a product designer who met in 30 Weeks in 2014. Reflecting about his time at 30 Weeks, Hollier reveals how the designer mentality was valued by the technology conglomerate:

> [They] had a hypothesis that designers can envision the future that relates to actual users and they're able to mock that vision up . . . in a way that would inspire the engineers, investors, and other partners you might need to make that a reality. That was . . . the model that the Google Creative Lab used.

At Google Creative Lab, designers do not strictly program or develop software; but their work still revolves around technology. The 'technological terroir' (Messari 2018) or local technology culture at Google Creative Lab mixes marketing, design, and technology innovation together to tell stories about the possibilities of Google inventions. One of the first projects Google Creative Lab created was the 'Parisian Love' Super Bowl Spot in 2009, which depicted a love story entirely made by screenshots of Google searches, which inferred the ubiquity and intimacy of Google's presence in the romantic lives of viewers. To create the advertisement, Google recruited five students from New York-based advertising and design schools that came to be known as the 'Google 5'. This arrangement later matured into the '5 initiative' where design students work inside Google Creative Lab for a year before returning to the industry.

Google Creative Lab has been called a 'brand development think tank' (Ryan 2013), which matches Google's reputation as a progressive thinking company with a change-favourable corporate culture (Steiber and Alänge

2013). The experimental nature of Google Creative Lab draws similarities to the British Broadcasting Corporation (BBC) News Lab, which Zaragova-Fuster and García-Avilés (2019) claim is part of a global innovation strategy that drives the diversity and quality of the BBC's products and services. Google Creative Lab connects the seemingly disparate professions of design, software development, and marketing together. According to Wong, Google Creative Lab adopts the workflows and practices that underpin Google software development and engineering—a non-hierarchical team structure, a prototype and iterative process to develop projects, an emphasis on user experience—and applies them to the marketing process (Iezzi 2010). Doing so has enabled Google to create a formal academy out of its own shadow, where budding Google creatives and technologists can work in awareness of popular critiques of the technology conglomerate. Caldwell (2014) calls this a 'shadow academy', where media industries reflexively emulate, incorporate, and mirror the oppositional modes scholars have used in the critique of these very industries. Whether in the form of Silicon Valley tech ethics or Google Creative Lab, the shadow academy is an example of how the industry has made media theorizing part of their brand.

The shadow academy can be seen as an extension of arts-based experimentation in organizations and as part of a broader project of corporate social responsibility. Berthoin Antal, Woodilla, and Sköldberg (2016) inform that, since the late 1990s, artists working in different mediums have collaborated with managers in large and small, public and private organizations to undertake artistic interventions or experimentations. These initiatives are motivated by diverse objectives that range from business-oriented development of employee creativity, branding, and innovation processes, to publicly oriented cultivation of corporate values beyond profit. On the one hand, managerial discourses may instrumentalize art for conservative purposes such as the improvement of existing business functions. On the other hand, technology corporations such as Facebook have more progressive purposes, orientating art in shared workspaces as possible modes of self-expression for employees to identify with (Turner 2018). Conversely, many artists look to businesses for platforms to 'critique society and to give voice to whatever lacks a voice' (Berthoin Antal et al. 2016, 4). Many artistic movements such as Futurism and the situationists strive for transformation of the social order—even if experiments can only be realized in the most limited of contexts. For this reason, Plant (2002, 40) describes artistic experimentation as 'a propaganda of the possible'.

In this sense, artistic interventions in corporate settings emerge from frictions between conservative tendencies and transformative imperatives. Berthoin Antal et al. (2016) relate these frictions to Boltanski and Chiapello's (2007) characterization of 'the new spirit of capitalism' in post-Fordism, where artistic critiques of capitalist systems are incorporated into those very systems in ways that feed back into capital accumulation. The artistic critique of capitalism has its roots in nineteenth-century bohemian Paris and perhaps reached its cultural apotheosis in 1960s and 1970s countercultural movements where authenticity, innovation, and creative endeavour were seen as under threat from big business and mainstream society (Boltanski and Chiapello 2007). These accounts emphasize how capitalism and its critique are not binaristic but synergistic, and that consumptive forms of resistance, in fact, drive the market economy. For example, Heath and Potter (2004) state that while slow living movements imagine a radical break from mainstream culture, they nonetheless perpetuate consumer capitalism.

While corporate collaboration may blunt the force of artistic critique, artistic interventions nonetheless retain resistive potential. Beyes and Steyaert (2011) explain that this is because the potential of such projects lies not in their overt politicization, but in their reconfiguration of the doable and sayable by creating experiential openings for instability and ambiguity. Schwab (2013, 117) maintains that artworks 'as epistemic things can never become fully transparent' and it is this structural incompleteness that engenders meanings and inspires politics. The Light Phone is not simply a commodity, yet not quite a work of art: it is a hybrid object of artistic intervention that is ambiguous enough to create an experiential opening into a possible world that is comfortingly familiar, yet tantalizingly phantasmic.

THE LIGHT PHONE: DISCONNECTION AS SENSATION

The Light Phone is a monochromatic mobile device with a matt e-ink display (see figure 6.1) and minimal functions that, according to its website, is 'designed to be used as little as possible'. As a consumer electronic in its second iteration, The Light Phone II focuses on core utilities such as calls, texts, and maps, while eschewing feeds, social media, advertisements, news, and email. Its website also states that The Light Phone II 'respects users' time and attention', cultivating intentional use over infinite scrolls, happiness over connection (The Light Phone, n.d.). For example, its promotional video visually depicts The Light Phone II as a choice between time on screen or life in a richly sensorial world of walking your kids to school, reading books in the warmth of sun, smelling flowers along the way, and sharing home-cooked meals with loved ones. Addressing users directly, the video asks, 'How will you choose to spend your life today?' and 'Is being so connected actually making us any happier?' Within this promotional imaginary, 'Going Light' is a branded lifestyle populated by racially diverse users, arts and crafts, slow food and communal meals, family and the outdoors—where the texture and

Figure 6.1　The Light Phone. *Source*: Light Phone (n.d.).

tactility of The Light Phone blend seamlessly into a nostalgic lifeworld of roller skates, ceramic mugs, Polaroids, and vinyl records.

This branding does not stand in for The Light Phone as a product per se, but for 'Going Light' as what Arvidsson (2006) calls a propertied frame of action that provides a context in which products are used. What branding accomplishes is the 'making and selling of immaterial things—feelings and affects, personalities and values—rather than actual goods' (Banet-Weiser 2012, 7). The Light Phone's branding is a propertied frame for what Stewart (2011) refers to as atmospheric attunement—a capacity to affect and be affected—that is palpable and sensory, material yet abstract. The Light Phone's everyday scenes of purposeful characters grounded in imagined storylines provide atmospheres 'that push a present into a composition, an expressivity, the sense of potentiality and event' (Stewart 2011, 452). By attuning ourselves to atmospheres built up from the resonance between branded imaginaries of Going Light, popular discourses about the techlash, dreams of escape, and plans for the future, we shape public feelings around disconnection into the forms of a life.

Going Light stretches across recollections of the past and ideas about the future, everyday losses and desires, linking mediated sensations of living well with daydreams of possible lives. Like many branded commodities, The Light Phone is a device for what Wolf (2014) calls world-building: an aesthetically cohesive imaginary world with rich, fully furnished ambiences that provide platforms for atmospheric attunement. The Light Phone builds a world screened in the faded colours of late summer, where the muted laughter of slow dinner parties drift between long hugs and pour-over coffee. This is a world of friends and family, where meaningful community trumps mediated connections, where matte and monochrome trumps smart and shiny. This is a world unburdened by smart devices, and saturated with sensory pleasures and wholesome feelings. The Light Phone's branded world is primarily mediated not through fully formed ideologies about disconnection, but through sensorial transmissions between memory and fantasy.

Seremetakis (1994) explains that sensorial cultures emerge dynamically from perception and memory, activated by shared landscapes of semantically dense objects and embodied acts. The slick groove of vinyl records, the crinkled weave of linen tablecloths, the dewy fuzz of flower petals are resonant textures saturated with meanings about authenticity, pleasure, and class that are mobilized by Going Light's brand of disconnection. These sensorially saturated yet mediated artefacts are passageways into entanglements between everyday material experience and cultural memory that make up what Stewart (2007, 2) calls ordinary affects: 'public feelings that begin and end in broad circulation, but they're also the stuff that seemingly intimate lives are made of. They give circuits and flows the forms of a life.' Sensorial culture—through which Going Light is articulated—is social and collective, yet is not reducible to language. Atmospheric attunements to Going Light— that potentiate alternative configurations of time, technology, and connectivity—are mediated by brands, yet are not reducible to branding.

When Aleena, one of the authors of this chapter, first encountered The Light Phone's online promotion, she was entranced. The website's background image of fluffy clouds centred around the single word 'light' reminded her of lazy days in the park spent with her sister when they were kids; another image of dusk on an open road fringed by distant mountain ranges superimposed by the text 'buy the phone' made her think about cross-country road trip inspiration pinned on her social media. It felt like a dream, like a memory—it felt good. The Light Phone transforms the politics of disconnection—of big tech, attention economics, and the techlash—into good feelings. Ahmed (2010) offers that contemporary discourses of self-help and positive psychology often equate feeling good with happiness. Within the brand of Going Light, happiness is a form of world-making that, according to Ahmed, shapes what coheres as a world, where certain objects proximate and the right people gather. The happiness projected by The Light Phone's world of handmade objects and authentic humans is, in Ahmed's terms, promissory. The Light Phone is not really a phone at all, but a feeling of Going Light; the ethereal pleasures of The Light Phone are derived not from actual use but from the imagined life in a promised world. Like self-help's circular logic of feeling oneself into states of happiness and New Age discourses about manifesting one's desires by channelling thoughts, beliefs, and emotions (Urban 2015), The Light Phone operates in a recursive loop in which the intoxicating imaginary of disconnection stands in for the need to disconnect at all.

Even with its US$350 price tag and optional $30 monthly mobile plan, for most people imbricated in social and professional structures that require constant connection, The Light Phone II remains an aspirational product. As Feldman reports in her chapter in this volume, many people see disconnected lifestyles as beyond their reach. Going Light exclusively is likely to be difficult for professionals who depend upon or value social connections in their jobs. The Light Phone's promotional imaginary operates through what Portwood-Stacer (2013) calls conspicuous non-consumption: a form of lifestyle politics drawing from consumer activism and neoliberal entrepreneurial selfhood that emphasizes creativity, empowerment, and flexibility. The Light Phone addresses users as entrepreneurs by attuning their sense of self to artistic ambitions or creative endeavours. The Light Phone falls in step with the neoliberal mantra to be creative that permeates our work, leisure, and institutions (Mould 2018). According to Hollier, creatively inclined customers were better prepared for the sudden change of lifestyle and sense of self in the absence of a smartphone:

> My initial hunch [was that] artists and other creatives that kind of have a passion already, they were the ones that you know were immediately able to Go Light, so to speak, and feel that anxiety that comes with leaving the smartphone with the things they already loved. Musicians Go Light and start playing piano and they forget about Instagram. But it was a little bit harder for people who maybe don't feel like they have that calling or thing that they're always doing.

For those without a passion project or a hobby, Going Light might be a painful exercise. Hollier mentions a customer who shared that Going Light triggered an existential crisis because of a realization that they lacked any actual hobbies or specific interests to pursue. Distinct from recreation, hobbies are productive forms of leisure (Gelber 1999) that feed into vocational passion—the obligation to 'do what you love'—which underlies exploitative labour practices in creative industries (Chia 2019). While the use of display art at Facebook's corporate headquarters is intended to provide a kind of architecture for employees to see themselves as artists (Turner 2018), The

Light Phone goes one step further, acting as a kind of litmus test to separate the true creatives from the pretenders. Within this ideology of disconnective creativity, stripping away smartphone connections reveals which users are primed to access positive psychologist Mihály Csíkszentmihályi's (1990) much vaunted 'flow' state, or the psychological condition of complete absorption in an activity. These conceptions of flow and hobbies commodify creativity as human capital.

In this sense, the creative forms of disconnection evoked by The Light Phone are exclusionary by design. Like creativity, the deployment of innovation as a construct is always strategic because it places individual actors in a competitive field of action that necessitates a certain order of response (Suchman and Bishop 2000). The Light Phone's developer discourses suggest that creativity is commodified as human capital by linking it to personhood—thereby revealing a politics of disconnection that is stratified by both class and race. While The Light Phone's economic exclusion is explicit, its racial exclusion through the aesthetic of whiteness is implicit. Analyzing cultural appropriation in food media, Alang (2020) offers that the contemporary aesthetic of whiteness channels organized clutter and effortless cool; it emanates from attractive, mostly millennial people, adorned by natural materials, handling artisan objects, bathed in natural light. This is also the taken-for-granted backdrop of The Light Phone promotional video, in which atmospheres for Going Light are channelled. In his landmark analysis of Western visual culture of film, photography, and painting, Dyer (1997) states that whiteness is constructed through luminosity: a purifying lightness that is unsullied by the corporeality of dirt, blood, passion, and even movement. The Light Phone operates within this moralized aesthetic register, purifying the incongruous distractions and relentless exertions of mobile connection into a symmetrical object within an effortless world.

Notably, the moral and symbolic power of whiteness lies in its invisibility as a norm; it is defined not by presence, but by absence. Lightness, and by association, whiteness, possesses ethical and aesthetic superiority because of its apparent non-particularity, as simultaneously everything and nothing. Since the translucence and normativity of whiteness is also a negation, it lacks distinction and character. For this reason, bodies of colour are frequently mobilized in visual culture to provide contrast to the aesthetic of whiteness (Dyer 1997), while global culinary influences are appropriated without due acknowledgement of origin or racialized inequities in Western food media to inject flavour into the white pantry (Alang 2020). Similarly, the aesthetic whiteness of Going Light mobilizes bodies of colour—casting Black, Brown, and Asian actors—to add earthy flavour to an ethereal palette of muslin drapes, twilit glassware, and stretched canvas. In other words, bodies of colour set The Light Phone's catalogue of desires into motion.

Going Light mirrors the aspirational structure of whiteness as an ideal that can never be attained. Just as to be absolutely white is to be a subject without hue or properties, The Light Phone cultivates a branded ambience that provides pleasure without satisfaction. Dyer (1997) qualifies that this paradox of whiteness as normative and negative, corporeal and transcendent, is a source of its representational dynamism and productivity. Just as this paradox is an engine of desire at the perpetual edge of resolution, Going Light is couched in an ambivalence that is aspirational in its world-making, yet mundane in its monthly mobile plan. Furthermore, The Light Phone is idealistic in its design philosophy against the attention economy, yet it is pragmatic in its manufacturing choices in the global tech industry. For example, Hollier admits that 'it's really a struggle and we don't have a lot of power to fully reinvent the manufacturing process or make a fair phone'. A fair phone is a telecommunication device that is built to minimize exploitative labour practices and environmental impact. Just as the paradox of whiteness is aesthetically generative, Going Light's ambivalence is a source of productiveness—an open-ended experiment with alternative modes of connection. Instead of peddling an empty promise of tech solutionism, The Light Phone was created by Hollier and co-founder Kaiwei Tang as an artistic intervention. The atmospheres and ambiences of Going Light tap into what Williams (1977) calls structures of feeling: social experiences in solution that linger at the edge of semantic availability, which do not need definition or rationalization to exert force in the world. The political force of Going Light's ordinary affects come into relief through contrast with disconnective experiments that do not cast sensory worlds, but condense worldly sensations into seemingly universal symbols. These experiments seek not to intervene in, but to protect the attention economy.

GOOGLE DIGITAL WELLBEING EXPERIMENTS: DISCONNECTION AS CONCEPT

Introducing Digital Wellbeing Experiments: a platform to share ideas and tools that help people find a better balance with technology. Try the experiments and create your own. Together we'll learn how to create better technology for everyone.

(Google Digital Wellbeing Experiments 2019)

Google's Experimental apps run on the Android operating system and include Post Box that holds all mobile notifications until a time specified by the user, who is encouraged to go through them at their own pace through an in-app interface. Another experimental app is We Flip, which is designed for in-person gatherings where everyone turns off their devices for designated periods of time to focus on face-to-face interactions. The platform cites Google researchers Aranda and Baig's (2018) research paper 'Toward "JOMO": The Joy of Missing Out and the Freedom of Disconnecting', presented at the Association for Computing Machinery's International Conference on Human-Computer Interaction with Mobile Devices and Services. The authors conducted a qualitative, mixed-methods study of mobile phone users in Zurich, Switzerland, and the San Francisco Bay Area, to 'inform opportunities for innovation in the mobile industry' (Aranda and Baig 2018, 19:2). By understanding experiences of mobile device overuse and non-use, Google's researchers hoped to innovate products and services encouraging people to moderate their usage habits in order to continue to use smartphones. In addition to time-tracking, notification management, and other tools that are built by the Android operating system as part of Google's Digital Wellbeing campaign, Experiments offers quirky apps for individuals to try, to play around with, to 'find a balance that's right for them' (Google Digital Wellbeing Experiments 2019).

Two apps by London-based design studio Special Projects stand out as encapsulations of big tech's strategy of 'experimentation' as a response to the techlash. The app Paper Phone uses an Android app to create a paper version of one's phone on a folded sheet of paper, that includes favourite contacts, maps and meetings, and even resources such as recipes and phrase books for activities like cooking and language learning. The second app Envelope is a paper sleeve that transforms the Google Pixel phone into a single-function device either for making phone calls or taking photos. This envelope must be torn open to restore the phone's original multi-functions. According to Special Projects, Envelope was inspired by basic phones with limited functions as a periodic alternative to a primary smartphone, which was also the original rationale for The Light Phone. Both Paper Phone and Envelope are visually promoted through stark minimalist aesthetics: both videos feature close-ups of the bleached whiteness of the Paper Phone and Envelope against a textureless grey studio background. The emphasis on the aesthetic and moral purity of whiteness is sharper than in The Light Phone's promotion. For example, Paper Phone and Envelope's designers appear in the promotional video wearing clinically white shirts; this sanitized monochromatic palette is punctuated only by the pastel hues of a perfectly shaped lemon framed by a terrazzo cutting board and pale pink polish of one designer's immaculately trimmed nails.

Unlike The Light Phone's sunlit vignettes of bodies of colour living, laughing, and loving, Google Experiments' studio lighting and pale protagonists provide a blank canvas for the evocation of cheeky artificiality and quirky sanitation. Distinct from the frisson of Going Light's luxuriant textures and diverse flavours, the sensations piqued by Paper Phone and Envelope are not of movement or expansion but of stillness. If The Light Phone's disconnective atmosphere is attuned through fuzzy synapses between memory and fantasy, then Google Experiments' ambience crystalizes the anxieties and ambitions of disconnection into a literal message to experiment. For example, Special Projects describe their apps as 'little concepts' and a 'little experiment' for taking a break from the digital world and finding personal balance with technology (Google Digital Wellbeing Experiments 2019). This aesthetic (of) restraint can be contextualized through conceptual art, which is understood by many critics as different from traditional art. Cray (2014) encapsulates that common understandings of conceptual art such as Marcel Duchamp's Readymades dematerializes the artefact to crystalize the idea. In other words, the urinal is decentred as an unremarkable medium for Fountain as an idea. This contrasts with the centrality of the materiality of other kinds of artwork.

In this sense, Paper Phone and Envelope can be interpreted as distilling the dense sensorial networks of disconnective atmospheres into a little concept: to try a little experiment with disconnection. For example, Envelope's promotional copy describes the app as designed to *'temporarily* transform your phone into a simpler, calmer device' (our emphasis). Similarly, Envelope's video states that 'the idea is to try to last as long as possible, before opening the envelope and getting your old phone back'. These experiential incisions in the temporality of connection are not meant to destabilize the status quo or imagine an alternate life and world with technology. Google's Digital Wellbeing Experiments are far from the big ideas proposed, for example, by tech ethicist Tristan Harris's now infamous 141-slide presentation 'A Call to Minimize Distraction and Respect Users' Attention' to fellow Google employees (Newton 2018). Instead, Paper Phone and Envelope pitch themselves as modest conceptual tools for re-calibrating device use towards normative standards of balance and continued usage.

The dematerialization of the object in conceptual art is not absolute but relative in its devaluing of the physical aspects of an artwork to focus on its conceptual aspects (Cray 2014). Similarly, Going Light's focus on the sensorially saturated atmospheres of disconnection is relative to Google's focus on the conceptual distillation of its small experiments. The variation of these strategies is instructive to understanding varying responses to the techlash. The Light Phone invites aspirational users to weave a personal tapestry from public dreams, fantasies, memories, and feelings about disconnection to potentially transform their relationship to digital devices. At variance with this, Paper Phone and Envelope do not weave a tapestry of disconnective desires; instead, Special Projects has surgically sliced and cauterized the fabric of connection to temporarily limit disconnection to an experimental lapse.

By conceptually distilling disconnection as an experiential lapse, Paper Phone and Envelope inoculate criticisms about the harms of constant connectivity and reinforce the norm of connectivity. As a disconnection strategy promoted by technology companies, Digital Wellbeing mobilizes what Mulvin (2018) describes as the language of prevention, inoculation, and hygiene. This can be seen in Google's Digital Wellbeing features on Android devices as well as Apple's Screen Time and Night Mode, which both have comparable features for tracking and restricting app usage and managing notifications to mitigate distractions. According to Mulvin, these disconnective features are a form of media prophylaxis, which emphasize harm reduction through self-care discourses that shift responsibility onto the individual without addressing the underlying cultural logics and business models of attention, engagement, and advertising.

By providing a platform for disconnective experiments and tools, Google Digital Wellbeing's message of balance through calibrated connectivity can be understood as part of Silicon Valley's integration of artistic critique of the attention economy to resist the techlash. By framing problems of constant connectivity within the language of tools for individual balance and calibration, Google Digital Wellbeing centres ethics in the world-building visions and practices of designers and technologists, not in social worlds or social contracts they develop technical systems for. These experiments rationalize the resistive potential of artistic endeavours into frameworks of organizational risk assessment. Furthermore, by incorporating and inoculating against critique about the harms of constant connection, these experiments are a way in which capitalism reshapes itself into less-objectionable forms, thus increasing resistance to similar critiques in the future (Boltanski and Chiapello 2005). In other words, Digital Wellbeing is Google's latest means to manage the brand, reinforcing how digital well-being acts as a social good to instil public goodwill (Beattie and Daubs 2020). The breadth of quirky Google Digital Wellbeing Experiments reinforces that the artistic critique of the attention economy has been integrated into the platform where ethical experimentation is institutionalized as brand management.

CONCLUSION: EXPERIMENTS IN DISCONNECTION

Using the problematic of disconnective experimentation, this chapter compared The Light Phone's branded sensations of lightness with Google Digital Wellbeing's concepts of balance. Both these disconnective experiments evoke the tactility of paper and the aspirational aesthetics of whiteness.

However, while Google's experiments frame disconnection as momentary, The Light Phone experiment grounds disconnection in the mundane. Google Digital Wellbeing Experiments may have a similar look and feel as The Light Phone. They may even share similar institutional incubation pathways. But their temporal deployments and politics of disconnection are critically different. Google's experiments limit disconnection to a gimmick, thereby inoculating criticisms about the harms of constant connectivity and reinforcing the norm of connectivity. The Light Phone's artistic experimentation create experiential openings for instability and ambiguity; however, by building a luxuriant world of mediated pleasures, the racialized aspiration of Going Light becomes an end in itself, instead of a means towards pursuing alternative configurations of time, technology, and connectivity across socioeconomic classes.

This chapter analyzed how the ethics and ethos of disconnective experimentation are institutionally, aesthetically, and politically imbricated. In so doing, this analysis presents a framework for the relational assessment of different disconnective experimentation. Artistic interventions operate not through overt political manifestations, but through the destabilization of dominant ways of seeing, doing, and thinking. In other words, artistic experiments such as Google Digital Wellbeing Experiments and The Light Phone should not necessarily be judged by Natale and Treré's (2020) criterion of political mobilization against cultures of connection. Instead, these experiments are more fittingly evaluated alongside Odell's (2019) call not simply for action, but for contemplation: resisting the attention economy happens first and foremost in the mind. Attention is not simply withdrawn from mobile devices and persuasive design techniques; attention must be cultivated elsewhere. Rather than Going Light or disconnecting from smart technology in a neoliberal framework of self-care, Odell demonstrates how to disengage from the profit motive that underlies the digital economy and demands our attention. For example, interacting with art and wandering through non-commercialized spaces such as public parks offer alternative sociotechnical environments that can both expand and deepen our attention.

Similarly, sensorially marked rituals of putting on records, sharing Polaroids, and brewing coffee can expand and deepen our attention. Seremetakis (1994, 13) emphasizes the political significance of everyday life in modernity for potentiating far-reaching historical transformations: 'Everyday life is also the zone of lost glances, oblique views and angles where micro-practices leak through the crevices and cracks of official cultures and memories.' In other words, the sensory structure of everyday disconnection imbricates the poetic and political. However, to resist the attention economy, these rituals and micro-practices must extend beyond cosseted branded worlds to confront the politicization of attention at the intersection of issues of public space, environmental politics, class, and race. In particular, this politicization must challenge the techno-aestheticization of whiteness as the default setting for human creativity, flourishing, and freedom (Hamilton 2018). Ahmed (2007) offers that whiteness is an orientation—not reducible to white skin—that puts certain objects, styles, capacities, aspirations, techniques, and habits within reach. As suggested by this analysis, the techno-aestheticization of whiteness in the sensory politics of Going Light frames disconnection through good feelings of an easeful life. What gets left out in this imaginary of disconnection are the ordinary feelings of discomfort that entrain bodies of colour. Therefore, politicizing race in disconnection entails more than dismantling the aesthetic of whiteness in branded ambiences of the techlash; it means centring discomfort in the sensory structure of disconnection.

Experimentation in response to the techlash such as Google Digital Wellbeing and The Light Phone may seem incommensurable with the culture of connectivity, yet these and other disconnection practices emerge from and are constitutive of that culture. These experiments with disconnection are what Hesselberth (2018) calls the 'constitutive outside' of the culture of connectivity: material, symbolic, and strategic forces that—in their resistance—are the condition of emergence of connectivity. The potential of disconnection, according to Hesselberth, is not in the rediscovery of age-old themes such as productivity or solitude, but in the possibility of creating an outside to whatever is being disconnected from. In other words, disconnection is not revelatory because it reminds us of the benefits of time spent alone, but because of the actual action of disconnection itself: the disengagement from something. To weaken the hold that the logic of connectivity has over society and individuals, we must assess the equivocality of this constitutive outside and weigh different disconnection practices against each other to understand their connections to each other, so that we may advocate some over others.

REFERENCES

Ahmed, Sara. 2007. "A phenomenology of whiteness." *Feminist Theory* 8(2), 149–168.

———. 2010. *The Promise of Happiness*. Duke University Press.

Alang, Navneet. 2020. "Stewed Awakening." *Eater*. May 20. https://www.eater.com /2020/5/20/21262304/global-pantry-alison-roman-bon-appetit.

Aranda, Julie H., and Safia Baig. 2018. 'Toward "JOMO" the joy of missing out and the freedom of disconnecting'. In *Proceedings of the 20th International Conference on Human-Computer Interaction with Mobile Devices and Services*. Barcelona, Spain, pp. 1–8.

Arvidsson, Adam. 2006. *Brands: Meaning and Value in Media Culture*. Psychology Press.

Banet-Weiser, Sarah. 2012. *AuthenticTM: The Politics of Ambivalence in a Brand Culture*. NYU Press.

Baym, Nancy K., Kelly B. Wagman, and Christopher J. Persaud. 2020. 'Mindfully scrolling: Rethinking Facebook after time deactivated'. *Social Media+ Society* 6 (2). doi:10.1177/2056305120919105.

Beattie, Alex, and Michael S. Daubs. 2020. 'Framing "digital well-being" as a social good'. *First Monday* 25 (12). doi:10.5210/fm.v25i12.10430.

Beer, Jeff. 2019. Why Google was the most important—and unconventional—brand marketer of the 2010s, *Fast Company,* December 30. Available at: https://www.fastcompany.com/90444095/why-google-was-the-most-important-and-unconventional-brand-marketer-of-the-2010s [Accessed 26 May 2020].

Berthoin Antal, Ariane, Jill Woodilla, and Ulla Johansson Sköldberg. 2016. "Artistic interventions in organisations." In *Artistic Interventions in Organisations: Research, Theory and Practice*, pp. 3–17. Routledge.

Beyes, Timon, and Chris Steyaert. 2011. "The ontological politics of artistic interventions: Implications for performing action research." *Action Research* 9 (1), 100–115.

Boltanski, Luc, and Eve Chiapello. 2005. *The New Spirit of Capitalism*, trans. *G. Elliott,* Verso. Caldwell, John T. 2014. "Para-industry, shadow academy." *Cultural Studies* 28 (4), 720–740.

Cray, Wesley. 2014. "Conceptual art, ideas, and ontology." *The Journal of Aesthetics and Art Criticism* 72(3), 235–245.

Crogan, Patrick, and Samuel Kinsley. 2012. "Paying attention: Towards a critique of the attention economy." *Culture Machine* 13, 1–29. https://culturemachine.net/wp-content/uploads/2019/01/463-1025-1-PB.pdf.

Csíkszentmihályi, Mihály. 1990. *Flow: The Psychology of Optimal Experience*. Harper and Row.

Deleuze, Gillies and Félix Guattari. 1987. *A Thousand Plateaus: Capitalism and Schizophrenia*. University of Minnesota Press.

Dyer, Richard. 1997. *White: Essays on Race and Culture*. Routledge.

Gelber, Steven M. 1999. *Hobbies: Leisure and the Culture of Work in America*. Columbia University Press.

Google. n.d. "Digital Wellbeing Experiments." Accessed December 31, 2020. https://experiments.withgoogle.com/collection/digitalwellbeing.

Google Digital Wellbeing Experiments. 2019. "Introducing Digital Wellbeing Experiments." Available at: https://experiments.withgoogle.com/collection/digitalwellbeing.

Hamilton, Jennifer. 2018. "Critical perspectives on whiteness and technoscience: An introduction." *Catalyst: Feminism, Theory, Technoscience* 4(1), 1–12.

Heath, Joseph, and Andrew Potter. 2004. *Nation of Rebels: Why Counterculture Became Consumer Culture*. Harper Collins.

Hesselberth, Pepita. 2018. "Discourses on disconnectivity and the right to disconnect." *New Media & Society* 20 (5), 1994–2010.

Iezzi, Teressa. 2010. Meet The Google 5, The Team Behind 'Parisian Love' Super Bowl Sport. *AdAge*. Available at: https://adage.com/article/special-report-super-bowl/meet-google-5-team-parisian-love-super-bowl-ad/146131.

Lewis, Paul. 2017. "'Our minds can be hijacked': the tech insiders who fear a smartphone dystopia." *The Guardian*. October 5, 2017. https://www.theguardian.com/technology/2017/oct/05/smartphone-addiction-silicon-valley-dystopia.

Light Phone. n.d. Available at: https://www.thelightphone.com/.

Metcalf, Jacob, Emanuel Moss, and danah boyd. 2019. "Owning ethics: Corporate logics, silicon valley, and the institutionalization of ethics." *Social Research: An International Quarterly* 86 (2), 449–476.

Monahan, Torin, 2015. The right to hide? Anti-surveillance camouflage and the aestheticization of resistance. *Communication and Critical/Cultural Studies* 12 (2), 159–178. doi:10.1080/14791420.2015.1006646.

Mould, Oli. 2018. *Against creativity*. Verso.

Mulvin, Dylan. 2018. "Media prophylaxis: Night modes and the politics of preventing harm." *Information & Culture* 53 (2), 175–202.

Natale, Simone, and Emiliano Treré. 2020. "Vinyl won't save us: Reframing disconnection as engagement." *Media, Culture & Society* 42 (4), 626–633.

Newton, Casey. 2018. Google's new focus on well-being started five years ago with this presentation, *The Verge*, May 10. Available at: https://www.theverge.com/2018/5/10/17333574/google-android-p-update-tristan-harris-design-ethics.

Odell, Jenny. 2019. *How to Do Nothing: Resisting the Attention Economy*. Melville House.

Phillipov, Michelle. 2013. "In defense of textual analysis: Resisting methodological hegemony in media and cultural studies." *Critical Studies in Media Communication* 30 (3), 209–223.

Plant, Sadie. 2002. *The Most Radical Gesture: The Situationist International in a Postmodern Age*. Routledge.

Portwood-Stacer, Laura. 2013. "Media refusal and conspicuous non-consumption: The performative and political dimensions of Facebook abstention." *New Media & Society* 15 (7), 1041–1057.

Ryan, Kevin, 2013. What Can the Average Marketer Learn From Google Creative Lab? *AdAge*, 19 April. Available at: https://adage.com/article/digitalnext/learn-google-creative-lab/240984.

Schwab, Michael, 2013. *Experimental Systems: Future Knowledge in Artistic Research*. Leuven University Press.

Seremetakis, C. Nadia, ed. 1996. *The Senses Still*. University of Chicago Press.

Steiber, Annika, and Sverker Alänge. 2013. "A corporate system for continuous innovation: The case of Google inc". *European Journal of Innovation Management* 16 (2), 243–264. doi:10.1108/14601061311324566.

Stewart, Kathleen. 2007. *Ordinary Affects*. Duke University Press.

———. 2011. "Atmospheric attunements". *Environment and Planning D: Society and space* 29(3), 445–453.

Suchman, Lucy, and Libby Bishop. 2000. "Problematizing 'innovation' as a critical project." *Technology Analysis & Strategic Management* 12 (3), 327–333.

Thorén, Claes, Mats Edenius, Jenny Eriksson Lundström, and Andreas Kitzmann. 2017. "The hipster's dilemma: What is analogue or digital in the post-digital society?" *Convergence* 25 (2), 324–339. doi:10.1177/1354856517713139.

Turner, Fred. 2018. The arts at Facebook: An aesthetic infrastructure for surveillance capitalism, *Poetics* 67, 53–62. doi:10.1016/j.poetic.2018.03.003.

Twenge, Jean M. 2017. *iGen: Why Today's Super-Connected Kids Are Growing Up Less Rebellious, More Tolerant, Less Happy—and Completely Unprepared for Adulthood—and What That Means for the Rest of Us.* Atria Books.

Urban, Hugh B. 2015. *New Age, Neopagan, and New Religious Movements: Alternative Spirituality in Contemporary America.* University of California Press.

Williams, Raymond. 1977. *Marxism and Literature.* Oxford Paperbacks.

Wilson, Mark. 2019. How the co-founder of Google Creative Lab turned it into a juggernaut, *Fast Company,* May 10. Available at: https://www.fastcompany.com/90 345911/how-the-founder-of-google-creative-lab-turned-it-into-a-juggernaut.

Wolf, Mark J. P. 2014. *Building Imaginary Worlds: The Theory and History of Subcreation.* Routledge.

Zaragova-Fuster, María-Teresa and José-Alberto García-Avilés. 2020. "The role of innovation labs in advancing the relevance of public service media: The cases of BBC news labs and RTVE lab". *Communication & Society* 33 (1), 45–61. doi:10.15581/003.33.1.45-61.

Chapter 7

From Digital Detox to 24/365 Disconnection

Between Dependency Tactics and Resistance Strategies in Brazil

Marianna Ferreira Jorge and Julia Salgado

This chapter proposes to examine the recent phenomenon of the digital detox, a kind of rehab for self-identified internet addicts, which comprises a variety of therapeutic offerings for all kinds of consumers. Offers range from self-help books for specialized courses, mobile apps to luxury resort lodging, from millionaire clinics to a variety of drugs to treat conditions that are increasingly common in our society, such as depression and compulsive disorders. They promise to appease some of the most damaging side effects or even permanently eliminate the harms of excessive internet use by encouraging 'conscious' consumption and promoting a 'happier', more 'balanced', and more 'productive' life. All this could be achieved, in theory, without great efforts and by enjoying some of the pleasures that capitalism provides.

To confront such widely disseminated discourses, we start from the hypothesis that such strategies are supported by advertising rhetoric and are often as profitable as they are temporary. After all, the lack of moderation in time spent in front of screens is characteristic of the network logic, and digital devices are built on the central objective of capturing attention and creating addictive behaviours, which turns any attempt at self-control into failure. Not surprisingly, the encouragement to do a detox tends to be engendered in an instrumental rationality that creates new problems instead of solving them, or even reinforces existing ones. What is sought, in most cases, is to optimize individuals' performance in order to adapt them to the precepts of capitalism, urging them to self-entrepreneurship, while voraciously consuming the unlimited offers available (Jorge and Sibilia 2019).

In short, what we suggest is that, far from serving as a means of resisting power mechanisms, the digital detox favours neoliberal interests and propagates the most desired lifestyles today. This is how the stimulation dynamics which replaced disciplinary repression—comprehensively addressed by French philosopher Michel Foucault (1987)—operate. Unlike in Foucault's modern society, the current biopolitical regime do not aim to oppress individuals, but aim to captivate them; they do not demand obedience, but generate dependence; they do not create embarrassment, but provide rewards (Jorge 2019). In fact, it is possible to observe constant stimuli to dependence on all kinds of products and services usually offered by the same means that propagate malaise. In some cases, it is assumed that each individual could (and should) fight against the sufferings arising from digital technologies use, while still enjoying their benefits.

Contrary to some theories according to which technologies are the 'cause' of changes in the ways of living (McLuhan 1969), this chapter addresses digital communications technologies as a sociocultural invention intermingled with many others (Crary 2014; Sibilia 2016). In this sense, we consider the technical artefacts, with which we have become 'compatible' in recent decades, as the *effects* and, at the same time, *instruments* of certain historical transformations (Foucault 1976). Such transformations comprise a set of new demands, desires, pressures, and discomforts, both at the individual and collective level, and produce sensitive impacts on the production of subjectivity and forms of sociability. By having their use naturalized, these devices contribute to the creation of new language games and repertoires of conduct, redefining the values and pleasures people hold dear, subverting the ways we experience time and space and inventing new bonds, imaginaries, and lifestyles.

On the one hand, digital technologies participate in the creation of this typically contemporary malaise, based on the lifestyles they propose and stimulate; on the other hand, the media, in a tactical alliance with the market and technology, produce explanations for the causes of such discomforts while offering solutions to appease them, promoting modulations in the interpretation of experiences and feelings. At a time of weakening of modern institutional references, the media plays the role of instructing people about the most appropriate ways of being and existing in the world, which tend to justify even greater market control of individual conduct. As with all the set of beliefs that exist in a given time, these truths are produced to the detriment of other sources of meaning, which are disqualified or ignored for not being adequate to the 'regime of power' in force (Foucault 2008).

Therefore, the proliferation of news stories about connection malaise and the digital detox strategy is emblematic. Through these narratives, we can observe a certain pedagogy of life that used to be produced primarily in traditional institutions. This is what Alain Ehrenberg (2010) calls 'assisted autonomy'. According to the author, the core values of our culture are freedom and autonomy but, paradoxically, the subjects of the twenty-first century have become increasingly helpless and disoriented, dependent on all kinds of specialized orientation, which submit them to new forms of social control and subjection.

As a counterpoint to the digital detox marketed through apps, retreats, and courses, we will analyze a more radical strategy of resistance to biopolitical entanglement: 24/365 disconnection. The expression 'disconnection 24/365' was inspired by Jonathan Crary's book *24/7: Late Capitalism and the Ends of Sleep*. More specifically, by the passage in which the author justifies not using the term "24/365" to characterize the current regime of power, because, contrary to the 24/7 logic, which is homogeneous and composed of 'incessant, frictionless operations', the expression 24/365 is 'an extended temporality throughout which something can actually change, and over which unexpected events can occur' (2014, 18). It is therefore a temporality that may create some openness to other possible ones, raising events, changes in rhythms and perceptions, as well as mechanisms that aim to escape control and to engender other ways of life. The aim is to understand how digital detox and the 24/365 disconnection differ and what they have in common, as well as their effects on the subjectivities in the second decade of the twenty-first century, mainly in Brazil. For that purpose, in November 2017, we conducted an in-depth interview with Brazilian artist Ana Rovati, who, a couple of years earlier, gave up internet connection artefacts for 365 days to experience the difficulties and benefits of an offline routine. Although the lack of internet access is a reality for about a quarter of the Brazilian population over 10 years of age, placing herself on the margins of society during that period was neither a decision caused by economic limitations nor an arbitrary imposition or obligation. Instead, it was voluntary, though not disinterested or free from other purposes, as we will see. This is the privilege of her social position and also its particularity.

The story we analyze is about someone who lived almost half of her life dependent on computer devices and, for one year, forced herself to live without them. Although the case analyzed here is peculiar and unusual, we consider that this experience provides us with a very particular perspective on connection and calls our attention to some characteristics that we might miss by adapting so fast to the continuous flows of information. From the cartography of a series of speeches, ranging from journalistic articles to an in-depth interview, we aim to reflect not only on the relationship between contemporary subjectivities and communication and information technologies, but also on the power grids that form us as subjects (Delfanti and Iaconesi 2016).

More than offering answers, the objective of this chapter is to raise questions, in order to offer clues to what we are becoming and, above all, what we are trying to resist. In this sense, the very resistance strategies employed today are also characteristic of a time and, as such, they can only be understood in the light of their time. As Italian philosopher Giorgio Agamben (2009) points out in his article, 'What is the contemporary?', those who truly belong to their time are those who neither perfectly coincide with it nor adjust themselves to its demands. That means that only those who are able to see beyond the lights and face the darkness and obscurity of their time—even though they are a product of that time—can really understand it.

Before we move on to the analysis, it is worth clarifying that we intend neither to assess the effectiveness of the strategies reported nor to offer a catalogue of good or bad 'solutions' for the dramas in question. Our aim is to explore the strategies and values that underpin the practices of disconnection. To this end, in the first part of the chapter, we analyse news stories on digital detox, focusing on Brazilian cases. In the second part, as a counterpoint to the critical apathy towards the subject nowadays, we reflect on Ana Rovati's unique experience, as an exception that proves the rule.

DETOX TO PERFORM

At the age of 15, F., a resident of São Paulo, had a personal history that still caused some astonishment in the first decade of the twenty-first century: he had a severe condition of digital dependence. After his parents' divorce when he was 13, F. stopped going to school and started spending a significant amount of time locked in his bedroom, from where he had unrestricted internet access. The teenager spent an average of 12 to 18 hours a day connected to the internet, having reached a maximum of 38 uninterrupted hours online. On three occasions, his mother's attempts to get him away from the computer culminated in aggressive behaviour. Upon being hospitalized, F. presented 'dysphoric humor, grandiose delusions, logorrhea, compromised pragmatism and no critical sense about his condition' (Stravogiannis and Abreu 2009, 78).

Today, in the prelude to the third decade of the third millennium, F.'s story no longer appears as surprising, even though it remains frightening. That is because, as research shows, the amount of time individuals spend connected to the internet increases progressively worldwide: while in 2011, the average time spent online was 1 hour and 15 minutes, in 2020, this increased to 3 hours. Social media platforms consume almost two-and-a-half hours of an individual's day.[1] In Brazil, the reality is even more worrying, since the country occupies the second position in the world ranking for the highest consumption of social networking platforms, with a daily average of 3 hours and 45 minutes in 2019.[2] Omnipresent smartphones, which became new body extensions for over 3.5 billion people—or 45% of the global population today[3]—intensify such excessive online consumption.

Stories like F.'s often appear as supporting evidence for campaigns such as the 'Digital Detox Challenge', promoted by the Ministry of Family in Jair Bolsonaro's administration. Making a linguistic pun, Minister Damares Alves states that 'the greatest challenge Brazilian families face is to reconnect', reinforcing the importance of the campaign. The proposal consisted of 24 hours without access to the internet and social networking platforms on 8 December 2019 so Brazilians could spend that time with their families. After the withdrawal period, participants were invited to record videos talking about their experience and, ironically, publish them on their social media pages. The minister herself, who posts four Twitter posts a day on average, failed the challenge on that day by tweeting the following: 'Until now, all of the Digital Detox participants are well and healthy with their families, with no abstinence crisis.'[4]

Although it is not yet categorized as a mental illness, it is increasingly noticeable that unbridled consumption of online content can generate dysfunctional individuals. Numerous media stories and reports are evidence of the phenomenon and present, in the form of 'self-help journalism' (Freire Filho 2011),[5] recipes to escape its deleterious effects. We can see an example in the article 'Detox Digital' on *IstoÉ* magazine (Lavieri 2020), which describes spa Botanique, one of the precursors of this type of 'exclusive service', the digital detox, in Brazil. For about 12,000 Brazilian Reals, one can afford a digital rehab in the fashionable Campos do Jordão region, the winter destination of São Paulo's elite. The two-night package includes a balanced diet, outdoor walks, massages, yoga sessions, manicures, pedicures, and other perks such as 'Atlantic Forest rain' and 'isotonic bath'. The handful of

---

[1] 'Internet usage worldwide—Statistics & Facts', Statista, accessed 9 July 2020, https://www.statista .com/topics/1145/internet-usage-worldwide/#dossierSummary__chapter1.

[2] 'Brazil ranks second in the list of countries that spend more time on social networks', Época Negócios, accessed 6 September 2019 https://epocanegocios.globo.com/Tecnologia/noticia/2019/09/b rasil-e-2-em-ranking-de-paises-que-passam-mais-tempo-em-redes-sociais.html.

[3] 'How many smartphones are in the world', BankMyCell, accessed 9 July 2020, https://www.ban kmycell.com/blog/how-many-phones-are-in-the-world.

[4] @DamaresAlves (2019, December 8) [Twitter post] https://twitter.com/DamaresAlves / status/1203741663606267904/photo/1.

[5] According to Freire Filho (2011), 'self-help journalism' is a category of journalism that, endorsed by specialists and based on real stories of overcoming adversity, promotes the idea that individuals can (and must) take actions and maximize their potential according to practical and rational guidelines.

analogue experiences aims to keep guests busy and divert their attention from their phones—since the hotel paradoxically allows smartphones and provides internet connection in all rooms. Still according to the report, only 30% of the guests get to effectively disconnect and spend their entire stay offline. The promise is that, after the short experience, customers can resume their activities in a more balanced and functional manner.

The same argument of searching for functionality is found on the Digital Detox Beach website:[6] 'The Digital Detox Beach is a great way to find balance between health, productivity and efficiency in a connected world.' Hidden in the Atlantic Forest in Paraty, in the south coast of Rio de Janeiro, the beach is only accessible by boat. The initiative promises 'the chance to pause and recharge, tuning and adapting our own rhythms to the rhythms of nature'. This way, 'when we return to our offices and everyday activities, we will be more productive, having gained a new perspective'.

In addition to the digital rehab tourism, there is also a growing demand for other types of services and products related to digital detox, as pointed out in a trend report sponsored by Fiep, the federation of industries in Paraná, Brazil.[7] After all, disconnecting for a few days on a paradise beach or a luxurious spa is one thing; it is quite another to be conscious about technological consumption on a day-to-day basis in our work and study routines. With services ranging from lectures, training, in-company (or in-schools) consultancy to two-day immersions for more radical detox, the Delete Institute[8] claims to be the first entity in Brazil specialized in digital detox. With a team of professionals led by behavioural psychologists, communicologists, and psychiatrists, the company offers a 'portfolio of products and services' for a diverse audience: from businessmen to children and adolescents, from high-performance athletes to school teachers. Acting as personal trainers, they promise to improve and optimize customer behaviour through training, games, handbooks, and even the visit of the company's mascot, *Deletinho*, in schools and companies. *Deletinho* is indeed the protagonist of the book 'Cartilha Digital' (something like 'Digital Guidebook'), in which he teaches children, through 12 steps, to make conscious use of digital technologies in their daily lives. The institute's website lists the benefits of their services[9] and leaves no doubt as to how instrumental rationality guides the company's objectives: 'greater efficiency and productivity', 'time management optimization', 'better interpersonal (professional, social, family, romantic) relationships', and 'shorter,

6 'Home', Praia do Detox Digital, accessed 2 August 2020, http://www.digitaldetoxbrasil.com/.
7 'Tendências 2019/2020 Sistema Fiep', accessed 11 January 2021, http://www.obshub.com.br/pub/tend/tendencias-2019-2020.pdf.
8 "Home", Instituto Delete, accessed 2 August 2020, https://www.institutodelete.com/home.
9 'Serviços', Instituto Delete, accessed 11 January 2021, http://www.institutodelete.com/servicos.

more productive and more focused meetings' would be some of the gains that can be achieved through the readjustment of technology use.

Instead of reflecting on why our daily activities are subjected to accelerated rhythms and constant demands, we are increasingly offered products and services that enable us to escape for a while, be it a luxurious weekend in the mountains, three days at a rustic Brazilian beach, or a 30-minutes meal without screens. Having lunch or dinner away from the distractions of the mobile phone, in fact, is one of the offerings of numerous applications designed to help us control time spent with smartphones. Mostly listed in the 'productivity' category on Apple Store and Google Play, applications such as Forest, Moment, Foco, and Get Off Your Phone, among others, set goals for time spent on social media, games, and news sites, as well as disconnect tasks sorted by time or activity to be performed. Almost all of them feature graphs with statistics, define goals to be achieved, and stimulate the user through motivational messages—tools and strategies typical of corporate productivity rationality and stimulation that feeds individual self-esteem. In practice, one compulsion is replaced by another under the effect of the same drug, in a continuous feedback.

The examples are many, as the phenomenon has been increasingly recurrent. What they all have in common is that the digital detox offerings neither seek a life 'free' from the power grids, nor do a critical analysis of the hyperconnection in order to understand the intentionality and strategic connections of this attention regime with the current economic system. In all these cases, technical devices are usually treated as determinants and protagonists of the problem in question, detached from the historical context that allowed its invention. Such simplifications, which tend to be based on a linear relationship of cause and consequence, end up impoverishing the debate and diverting attention from any political action that could be more effective. There is neither questioning of the reasons why we (and especially young people) are all irremediably connected nor any attempt at creating alternatives to constant connection. What we witness is, simply, pedagogical content about how not to let excessive consumption of internet devices hinder our social and professional performance. We learn, through tips, guides, apps, and experimental spaces, to embrace the connection—provided we are still functional and productive. What the discourse in those media stories and in contemporary common thinking often disapproves is not hyperconnection or entertainment subsidized by capitalism, but low productivity, lack of self-esteem, and unhappiness.

DISCONNECT TO CONTEMPLATE

Another emblematic case to be analyzed, which contrasts to this widely disseminated reality endorsed by the perverse biopolitical imaginary, is that of

Brazilian photographer Ana Rovati, who, in December 2015, embarked on the mission of staying offline for one year. Her self-imposed disconnection was the premise of OFF-LINE, an artistic initiative that the artist proposed as her final project for a master's degree in Spain. In the project she questions the sociability dynamics dictated by the logic of hyperconnection. 'The issue of contemporary relationships and how we engage with the world is something that interests me a lot and I found in disconnection a way to talk about it,' she says. The proposal did not include any type of exception. She did not allow herself to use internet connected devices, not even enjoy their benefits through other people, for a whole year.

Before she had the final version of the proposal, Ana approached elderly people on the beaches of Rio de Janeiro, expecting to obtain accounts from the 'last off-line generation'. But her creation only came to light when she understood that it would be necessary to experience disconnection to fully understand the impacts of being offline. More specifically, she would have to gain distance to be able to see the effects of digital technologies on contemporary subjectivities and our relationships with ourselves, with others, and with the world.

The decision was not simple and generated all sorts of sentiments of fear, anxiety, and denial. The photographer says the idea was difficult to accept at first, because she feared the consequences of that choice, but the final decision came from a conversation with her mother. Here is a very symptomatic case of these contemporary dynamics, as she recounts: 'When I moved to Europe, my mother didn't cry, but when I told her I was going to leave the Internet, she started to cry.' Her mother, who is a university professor and has always supported her daughter in her studies, received the news with concern and tried to get her to give up the idea. Her distress, in that case, was not to be far away from her daughter, but to lose the possibility of her image presence at any time of the day. 'For me, that was the answer,' says the artist.

So, on 2 December 2015, Ana embarked on a one-year journey without access to any online device. At the age of 30, living in two large urban centres (6 months in Madrid and 6 months in Rio de Janeiro), she abandoned her smartphone, email, WhatsApp, Google, Facebook, Skype. She recounted her experience and her resultant reflections on various aspects of contemporary life, in an in-depth interview conducted in November 2017.

At the time, Ana shared the main difficulties she had to deal with during that period: the first one was more related to the economic sphere, the second one to the social and affective spheres, and the third to the political one. 'I was off-line and the big crisis was how to keep my life going, because I didn't know how I was supposed to pay my bills.' By the time she decided to study her master's in Madrid, the Brazilian artist had not yet conceived the artistic project and therefore she did not anticipate that she would be offline for so long. She expected, then, to carry out freelance photography work in the Spanish capital to complement her income. The problem is that the project made that impossible, for a very essential reason: she did not have the means to do so. Without internet access, she wouldn't be able to share photos and make contacts with the required agility. An employer would hardly accept those restrictions. Trying other fields has also become a challenge. How to get a job without accessing the internet? How to be seen, found, contacted, without an email address, a WhatsApp number, an online portfolio? Ana then realized that her absence from the digital world excluded her from a social reality in which she inhabited until that moment:

> I was automatically put to the margin. I stayed off-line and was deleted. My feeling is that the world was telling me: You don't want to be part of how we want you to be? So, fall off! We have no interest that you consume, because you do not have the means to consume.

The artist is aware of the fact that such marginalization, experienced by her voluntarily, is imposed on a large portion of the population, who are simply deprived of access to the Internet and, with this, of many possibilities there. 'If before I could upload my resume to a jobs list website, without the internet I had to print it and deliver it in person at specific less crowded hours.' Limited to the analogue world, the list of job options included activities such as waitress, cleaner, manicure, massage therapist. 'In economic terms, many doors were closed in my life. I entered another category of remuneration, even though photographers don't earn much money . . . anyway, options get limited, my horizon of possibilities changed.' After three months of being unemployed and with her savings coming to an end, Ana considered giving up the project. She finally got a job as a waitress at a local bar, which allowed her to make ends meet.

Not only did the decision not to use technological devices of control and visibility threaten her with lack of money and economic failure, but it also presented the risk of invisibility and social non-existence. The second big challenge in her offline journey comes from this fact. Although she considered herself quite sociable and had good friends, Ana saw herself disappear from interpersonal relationships: 'That makes you wonder if you make any difference in anyone's life.' In the current business logic merged with that of the spectacle (Debord 1997), each individual is what they show in the visible sphere (Sibilia 2016). Therefore, online absence would weaken one's presence in the world, making their image disappear from the newsfeed and, consequently, from friends' and acquaintances' minds: 'You are no longer a part of other people's everyday lives since they no longer see your image and simply no one invites you to anything.'

This weakening in social connectedness also relates to the third challenge faced by the artist, resulting from the general misunderstanding of why she decided to spend such a long time offline: 'I felt alone in my world view. People didn't know what I was talking about. I sounded crazy all the time.' Captured by the dynamics of the here and now and unable to take a distanced look at their own present, the people she met over the 12 months of the experiment did not see any logic in her attitude. Unlike the celebrated three-day digital detox to 'detoxify' habits and regulate performance, the artistic (and political) act of questioning the individual and collective submission to uninterrupted digital flows through a long and radical disconnection became incomprehensible—a gesture that, for most people, could be comparable to self-injury practices. Alternatively, long and radical disconnection is seen by some as a resource that could only be justified by a possible trauma or by a certain hermit tendency and therefore not worthy of importance and attention.

Although the loss of interpersonal relationships was massive—Ana estimates she lost contact with about 90% of her friends and acquaintances—the artist says that the bonds that remained were strengthened. She also became closer with her parents. In an attempt to resist the imperatives of the digital networks, what was strengthened, above all, were family ties, while friends became increasingly scarce. 'My parents' first phone call was the most beautiful thing. That is because before the experiment I was always available. I turned on the computer and everything was already connected. My mother was always online, so was my sister.' Even though her parents were thousands of kilometres away, the illusion of presence guaranteed by both instant communication applications and online social networks meant that the artist felt the conversations were always rushed, superficial, and fractured, competing with so many other stimuli throughout the day, in the day-to-day run. 'We had access to one another all the time, we had the opportunity to connect all the time, but you just never make that connection count, you are never really into it,' she reflected. 'When you know you can get in touch with that person at any time, you end up not paying so much attention.'

Because it was certain that contact could be established at any time, online chats followed the same dynamics as all others, without great efforts or motivation for deeper conversations. Phone calls, on the other hand, were expensive and demanded time availability and listening disposition—two increasingly scarce resources in today's hectic, tiresome, self-administered, and overstimulated routines. 'I was no longer accessible. That was the great change,' says Ana. She expressed that such a step was crucial to stopping the flow of self-referent images and empty words, which are characteristic of online dynamics, and provided conditions for further elaboration of lived experiences. 'The first time my parents called me during my offline period was beautiful. They got together so we could talk, something that never happened before. And for the first time they paid attention,' she deduced. 'We had a 15-minute conversation that was much more intense than all daily conversations we had before,' Ana recalled.

She recounts starting to perceive that same intensity in other moments of her new, more attentive and dedicated routine: 'Everything in my life became intense. It was like I felt everything more—more sincere, more attentive. Because it is about dedication, right?! We live in a time when no one has time, no one is dedicated.' Since contemporary society is populated with varied fast and uninterrupted flows, we would lose the ability to answer a phone call without distractions, or to walk on the street contemplating the landscape, instead of the usual bowed head and eyes fixed on the smartphone. Or even writing a letter in a reflected manner, under the cadence imposed by handwriting, while inserting fragments of songs, stories, photos, and memories on paper. 'It is as if you open up the opportunity for people to show things that we do no more,' she reflected. 'For me it means to feel loved. I felt loved when I received a letter like this. I thought: "they're doing it for me,"' she added before concluding: 'I exchange a mindful phone call or a letter like that for a week without mindless communication.' Ana was emphatic about her increased ability to be affected: 'Having been disconnected made me see the world more clearly and more sensitively. It's like I had been "in full bloom", open to the world and more confident about myself.' That statement does not seem to be a matter of chance.

THE LIMITS OF UNLIMITED PLEASURE

In a context where the imperatives of absolute connection and unbridled consumption predominate, hyperstimulus walks hand in hand with impoverished experiences (Crary 2014). In this regard, it is appropriate to resort to some reflections from Italian philosopher Franco Berardi (2005; 2019). According to the author, it is possible to extend the period of exposure of human organisms to information overload resulting from digital artefacts, or even to accelerate the reaction time to media stimuli. However, the human brain is limited and experience cannot be intensified indefinitely. Acceleration causes a reduction in the very consciousness of stimulation along with loss of sensitivity, which compromises perception, empathy, and ethics. As a result, experiences are not elaborated, leading to the loss of the singularity of events and anesthetizing of the body to the alterities that gravitate around us. It also produces a deterioration of the possibilities of thought and the ability to create forms of expression and meaning, caused by a continuous process of desensitization, homogenization, and redundancy of receptive capacities

(Crary 2014). In fact, all stimuli become similar and get blurred in the same fluidity—without concreteness, recognition, or distinction.

The effects of this superfluidity on subjectivities are many and they are going to be addressed briefly in the following lines. We base our argument on Brazilian psychoanalyst Teresa Pinheiro's (2012) clinical experience. According to the author, one of the main symptoms of the current malaise comes from the impoverishment of experiences and narratives about life itself, that is, the inability to create for oneself a substantial and linear history, with past, present, and future. Patients arrive in the clinics without any manifestation of the unconscious to be analyzed and usually present an empty and abstract feeling of anguish or even serious signs of depression, whose causes they do not know. They have difficulty understanding themselves and interpreting the meaning of their feelings, besides demonstrating a sense of strangeness about the perceptions and sensations of the body itself. Moreover, relationships with the past, with dreams, lapses, and imagination are nearly absent; they also present a superficial approach to the present and difficulty in projecting themselves into the future. 'If what they want is not reachable instantly, then it is not worth it,' Pinheiro examines (2012, 24). Objects of desire, in their case, are as volatile and disposable as the current needs of consumer society, and therefore, they cannot last. Fragile and without a solid inner universe, these individuals need constant evidence of their own existence: be it the recognition from others, their own reflection in the mirror, or somatic manifestations on their bodies. In short, all of these are means of creating an external narrative about oneself. Otherwise, they are depressed.

Therefore, these subjectivities are increasingly adapted to the dizzying rhythms of financial capitalism, and are built on two central vectors: visibility and connection. To do this, they need to be legitimized by the recognition of others, which gives them meaning, consistency, and, above all, the very feeling of being alive or necessary in the world. In this scenario, it is no surprise that new forms of anxiety, such as those generated from the search for social approval, are generated and intensified, especially when subjects face the accusing silence of social networking platforms on digital devices.

'The promotion and adoption of wireless technologies, and their annihilation of the singularity of place and event, is simply an after-effect of new institutional requirements,' as Jonathan Crary points out (2014, 40). The use of these devices and appliances has impacted sociability and has redefined the individual experience and perception, submitting them to rhythms, speeds, and forms of accelerated and intensified consumption, as well as to new systems of continuous control and submission. The fruition time of any situation—a concert, dinner with friends, a trip—is fragmented in ephemeral moments and then captured in dispersing flows. These, in turn, do not eliminate experiences, but impoverish them, subjecting bodies to the speeds of transformations and instant communications, as well as to planned obsolescence and infinite acceleration of info-stimuli. Instead of the full enjoyment of the present moment, Ana calls attention to a fragmented consumption of the now, which would function as a record rather than an experience: 'It seems that people forgot how to live the experience. They constantly seek to tell others about an experience that didn't exist, because they were actually busy recording it, not experiencing it.' The artist believes that the constant recording of moments—the favourite song, the gourmet dish, a selfie at the tourist spot—feeds a 'drive, this urge to tell your story all the time', usually duplicating the advertising aesthetics.

And what kind of story are people telling? Plots, scenarios, and characters certainly vary, but the message is the same: a sort of happiness that is only real as long as you publicize it. Social media platforms are important allies in this process, allowing users to create various strategies of visibility and performance, through a mindful 'curatorship of the self' (Sibilia, 2016). Thus, each individual is encouraged to build attractive profiles in platforms such as Facebook, Instagram, and TikTok, that can deliver the best effects to a broad audience, in order to ensure the desired likes or followers. For that purpose, it is essential to make constant individual efforts, both to attribute value to oneself and to manage a good reputation as well as monitor the uninterrupted flow of posts, in order to maintain virtual contacts, reciprocity in likes, the feeling of belonging, and, above all, the guarantee of some social relevance.

'In the era of compulsive and compulsory happiness', there are plenty of 'roadmaps to achieve of happiness' (Freire Filho 2010, 17, 23), providing the contemporary consumer with the most diverse products and services that supposedly guide them towards the conquest of the dreamed well-being state: from self-help books to motivational workshops and private coaching sessions. But our era is not only that of imperative happiness, but also of a continuous spectacle, which has in the connection technologies their stage. As Christian Ferrer (2010, 178) states, 'Performances that appeal to the sense of sight depend on the accuracy of technologies, their ability to capture visual attention and to facilitate it with images of happiness, where there is invention, surprise, eroticism, relief.' Thus, the dependence created in the triangulation 'Happiness—Visibility—Technology' brings to light a world in which invisibility and rejection of information and communication technologies necessarily imply a state of solitary unhappiness. Contrary to this perspective, Ana gave a statement that may sound somewhat paradoxical: 'Before, I could get in touch with everyone, but I felt lonely.' From the experience of disconnection, 'being alone' gained new connotations and turned into 'being with oneself'. Not in the identity sense and unaffected by the other, but vulnerable to the otherness of the world that they inhabited (Rolnik 2018). It is, above all, a 'populated solitude', as Deleuze (1992) puts it. About the transformation of the feeling of loneliness experienced throughout the process, the artist reported the following:

> At first, I felt solitude, because I reduced the amount of contact drastically, but I do not know if that was loneliness afterwards. It was being alone, but not solitude. I did not feel abandoned, I felt in my own company. You change the perspective. I became a good company for myself. It was a readjustment of life, in which I adapted to silence, which is important for the understanding that excessive connections do not mean company, hundreds of likes do not mean affection. (Ana Rovati, unpublished interview, 7 November 2017)

According to Ana, in the midst of the desire for more connection, it is possible to observe the inability for critical and reflective thinking about the contemporary world. 'Having experienced disconnection made me realize how blind and close-minded we are, only following in the frenetic flow of consumption and production, that nonstop rhythm which is the hyperconnection.' In fact, the inability here is doubled: We are incapable of realizing our inability to self-control.

It is not by chance that the term 'addiction' is increasingly used to refer to our complex relationship with the devices we are focusing on. What provokes the malaise is the difficulty of limiting the amount of time spent online, as a voluntary and individual strategy that usually fails. Far from being a prohibited activity for being immoral or illegal, the connection is hyper stimulated. However, it is recognized that its 'excessive' use ends up jeopardizing other areas of life and affecting good performance by reducing productivity. Yet, the malaise of the present can be said to stem from this very fall in the prestige of law and duty, and the related decline in the perceived value of the self-control that used to be embraced in service of a superior cause. This is an instance so far removed from the rigours of the super-ego that it almost seems like its opposite. Instead of being caused by self-censoring moral limits, now the drama stems from the lack of limits and the incapacity for self-control (Jorge and Sibilia 2019, 1432).

However, neither does prolonged disconnection seem to be the definitive solution to acquire such criticism, nor does it provide immunity to the business logic. A rich list of individuals—mostly young, white men—who suspend internet use for a period of time and then monetize their experience through books, courses, and motivational talks shows us how disconnection is not always enough to escape the connection logic. A notable example of this is that of Levi Felix, an American man who, in 2008, grabbed his backpack and left with his girlfriend for a sabbatical experience around the world.[10] The decision occurred after Felix was hospitalized due to

---

[10] 'Como o corpo reage ao vício digital', *Superinteressante*, accessed 14 January 2021, https://super.abril.com.br/especiais/detox-digital-o-corpo-reage-ao-vicio-online/.

an exhaustion crisis, caused by a strenuous work routine in a technology start-up. During the two-and-a-half years he lived outside the country, he lived in places such as an island in Cambodia, without a cell phone and no internet connection. Upon returning to the United States, Felix recounts realizing that digital devices and gadgets were everywhere, expanding their consumer market from technicians, bloggers, and media-hungry to society as a whole.

In an attempt to solve the problem, in 2011 Felix started the Digital Detox, a pioneer company in the digital purification movement, whose motto is 'disconnect to connect'. Although the intention, at first sight, seems to be a noble one, it is symptomatic, and rather worrying, that the experience of overwork and the subsequent technology-free experience has derived in such an impoverished conclusion and in such a little transgressive solution. In short, Felix's idea—or rather, the opportunity he envisioned—was to take profit from those in a similar situation to the one he lived years earlier.

Similarly, another of his ventures is Camp Grounded, a playful and analogue summer camp for adults, with the promise of transporting them to the holiday camps of the old days. Among the activities included are 'games, counselors, yoga, friendship bracelets, camp dance, talent shows, typewriters, capture the flag game, classical booths, colorful wars, star observation, healthy gourmet meals, campfires'. In short, stimuli, stimuli, and stimuli. On the company's website, from where we collected the information mentioned earlier, there are no questions about the prevailing morality. Instead, all responsibility for the accelerated and dispersed routine lies in the individuals themselves and the technical apparatus. In 'Technology Retreats and the Politics of Social Media', anthropologist Adam Fish states:

> I argue that technology retreats depoliticise social media by placing the responsibility of limiting Internet use on the individual, and rewarding limited use with hedonistic and spiritual experiences. My concern is that this softens the political potential of media resistance with leisure and recreation. (2017, 364)

It is possible to observe that the logic is both that of stimulus and that of immediate, disposable, accelerated, bored, and little reflected consumption. All of these are symptoms that align with the neoliberal rationality characteristic of present days, in which the unproductive 'waste of time' seems inconceivable and any breach for leisure and rumination becomes unbearable, as well as the possibility of reflecting on the experiences of malaise that may manifest physically. Brazilian philosopher Paulo Vaz (2010) points out that, just like theatre represents the spectacle, the hospital is an institution that functions as reference of the current therapeutic culture. That is because, unlike in modern times, when suffering was conceived as a 'natural' condition of the human being or even as a valid strategy of self-discovery and learning, nowadays malaise are seen as failures or even meaningless waste of time and therefore, demand individual action. The hospital—an institution that represents not only health houses and medical professionals, but also the pharmaceutical industry—indicates that avoiding suffering is not only possible, but above all desirable.

In fact, in search for being constantly active and managing oneself as a profitable capital, human activities and relationships are now managed by a utilitarian and pragmatic logic, guided by cost and benefit calculations, by the ranking of skills and high performance in all instances. 'The rhythms of technological consumption are inseparable from the requirement of continual self-administration,' says Crary (2014, 54). In this way, there is an unprecedented spread of instrumental rationality beyond the barriers of the economical sciences and the structures of companies, spreading throughout all the domains of human life. And, in this rationality, the idea of balanced online consumption is sold just like aspirin to treat bacterial infection: to medicalize and capitalize.

I thought I was not addicted, but now I think I was. I think we all are. There are few people who have detachment, who find a balance. Because these artefacts are not intended for balance, but to generate stimuli all the time and capture attention. And I don't think 'the Internet' is the problem. The internet is very symbolic of this process and of our new ways of living, but it is an economic and political issue, on the macro level, in which we are so implicated that we do not realize (Ana Rovati, unpublished interview, November 7, 2017).

As our final considerations, we consider Ana's experience to be quite symptomatic of contemporaneity. While the power of her gesture and the daring of the lifestyle she created for herself are undeniable, the impetus for emancipation from the tentacles of post-industrial capitalism remains restricted to the limits of the capital and the tyranny of purpose as it needs productive justifications to be validated—and nothing more indicative than the determination of a period (one year) for an experience that served as a case study for her master's project. Even though she may be able to take a distanced look at it, she is still a product of that very logic. Therefore, it is important to emphasize that the business logic, to a greater or lesser degree, has managed to (almost) absorb everything: including the attempts of resistance. Even where there seems to be a more radical transformation effort, there are certain catches and distortions that prevent individuals from perceiving power relationships.

In the midst of the 'noise' that prevails in today's turmoil, when the networks cross all walls, it is important to draw on the power of thought. That means to create tactics to 'resist' the market flow and the saturation of senses caused by (dis)connection, well-being, and visibility imperatives, having the digital detox as a paradigmatic case. That is the power of the 24/365 temporality: allowing subjectivities to venture into other rhythms, movements, affections, and values, capable of sedimenting the experience and of dearticulating the dominance of dictatorial forces that weaken our ability to act. Furthermore, it favours the invention of underground and combative existence, willing to create breaches, circuit breakers, and new tools, even though knowledge always tries to penetrate them and power tries to appropriate them. 'It is at the level of each attempt that the resistance capacity is evaluated or, on the contrary, submitted to a control,' warned Gilles Deleuze (1992, 218), launching the following clues: 'The key thing may be to create vacuoles of noncommunication, circuit breakers, so we can elude control' (1992, 217). In light of the flashes presented in these pages, we bet on the polyphony of silence, boredom, and loneliness, as well as on the alliance with subversive artistic manifestations and with other joyful encounters, capable of decolonizing the desire and activating vital forces. To see new possibilities, it is still necessary to be careful in the face of each stimulus, to open up to the unthinkable and the sensitive, to germinate new existential possibilities, and to free our lives from social, political, and historical ties.

REFERENCES

Agamben, Giorgio. 2009. *O que é o Contemporâneo? e outros ensaios*. Chapecó: Argos.

Berardi, Franco. 2005. *A Fábrica da Infelicidade: trabalho cognitivo e crise da new economy*. Rio de Janeiro: DP&A.

———. 2019. *Depois do Futuro*. São Paulo: Ubu Editora.

Crary, Jonathan. 2014. *24/7—Capitalismo Tardio e os Fins do Sono*. São Paulo: Cosac Naify.

Debord, Guy. 1997. *A Sociedade do Espetáculo*. Rio de Janeiro: Contraponto.

Deleuze, Gilles. 1992. *Conversações*. Rio de Janeiro: Ed. 34.

Delfanti, Alessandro and Salvatore Iaconesi. 2016. Open Source Cancer: brain scans and the rituality of biodigital data sharing. In *The Participatory Condition in the Digital Age*, edited by Darin Barney, Gabriella Coleman, Christine Ross, Jonathan Sterne and Tamar Tembeck, 123–144. Minneapolis, MN: University of Minnesota Press.

Ehrenberg, Alain. 2010. *O Culto da Performance*. São Paulo: Ed Idéias & Letras.

Ferrer, Christian. 2010. "Consumo de espetáculo e felicidade obrigatória: técnica e bem-estar na vida moderna.' In *Ser Feliz Hoje: reflexões sobre o imperativo da felicidade*, edited by João Freire Filho, 165–179. Rio de Janeiro: Editora FGV.

Fish, Adam. 2017. "Technology Retreats and the Politics of Social Media." *TripleC* 15 (1): 355–369.

Freire Filho, João. 2010. *Ser Feliz Hoje: reflexões sobre o imperativo da felicidade.* Rio de Janeiro: Editora FGV.

————. 2011. "O poder em si mesmo: jornalismo de autoajuda e a construção da autoestima". *Famecos* 18 (3): 717–745.

Foucault, Michel. 1976. *História da Sexualidade I: a vontade de saber.* Rio de Janeiro: Graal.

————. 1987. *Vigiar e Punir: Nascimento da Prisão.* Petrópolis: Vozes.

————. 2008. *Microfísica do Poder.* Rio de Janeiro: Graal.

Jorge, Marianna Ferreira. 2019. *A Droga da Conexão: transformações no mal-estar moderno e nas estratégias de resistência.* Tese de doutorado. Universidade Federal Fluminense.

Jorge, Marianna Ferreira and Paula Sibilia. 2019. "The Online 'Addiction' as a Malaise of the 21st Century: From Repression by the Law to 'Free' Unlimited Stimulation." *International Journal of Psychoanalysis* 100 (6): 1422–1438.

Lavieri, Fernando. 2020. "Detox Digital." *Istoé*, February 14, 2020. URL.https://istoe. com.br/detox-digital/.

McLuhan, Marshall. 1969. *Os Meios de Comunicação como Extensões do Homem.* São Paulo: Cultrix.

Pinheiro, Teresa. 2012. "O modelo melancólico e os sofrimentos da contemporaneidade." edited by Julio Verztman, Regina Herzog, Teresa Pinheiro and Fernanda Pacheco-Ferreira, *Sofrimentos Narcísicos*, 17–38. Rio de Janeiro: Cia de Freud, UFRJ.

Rolnik, Suely. 2018. *Esferas da Insurreição: notas para uma vida não cafetinada.* São Paulo: n-1 edições.

Sibilia, Paula. 2016. *O Show do Eu: a intimidade como espetáculo.* Rio de Janeiro: Contraponto.

Stravogiannis, Andréas and Cristiano Nabuco de Abreu. 2009. "Internet Addiction: A Case Report." *Revista Brasileira de Psiquiatria* 31 (1): 78–79.

Vaz, Paulo. 2010. "A vida feliz das vítimas". In *Ser Feliz Hoje: reflexões sobre o imperativo da felicidade*, edited by João Freire Filho, 135–164. Rio de Janeiro: Editora FGV.

Part IV

DELAYING DISCONNECTION

Chapter 8

Overcoming Forced Disconnection

Disentangling the Professional and the Personal in Pandemic Times

Christoffer Bagger and Stine Lomborg

INTRODUCTION

Following the outbreak of the Covid-19 pandemic in 2020 and the subsequent lockdowns imposed by governments across the world, a major part of the workforce in the Global North was ordered to 'work from home'. Consequently, the struggle between work and personal life was turned upside down, as was the public, normative framing of digital media. Just a few months earlier, digital media were largely blamed for creating work/life balance problems for white-collar workers. However, the lockdown meant that this was no longer a matter of an 'overflow' (Bailyn 1988) or a 'spillover' (Berkowsky 2013) of work into 'life'—but rather a complete relocation of 'work' into the domain of the personal. Now these media were able to offer a ready-made solution for making this transition work and for facilitating the coordination of work tasks and daily social contact that many people missed. Even before the lockdown, digital technologies played a dual role in both structuring everyday life and making people available across all their different life roles and domains (Beckman and Mazmanian 2020). However, with the lockdown, the semi-stable situation whereby activities and expectations more or less fell into specific contexts of 'home' or 'work' (Nippert-Eng 1996) came under pressure. As a result, individuals and households were faced with the challenge of creating and re-organizing day-to-day routines on a micro-scale, with these routines relying more than ever on digital media to continue functioning.

The pandemic informs two areas that were already of interest to media studies and turns them upside down: the first is that of 'digital disconnection' literature, which often frames disconnection from digital communication as both voluntary and beneficial (Syvertsen 2017) and which is often cast as a pushback on the encroachment of digital media in everyday life. The second area covers studies looking into remote working, which has found that the ability to work outside the traditional office can be conducive to inclusivity, productivity and even personal well-being (Anderson, Kaplan and Vega 2015). Rather than constituting a conscious disconnection from specific technologies (Karppi 2018), or emphasizing a turn to face-to-face interaction (Turkle 2015), the lockdown in response to the Covid-19 pandemic represented a disconnection *from* co-present interpersonal communication. Now mediated communication was the only available option outside the immediate household. We argue that this is best understood as a type of *forced disconnection*. The response to this disconnection was an intensified connection to and through digital technologies in order to make things work. However, overcoming this forced disconnection has had the effect of pulling us all deeper into the rabbit hole of an ideology of connectivity and optimization of self, work, and life (Kristensen and Banke 2019; Moore 2018). Connection and disconnection are not merely opposites, but deeply entangled (Kaun and Schwarzenegger 2014). Indeed, the forced disconnection experienced during the pandemic, ironically, would not have been possible without a prior reliance on digital communication infrastructures through which people were subsequently forced, or at least strongly urged, to *connect*. In this chapter, we unpack the notion of forced disconnection, exploring its key characteristics and experiential qualities in the specific context of the pandemic lockdown through examples drawn from a small interview study with knowledge workers employed in companies using the enterprise social medium Workplace from Facebook. We argue that the primary difficulty of forced disconnection in this particular situation lies in establishing temporal, spatial, and contextual boundaries between the different domains of everyday life once digital communication becomes the default mode of connection to the outside world.

APPROACH AND METHODOLOGY

To empirically illustrate how the forced disconnection of the pandemic lockdowns necessitates a reliance on communication media, we draw on examples collected as part of a broader empirical study into the role of so-called Enterprise Social Media (ESM) (Leonardi, Huysman, and Steinfield 2013) in changing boundaries between the domains of 'home' and 'work', leading to a blurring of professional and personal modes of communication. More specifically, this study evolved around Workplace from Facebook, a product that has so far received little public attention, while Facebook itself is perhaps the most popular social media platform *to disconnect from* (Baym, Wagman, and Persaud 2020; Karppi 2018). Workplace from Facebook is a social media platform aimed at enabling people to connect and collaborate at work. The platform was launched in 2016, and mimics the design and functionality of the public Facebook platform. The study, conducted by the first author, was done in Denmark, a Nordic welfare state with a highly advanced digital infrastructure and near-total penetration of internet connectivity among the population (Flensburg and Lai 2020).

The primary data material for this chapter comes from nine purposively sampled qualitative interviews carried out by the first author. Interviewees were young Danish so-called knowledge workers affected by the pandemic lockdown, all recruited via network sampling. Ages of the interviewees ranged between 18 and 36. Eight were Danes living and working in the greater Copenhagen area, with one English person residing in the UK. Interviews were conducted between March and July of 2020 and focused on what role communication media play in how the interviewees' structured and shaped a 'new normal' everyday life.

In these conversation-style interviews, we asked the respondents to reflect on how the lockdown had changed the nature of their communication with colleagues and business connections, probing specifically into the use of Workplace, but also paying attention to how other media had taken on new functionalities. We also asked our respondents to imagine if anything they might have learned about themselves and their working habits and routines during lockdown might continue even after restrictions are eased, in an attempt to outline how they might imagine their future working life. Sometimes the conversation moved on naturally to how they now maintained contact with their friends and family, and we allowed the interviews to develop naturally and organically, recognizing that the interview itself played a part in reconnecting to a social world beyond the home. Aside from these interviews, we drew on published material and webinars co-produced by Workplace, designed to give tips on best practice during the pandemic. These led us to observe how Facebook tried to position their ESM as a primary communication tool for both collaboration and sociability at work during the pandemic and ensuing lockdown.

It should be noted that of course not all professional lives were affected equally by the outbreak of the pandemic. In the bigger picture, having to work from home can be seen as a luxury problem: around the globe, people have lost their jobs and businesses or been forced to the work on the frontline of the pandemic with an associated higher risk of exposure to Covid-19. The latter category includes drivers, medical staff, caregivers, and other employees critical to society continuing to function. As argued by some scholars, we should be careful not to universalize experiences of the crisis (Milan and Treré 2020;

Karppi 2021, xiii), nor should we assume that struggles of disconnection as such are the same everywhere (Natale and Treré 2020). The empirical analyses in this chapter thus reflect the struggles of home and work from the point of view of generally privileged knowledge workers in a welfare state.

We were interested in our present sample for both ethical and practical reasons. The ethical reasons included not wanting to place an additional burden on people with familial care responsibilities exacerbated by the lockdown or on people in particularly precarious work situations who might be at risk of losing their livelihoods during the lockdown. For related reasons, we sought out people without familial carer responsibilities. This is a limitation of the study—one we shall return to in the discussion—but also a product of the challenge of doing research, ethically, in an unprecedented global emergency. The practical reasons include our interest in building on previous research aimed at understanding the knowledge worker as being particularly enmeshed in digital communication technologies, to the point that these blur the boundaries between work and other domains of life.

Researching younger (18–36) knowledge workers also offers a number of advantages. Not only is this a group which is often seen as being particularly engaged in their careers (Petersen 2020), but one which we also expected would be particularly hard hit by the loss of the workplace and colleagues as sources of sociability in everyday life. The lockdown might leave these people physically isolated, with at best housemates or domestic partners for company.

Hence, looking at their experiences may be particularly informative in the context of developing an understanding of 'forced disconnection'. The data was analysed first through a process of open coding, which iteratively morphed into thematic coding (Bryman 2012). Within the coding process, special attention was paid to how our respondents described their new practices in the state of lockdown, and what hopes and dreams they expressed for their future work life practices. We compared our findings with the existing literature on digital disconnection and digital nomadism (discussed below) and paid special attention to how our respondents negotiated advantages and disadvantages of the lockdown, according to spatial, temporal, and contextual dimensions.

This process led us to develop the notion of 'forced disconnection', which was also partially inspired by the repercussions the pandemic had on shaping this research. Not only did it inspire us to carry out this particular sub-study rather than another kind of study, but also put into stark relief both our relationship to our respondents and our mutual relationship as researchers. In an immediate sense, our own homes were no longer places that were separate from our work (if they ever had been), nor did they constitute places where we were necessarily separate from our respondents. Just as the homes and work of our respondents were intertwined, so were our own 'homes' and the 'fields' we were working in now fused together via digital media (Kraemer 2016). Just as the people we interviewed talked to us remotely right out of their own homes, so did we. And just as they had lost neutral 'third places' which might have proved essential for professional interactions, so had we (Hemer 2012). And just as they felt the realm of the professional now also consisted of a large amount of communication pertaining to the personal, so did we (Benmore 2016).

THE PANDEMIC, THE PROFESSIONAL DOMAIN, AND 'PERPETUALLY ON' MEDIA

The Covid-19 pandemic and the subsequent lockdown measures, which started in 2020 and are still ongoing as we put the finishing touches to this chapter, have brought with them many material, political, and social changes affecting a wide variety of contexts. Put simply, how far a person and their family were at risk from the virus, their life circumstances, and the physical context of the home now set the parameters for what is possible and desirable for them to achieve at work. The lockdown measures taken in March 2020 in Denmark—like in many other countries—included requiring all non-critical staff in the public sector and large parts of the private sector to work from home. Cafes, restaurants, fitness centres, and retail shops were closed, as were schools and childcare centres. Hence, while Danes were allowed to go outside and meet in small groups, most day-to-day life revolved around the home during the period the study investigated. In this new normal, individuals have to navigate around a number of issues including taking appropriate preventive measures—managing unexpected financial burdens; maintaining social contact with family and friends; handling anxieties related to the uncertainties of an unprecedented and unknown pandemic; home-schooling children—all the while transitioning work activities to the home sphere.

In the early phases of the pandemic 'social distancing' became the *de facto* moniker for a range of strategies which included limiting how many people you could meet up with face to face and minimizing out-of-home activities. These strategies went hand in hand with temporary shutdowns of public areas such as libraries, restaurants, and educational institutions, otherwise known as 'lockdown measures'. Offices and other workplaces were also shut down with the justification that proper physical distancing and sanitization measures could not be implemented given the physical constraints.

As the WHO later stated, the term 'physical distancing' might have been a more precise description for these strategies, as the loss of social interaction per se was *not* the point (World Health Organization 2020), and researchers were quick to point out the dangers associated with neglecting the social aspects of life (Yip and Chau 2020). In fact, social interaction—and communication—was still a crucial part of everyday life. This interaction was, however, heavily reliant on digital communication technologies (Kemp 2020).

In the context of this study, we consider the reconfigurations of communication in the wake of the pandemic lockdown to be a question of 'boundary work' (Nippert-Eng 1996). This term helps us understand how boundaries between different domains of life (usually 'home' and 'work') are constructed and maintained through spatial, temporal, psychological, and emotional means. Sometimes these means overlap, as in the case of the commute between home and work, which may be a temporal, spatial, and emotional passage. These boundaries can be subject to planned reconfigurations, such as the pursuit of more leisure via, for instance, tourism (Ferreira and Lampinen, this volume) or a complete reconfiguration of work and home life, an extreme example of which is digital nomadism (Woldoff and Litchfield 2021).

Being confined to the home during lockdown, coupled with the individual's perpetual availability through 'always-on' digital technologies, led to a unique challenge to these boundaries, and perhaps particularly so for people we may term knowledge workers. These constitute a category of employees who—research has shown—are already heavily engaged with digital communication technologies which challenge the boundaries between home and work (e.g. Gregg 2011; Mazmanian, Orlikowski and Yates 2013).

FORCED DISCONNECTION AND RECONNECTION THROUGH DIGITAL MEDIA

For media and communication studies, as well as for general sociological research on boundary work, the unprecedented circumstances of a lockdown inform two ongoing discussions in the scholarly literature: 'digital detoxing' (Syvertsen and Enli 2020) and 'digital nomadism' (Woldoff and Litchfield 2021). These concepts present very different takes on the 'always-on' potential of digital communication technologies, and we explore them in the following section to help unpack what we term 'forced (dis)connection', as related to the Covid-19 pandemic.

In the 'detox' literature, disconnection from social media and digital technologies as such is seen as a way to more fruitfully engage or reconnect with one's surroundings and oneself (Syvertsen and Enli 2020). What we may lose in disconnecting from digital technologies is regained by slowing down and being mindfully present in the here and now. Even temporary disconnection is seen as having advantages in terms of mindful engagement when we go back to our digital media again (Baym, Wagman, and Persaud 2020).

However, while research has not always found this type of disconnection to be unproblematic for the end user, it is usually the result of a voluntary choice (Jorge 2019; Portwood-Stacer 2013; Syvertsen 2017). The available media are, in a sense, perceived as the problem. We contend that problems of constant connectivity that people experience are not just related to the media in question, but more fundamentally concern the various and often conflicting demands that different aspects of everyday life impose on us (Gregg 2011). Work, leisure, housekeeping, political engagement, childcare, entertainment, health, socializing, and so on compete for our time and attention and create different structural conditions and expectations for each of us in our digitally tethered day-to-day lives (Beckman and Mazmanian 2020). Disconnection may, so to speak, serve as a strategy for redrawing boundaries around specific contexts in space and time as we go about our daily lives.

In the other body of literature, which is a loosely knit grouping of organizational and management studies, with elements from leisure and media studies, attempts at 'remote working' are often eyed with suspicion (Anderson, Kaplan, and Vega 2015); nonetheless, such attempts have found their ideal expression in terms such as the 'digital nomad'. Such a nomadic work life is characterized by independence from any physical location, only tethering the workers to their workplace(s) through a laptop and a sufficiently reliable internet connection (Reichenberger 2018; Thompson 2019). This nomadic style of disconnection from physical locations has been shown to risk producing 'workplace isolation' among remote workers in particular (Hickman 2019). Indeed, people who engage in nomadic work stress their own need for a community or 'tribe'' of like-minded individuals to which they can belong (Woldoff and Litchfield 2021). This shows us that social isolation is a risk even among people like the nomads who may be said to belong to the most aspirational and mobile class of workers (Polson 2020).

One group of digital platforms that have been developed to try and combat such problems of isolation are the so-called ESMs (Leonardi, Huysman, and Steinfield 2013), which allow employees to connect across space and time. These platforms claim to have a positive influence on the social side of work and information-sharing (Miller 2016; Treem and Leonardi 2012), as well as generally fostering a sense of community in the organization (Uysal 2016). In other words, these platforms seem ideally positioned to facilitate the type of social belonging often associated with professional domains which may be sorely lacking during a lockdown. Indeed, Workplace, the platform used by all the organizations our sample members were employed by, has been developed by the Facebook company, and deliberately mimics their other, more popular platform. This in and of itself also presents a possible source of tension, as Facebook is both among the most frequent targets of disconnection studies (Karppi 2018; Vaidhyanathan 2018), and at the same time is regarded as a common, everyday platform for mediated sociability (Lomborg 2014). Judging from the many webinars available on using ESMs in general and more specifically for coordinating tasks and socializing at work during the pandemic, Facebook (and other platform providers) have seized the moment to brand and expand the reach of their ESM. Facebook, for example, argue that Workplace provides a vital source of connectivity and meaning in everyday life during a lockdown, thereby offering a technological solution to a *forced disconnection* from the physical encounters of normal co-located work life.

We use the notion of a *forced disconnection* as a media agnostic description for a situation where the individual's habitual means of interacting and communicating with the surrounding world have been cut off. In other words, this is a spatial, temporal, and social disconnection that individuals must manage and make sense of. Crucially, this disconnection is not—at least not primarily—the result of aspirations and a deliberate effort on the part of the individual as research into media refusal or digital disconnection has found (Portwood-Stacer 2013; Hesselberth 2018). Neither is this disconnection usually the result of planned organizational policies nor of individual aspirations towards more autonomy, such as the extreme case of the digital nomad. In other words, the goals of optimizing individual well-being or increasing organizational flexibility are not, as they normally would be, the primary drivers of change. Instead, exigent circumstances, in this case a pandemic, have led to a situation where spatial, temporal and social routines have largely been suspended. This has had the potential to disrupt established orders of meaning and, in this particular case, has accelerated a dependence on digital communication platforms, now even more prominent in people's home context. In this Corona virus situation, the forced disconnection also led to a *forced connection* to digital platforms from home. With opportunities for socializing and communicating co-presently currently at a minimum, this has resulted in greater reliance on digital technologies such as social media, video chat platforms and streaming services. This dependence on digital communication platforms to perform work tasks, while simultaneously juggling the increasing demands on personal lives, makes it imperative to investigate how to optimize the way we organize work, and perhaps how we organize our lives. We will discuss this further as we turn to our empirical findings in the next section.

ANALYSIS

Life, Interrupted and Restarted

As already outlined, the Covid-19 lockdown measures led to a forced disconnection from the regular patterns of everyday life for our respondents.

Chronologically, this was first evident in the sudden changes that occurred in their everyday settings and locations at very short notice. For example: one 28-year-old woman travelled hundreds of miles in order to relocate to her parents' home. A 28-year-old man was suddenly called home from the United States and had to figure out how to manage the lockdown situation together with two housebound housemates. Yet another man (30-years-old) had to navigate the new restrictions in the middle of moving in with his partner. In short, the pandemic represented a shift in people's circumstances that happened almost overnight and which had far-reaching repercussions.

At the time we interviewed them, most of our respondents had settled into some routine involving a degree of new normality. The details varied from case to case, but in general they all described themselves as having established new routines, though they all expressed dissatisfaction with certain aspects of their new everyday lives (aside from being frustrated with the pandemic per se).

In a tangible, physical sense, the Covid-19 lockdown measures meant that our respondents were physically disconnected from most of their extended networks. As we will demonstrate later in the analysis, the lockdown also forced a change in the usual temporal and social boundaries, with these social shifts being expressed in the reconfiguring of work-related communicative contexts. In order to 'get some spare time—*even though* you're working from home' as one respondent pointedly put it, the people we talked to were largely left to their own devices. While working from home certainly had its advantages, it also involved missing out on a lot of scaffolding and structuring of work tasks, and this resulted in people experiencing problematic losses of boundaries (cf. Nippert-Eng 1996). In the following section, we investigate the loss of spatial, temporal, and social routines in turn to unpack the core experiential dimensions of forced disconnection. For each dimension, we examine to what extent the ESM Workplace was utilized in structuring these new boundaries and in structuring the forms and practices of connecting.

Spatiality

What all the people we talked to had in common was that the home had attained a new central position in their everyday life. While the home was never *not* important, it now became the physical site where most activities were carried out throughout the period of the lockdown—this was perhaps the most salient manifestation of how the lockdown blended professional and personal life. Everything now generally took place in the home. One respondent in particular described how he had difficulty maintaining the temporal boundaries between his work and home life for the first time ever in his career, since the dinner table in his shared apartment was now permanently occupied by his own and his housemates' bulky work computers (man, 29, two housemates).

Reactions to the lack of variety in the physical surroundings were varied, but the general trend was to attempt some sort of boundary creation and management within the home. The early days of the pandemic might have seen our respondents working while 'sitting with their porridge' (man, 29, co-habiting), but this was now something they actively sought to avoid. In this, they all described how they introduced the norm of setting boundaries between the domains of the personal and the professional—even if this was difficult. The most extreme example of this was perhaps the respondent who was in the middle of a move during the lockdown (man, 30, co-habiting). He refurbished the old, empty apartment as a makeshift office, to which he commuted for work until the new owners received the keys. We can hardly think of a better illustration of how someone can value the spatial and temporal boundaries which a dedicated workspace provides.

The problem of resituating the domain of work into the home was exacerbated by the lack of 'third places' such as bars, restaurants, libraries, and cafes. All our respondents lamented the loss of these institutions. While third places are usually thought of as existing purely for social purposes (Oldenburg and Brisset 1982), they might also have served as alternative spaces for getting work done (Sayers 2009). Neither of these third-place functions were available to our respondents during the most restrictive periods of the lockdown, and they clearly missed them both.

Facebook's *Workplace*, the ESM platform of particular interest in our interviews, was offered as a space for ambient intimacy—if not *pure* sociability—during the lockdown period. This was a behaviour which was actively encouraged, indeed heavily promoted, during lockdown by the makers of Workplace through their webinars and published materials. A specific practice that the Facebook ambassadors encouraged—with their own company as an example—was the creation of specific fora (groups) to share photos of home offices, 'working from home meals' (usually understood to be much 'sadder' than the office canteen) and pets. While this practice had been adopted by several of the companies our respondents were employed in (in one case modified to 'show us your fridge'), none of our interlocutors had actively participated in sharing photos of their home offices (or fridges). Nonetheless, the fact that employees were encouraged to share personal photos, and so on highlights a point which we shall return to in the discussion—that of digital, work-related technologies being utilized in a domestic context, in this case by making the home available online (documenting and sharing it) in an ostensibly professional context. Here it might be worth considering that the connections created by digital platforms may not only be *forced* (though to some degree they certainly are), but may also be *forged*

(Van Dijck 2012, 164). Following Van Dijck, we suggest that the affordances and normalized behaviours on specific social media platforms make those same platforms 'not transmitters but rather *producers* of sociality' (cf. Van Dijck 2013, 150, my emphasis).

Another factor which exacerbated the lack of spatial boundaries were the other people in the household, for example, housemates and parents. These cohabitees represented a difficulty that had to be navigated in order to ensure some degree of privacy. One respondent (man, 18, living with parents) described how his frequent video chats with close friends (in lieu of meeting up physically) were soured by him being all too aware that his parents were just one thin wall away. But the digital environment is always embedded in physical surroundings—and these sometimes make it very difficult to simulate a third place. In this way, work has not only invaded the space of the home and compromised the privacy that is usually expected in the home. 'Home' may in turn also be eroding the possibilities of recreating a third place. Thus, the social interactions often found in third places might have moved into the digital spaces, thus exemplifying *forced connection* to overcome the forced disconnection. Even so, the actual spatial surroundings—and the people and other domains which occupy it—are still ever-present. We shall return to this point in our discussion.

Temporality

The general conditions prevailing during the lockdown led to a different relation to time on a macro scale: 'time flies' as one respondent remarked as he confirmed he had been working from home for just over two months. The lockdown conditions also facilitated new ways of managing time on a more day-to-day basis. This manifested itself in ways our respondents found both positive and negative.

One respondent (woman, 27, co-habiting) found herself free to work on a personal schedule that she would have found impossible during the times when she was required to work in her usual office space. 'What kind of slacker shows up at 11' she imagines her co-workers saying if her new habits were to be adopted in the physical office. What she described is a way of reconnecting to her own 'authentic' routines and practices according to her own temporal rhythm. Being connected through digital devices (as opposed to being in the physical office space) allowed her to structure her day as she wished and avoid the judgement (as she perceived it) of her co-workers and peers. This is just one illustrative example of how digital technologies might play a positive role in structuring a better everyday life. This respondent had been freed from the normative temporal constraints of her surroundings. Not everyone was as fortunate.

Another respondent—the one who had been recalled from the United States—was also on a very different time schedule as a result of this interruption. In his case, this had far less to do with choice than with necessity, as all his meetings were now with people in a very different time zone. This highlights the fact that organizational and relational demands constitute strong forces in structuring communicative habits. This is, however, not simply reducible to 'perpetually on' technologies creating 'perpetually on' norms.

Workplace, too, played a role in shaping time. While ESMs are mainly conceived of as facilitating asynchronous or semi-synchronous communication, our respondents reported an increase in live-streamed content, especially from corporate leadership. This suggests an organizational emphasis on 'liveness' or synchronous communication during lockdown. We attribute this to a general desire by both management and the organization to present themselves as a 'live' organization, with a strong presence vis-à-vis employees during the lockdown, thus attempting to counteract the struggles that 'virtual organizations' experience, such as lack of social stimulation, informality, and improvisation (Plesner and Husted 2020, 94–5). We regard the emphasis on synchronous meetings and social media interactions to be a result of this.

While our respondents mostly felt that this showcased Workplace as a means of top-down communication, this is congruent with wider trends in communication use during the pandemic which saw an increase in social media use, but an even bigger increase in synchronous digital communication use overall (Nguyen et al. 2020). We might see this as a deliberate effort to recreate the temporal boundaries of working life, and serves to underline the centrality of working life to the everyday experience of living (cf. Gregg 2011). During the pandemic, it might even represent a primary resource for socialization, leading to a renegotiation of what types of communication the domain of the professional is supposed to utilize, but also to a reliance (forced connection) on particular types of communication platforms, most prominently those that support synchronous modes of communication (e.g. videoconferencing, but also enterprise social media).

Communicative Contexts

Workplace from Facebook also seems to constitute a communicative context in the everyday lives of our respondents. While the webinars and promotional materials published by Facebook in the initial months of the pandemic demonstrated how the platform Workplace was designed to be used as a meeting forum, with the aim of re-creating the conversational and connected aspects of organizations, this was not an experience echoed by our respondents. Rather, they talked about how they were not particularly keen on the organic, conversational content on Workplace. While the management and communication staff in their respective companies were active users during the lockdown, the employees in general were not, at least not according to the testimonies we received.

We attribute this in part to a lack of ambient activities in people's lives during the lockdown, which meant that there was very little to discuss in terms of 'water cooler' conversation. This was evident both in the asynchronous communication on Workplace and in the many virtual meetings that were now being held. 'It's not easy chatting [with your colleagues] about how the football match went when there are no football matches being played' as one respondent put it during the strictest part of the lockdown. This is another way in which *forced disconnection* manifests itself—areas of life not immediately associated with co-present interaction (such as sports matches and other world events) were missing and so couldn't play a role in the communicative rituals of everyday life.

In general, with the absence of the informal and unstructured interactions that were typical of office life, our respondents described how their teams and colleagues increased both the frequency and the breadth of structured communication. In a quantitative sense, this manifested itself in the increased number of virtual meetings, phone calls and emails. This increase in communication would sometimes feel at odds with how our respondents' wished to optimize their own, uninterrupted workflows, but they generally understood it to be a necessity.

In terms of breadth, these mediated conversations also involved frequent discussions about the well-being of others. Both mental and physical health were frequent subjects of discussion, becoming a new communication ritual during lockdown. We interpret this to mean that our respondents felt that the broader communicative context of the professional per se had to accommodate *more types of communication* during the lockdown—specifically about the well-being of oneself and one's colleagues. While this expansion may be seen ostensibly as an expression of care and may have been intended as a means for communicative cohesion—it was in fact met with some exasperation. This was expressed most clearly by two of our respondents. One (the same one who talked about the football matches) said that he felt that there was a lot of irrelevant chit-chat at many meetings—and suggested that those who felt a need to catch up 'start the meeting five minutes earlier' to get it over with (man, 28, two housemates). Another expressed more complex reflections in which she weighed the pros and cons of these newly ritualized phatic communications:

> I know it's really important to maintain social contact and to support one another because it is really difficult, and I do have colleagues who have young children and I think that for them it's really nice to know that they are supported

by the rest of us in the team. It's just that I'm thinking 'do we need to spend half an hour on video talking every day?' (woman, 28, single)

The above quotes illustrate a central theme of the forced disconnection we have studied and appears to be a consequence of transitioning all work-related activity to digital platforms: that this new form of sociability can feel forced and actually distracts people from what they feel is the real purpose of their jobs—performing the tasks that they and others find valuable, measurable or take pride in. Viewed through this lens, bounding the 'personal' off from the 'professional' becomes just as important for the individual as keeping the professional separate from the personal.

This is not to say that the forced disconnection led our respondents to avoid sociability in their time at home. On the contrary, several of them reported checking in on friends and acquaintances through messages on social media, and often this led to them picking up the phone or otherwise engaging in conversations with people they might otherwise not have spent much time interacting with. In this way, the lockdown afforded an opportunity to connect more with people in the realm of the personal, if not the professional. Notably, this was *not a forced connection*, but something they reported doing voluntarily and happily.

In the domain of the professional, the forced disconnection was more likely to afford an opportunity for uninterrupted work, free from the perceived distractions of office life. Here, our respondents refer to a common thread in popular discourses on modern working life, covering the design of office facilities, the structure of the working day and the pervasiveness of (distracting) digital media. This in turn has led to the emergence of a regular industry of self-improvement books and narratives (Gregg 2018). In short, the disconnection *from* distractions (usually in the form of chatty colleagues or addictive media) will lead to a deeper connection with one's tasks (Reagle 2019). This represents a central tension between the two key challenges that knowledge workers face during the pandemic lockdown: the struggle to optimize work and work tasks and the struggle to feel a sense of social belonging in a professional context. All of this, it seems, becomes more difficult when the normal spatial and temporal bounds of the professional realm disappear.

LOOKING AHEAD: HOME-HOME CONFLICT, DIGITAL MEDIA ENCROACHMENT, AND THE FUTURE OF WORK

Our analysis of forced disconnection highlights something which we imagine will become a recurring theme in the study of work patterns in the future:

the boundaries not only between work and personal life within one's own home, but also at the *boundaries between one's own home and the homes of others*. In a situation where people were not only barred from access to their offices, but also lacked any sort of 'third place' (cafes, libraries, co-working spaces) in which they could create their own 'bubble' of professionalism and creativity (cf. Fast and Jansson 2019), the home becomes a forced site for the domain of the professional even more than previously.

As one interviewee put it. 'you're reminded of it constantly, that you're communicating from your home to someone else's home' (woman, 28, single). One result of this is that people very consciously reconfigure the visible and audible spaces in their homes that are accessible to others (such as hiding ironic paintings of Russian dictators that would simply require too much explanation in a client meeting); it has also led to a heightened awareness of the everyday goings-on of the living spaces of colleagues and business connections. In our study, this manifested itself, for example, in our childless respondents' reactions to the antics of their colleagues' children and pets: although they showed some sympathy, they also felt exasperation, especially when such antics were perceived as an interruption. This is a specific example of what we believe is a more general problem: that the home, a physical space which has had to become the domain of *both* the professional and the personal, is potentially an unruly space that is not necessarily fit for the purpose of maintaining contemporary boundaries of professionalism. This is especially evident in the discomfort that was reported by our respondents— such as the one quoted at length above—of having their homes exposed to the outside world, and, conversely, being able to see into other people's homes.

One of the acknowledged advantages that the domain of work offers is that of general and overt recognition, in contrast to the often overlooked toil involved in house- and care-work (Hochschild 1998). This disparity is felt especially strongly in cases where relatively well-educated knowledge workers, such as our respondents, are relegated to the domestic sphere and excluded from the domain of the professional (Orgad 2019). The home risks becoming just another task subsumed under a broader heading of 'work', and being entangled in a web of media-facilitated and -facilitating coordinating activities that enable working life (Beckman and Mazmanian 2020). Insofar as the home must offer an 'appropriately' visible and functional setting, it must be professionalized and domesticated. If this turns the home into a *doubly* unrecognized domain—neither recognized as a support structure for 'work' nor as its de facto setting of the (mediated) activities of work—then this is obviously a negative development. From a media studies perspective, we must now consider media as both facilitating the integration of domains (Gregg 2011) and as avenues for the necessary *recognition work* (Fast and Jansson 2019) that a sustainable remote work situation would necessitate.

We propose the notion of *home-home conflict* to describe the phenomenon of increased permeability *between* and reliance *upon* more or less professionally arranged homes. In contrast to previous concepts used in the literature on everyday life, such as 'home-work conflict' or 'home-family conflict', the notion of the home-home conflict does not describe a dichotomy between two domains within the life *of a single person*. Rather it emphasizes how the home domains of two different people might conflict and clash without the concrete temporal, spatial and contextual boundaries of the professional as an intermediary.

In this case, the professional organization, with its physical boundaries and routines—and to some extent maybe even its temporal and social routines—has disappeared as a marker of the domain of the professional. Instead, professional interactions occur *from one home to another*. This may present a number of problems in and of itself, such as the loss of the Goffmanian 'backstage' (Goffman 1978), or an increased amount of 'spillover' between an individual's professional and personal domains within the home (Berkowsky 2013). This also fundamentally changes what kind of domain the home is allowed to be. Furthermore, it may involve a greater reliance on digital platform providers, even if these have been the subject of much criticism (e.g. Vaidhyanathan 2018; Zuboff 2019). In fact, it could be said that the lockdown is providing an ideal opportunity for these platforms to further encroach on even our most intimate living spaces, including our homes, and exploit them for profit. Any sort of resistance on an individual basis is made extremely difficult under the circumstances brought about by the pandemic. In a lockdown scenario such as the one we are currently experiencing, even as we finalize this chapter, the individual may be stuck between a rock and a hard place. The traditional types of digital disconnection may result in professional and social isolation, while connection may mean relying on technologies which they are highly critical of.

In sum, a home-home conflict describes both the meeting of different homes in a professional context, and the potential for conflict within the home. Homes are often occupied by several people, and the often opposing visions of what *kind* of home it is to be—and how it is to be demarcated from other domains (e.g. the professional)—can potentially become a source of tension. While our study sample was limited to mainly childless professionals, other research on work during the pandemic has demonstrated how the situation has increased existing professional inequalities between men and women (Beckman and Mazmanian 2020; Orgad 2019), probably due in part to an uneven distribution of domestic and care duties (Collins et al 2020; Reichelt, Makovi, and Sargysan 2020; Squazzoni et al. 2020).

Irrespective of when the pandemic ends, experts across the globe expect remote work to play a fundamental part in society for the foreseeable future.

Thus, even if quarantines and lockdowns ease, the likelihood is that workers will still be left with the problem of optimizing their own lives—both personal and professional—within a limited space. Applying the concept of home-home conflict, we suggest that there is an urgent need for the continued study of boundary work in order to understand the communicative and social implications of the home having to forcibly perform the 'double duty' of being both the domain of the professional and the personal.

CONCLUSION

In this chapter, we have discussed disconnection as a forced structural circumstance which has separated individuals from their usual spatial, temporal, and social routines. Under the Covid-19 pandemic, when face-to-face encounters were severely restricted, digital communication technologies played a vital role in maintaining connections and continuing the daily routines of work, school and so on. Our analysis of forced disconnection and the increased reliance on digital connectivity to collaborate and push back against social isolation adds a new and media agnostic perspective to the scholarly discussions and public ideas of 'detoxes' from and connections to social media. Forced disconnection may mean people being forbidden to meet face to face, as we have seen in this chapter. However, it may also take the form of specific (distractive) websites or devices being forcibly shut down while using digital technologies provided by the workplace, or be the result of breakdowns in infrastructure that cut off digital or other means of communication altogether. Similarly, how people overcome forced disconnection may rely on whatever substitute means of communication are available. Disconnection, then, is not merely a matter of turning away from digital media as part of nostalgically longing for purely analogue forms of connecting with oneself and others. We may also understand disconnection as the act of selecting the optimal mode of communication from a range of alternative modes of communication (e.g. synchronous or asynchronous, one-to-one, many-to-many) in order to connect and get things done in a given context at a given time (Helles 2013).

For our respondents, the ESM Workplace from Facebook did not play the central, structuring role for the professional that Facebook intended it to. However, the communicative context of the professional per se expanded significantly. This meant that the domain of the professional was often experienced as all-encompassing, eclipsing spatial boundaries, temporal boundaries and hitherto delineated social contexts. This last point caused our respondents particular chagrin, which suggests that boundary work to maintain some separation of contexts remains a valuable practical and analytical category for disconnection research, as well as for studies into the future of work.

Our analysis of forced disconnection engages with the longstanding and ongoing struggle to establish boundaries between home and work through communicative practices, as manifested by, for example, people's attempts to balance their professional and personal or sociable types of communication during the pandemic lockdown. Working from home thus raises questions about both the kind and depth of (re)connection facilitated by digital media. We found that the forced disconnection—in these cases—might provide an opportunity to connect deeply with one's work as an optimizable *process*. What was more difficult was navigating a sense of social connection when most of the routine and ritualized interactions with colleagues and co-workers were gone, as was *setting boundaries* between different domains when people were left to their own devices. This boundary-setting can become even more difficult when utilizing live video chat services and ostensibly sociable social media for work purposes, as has been observed under the current pandemic circumstances.

If future professional interactions are more likely to take place directly between two homes, this may well lead to further future complications and necessitate a renegotiation of boundaries between the professional and the personal. In this way, the 'forced disconnection' manifested itself as a dual struggle: trying to fulfil the desire for professional optimization while making it harder to achieve sociability without compromising on the integrity of the domain of home—so giving in to both professional pressures and to digital service providers and social media platforms which we might otherwise want to resist.

FUNDING ACKNOWLEDGEMENTS

This research has received funding from the Danish Independent Research Council Grant no. 8018-00113B.

REFERENCES

Anderson, Amanda J., Seth A. Kaplan, and Ronald P. Vega. 2015. 'The Impact of Telework on Emotional Experience: When, and for Whom, Does Telework Improve Daily Affective Well-Being?' *European Journal of Work and Organizational Psychology* 24 (6): 882–897.

Bailyn, Lotte. 1988. 'Freeing Work from the Constraints of Location and Time'. *New Technology, Work and Employment* 3 (2): 143–152.

Baym, Nancy K., Kelly B. Wagman, and Christopher J. Persaud. 2020. 'Mindfully Scrolling: Rethinking Facebook after Time Deactivated'. *Social Media+ Society* 6 (2): 2056305120919105.

Beckman, Christine M., and Melissa Mazmanian. 2020. *Dreams of the Overworked: Living, Working, and Parenting in the Digital Age.* Stanford, CA: Stanford University Press.

Benmore, Anne. 2016. 'Boundary Management in Doctoral Supervision: How Supervisors Negotiate Roles and Role Transitions throughout the Supervisory Journey'. *Studies in Higher Education* 41 (7): 1251–1264. doi:10.1080/0307507 9.2014.967203.

Berkowsky, Ronald W. 2013. 'When You Just Cannot Get Away: Exploring the Use of Information and Communication Technologies in Facilitating Negative Work/ Home Spillover'. *Information, Communication & Society* 16 (4): 519–541.

Bryman, Alan. 2012. *Social Research Methods*, 4th edition. Oxford, New York: Oxford University Press.

Collins, Caitlyn, Liana Christin Landivar, Leah Ruppanner, and William J. Scarborough. 2021. 'COVID-19 and the Gender Gap in Work Hours'. *Gender, Work & Organization* 28 (S1): 101–112. doi:10.1111/gwao.12506.

Dijck, José van. 2012. 'Facebook as a Tool for Producing Sociality and Connectivity'. *Television & New Media* 13 (2): 160–176. doi:10.1177/1527476411415291.

———. 2013. 'Facebook and the Engineering of Connectivity: A Multi-Layered Approach to Social Media Platforms'. *Convergence* 19 (2): 141–155. doi:10.1177/1354856512457548.

Fast, Karin, and André Jansson. 2019. *Transmedia Work: Privilege and Precariousness in Digital Modernity.* Routledge.

Flensburg, Sofie, and Signe Sophus Lai. 2020. 'Networks of Power. Analysing the Evolution of the Danish Internet Infrastructure'. *Internet Histories*, May, 1–22. doi: 10.1080/24701475.2020.1759010.

Goffman, Erving. 1978. *The Presentation of Self in Everyday Life.* London, UK: Harmondsworth London.

Gregg, Melissa. 2011. *Work's Intimacy.* Cambridge, MA: Polity.

———. 2018. *Counterproductive: Time Management in the Knowledge Economy.* Duke University Press.

Helles, Rasmus. 2013. 'Mobile Communication and Intermediality'. *Mobile Media & Communication* 1 (1): 14–19. doi:10.1177/2050157912459496.

Hemer, Susan R. 2012. 'Informality, Power and Relationships in Postgraduate Supervision: Supervising PhD Candidates over Coffee'. *Higher Education Research & Development* 31 (6): 827–839. doi:10.1080/07294360.2012.674011.

Hesselberth, Pepita. 2018. 'Discourses on Disconnectivity and the Right to Disconnect'. *New Media & Society* 20 (5): 1994–2010. doi:10.1177/1461444817711449.

Hickman, Adam. 2019. 'Workplace Isolation Occurring in Remote Workers', PhD Thesis. Minneapolis, MN: Walden University College of Management and Technology.

Hochschild, Arlie Russell. 1998. *The Time Bind: When Work Becomes Home and Home Becomes Work.* New York: Metropolitan Books.

Jorge, Ana. 2019. 'Social Media, Interrupted: Users Recounting Temporary Disconnection on Instagram'. *Social Media+ Society* 5 (4): 2056305119881691.

Karppi, Tero. 2018. *Disconnect: Facebook's Affective Bonds*. Minneapolis, MN: University of Minnesota Press.

———. 2021. 'Studies in Disconnection: On the Fringes of COVID-19'. In *Undoing Networks*. S.l.: University of Minnesota Press.

Kaun, Anne, and Christian Schwarzenegger. 2014. '"No Media, Less Life?" Online Disconnection in Mediatized Worlds'. *First Monday* 19 (11). doi:10.5210/fm.v19i11.5497.

Kemp, Simon. 2020. 'Report: Most Important Data on Digital Audiences during Coronavirus'. *Growth Quarters | The Next Web*. 24 April 2020. https://thenextweb.com/growth-quarters/2020/04/24/report-most-important-data-on-digital-audiences-during-coronavirus/.

Kraemer, Jordan. 2016. 'Doing Fieldwork, BRB: Locating the Field on and with Emerging Media'. In *EFieldnotes: The Makings of Anthropology in the Digital World*, edited by Susan W. Tratner and Roger Sanjek. Philadelphia, PA: University of Pennsylvania Press, pp. 113–131.

Kristensen, Dorthe Brogård, and Signe Banke. 2019. 'The Datafication of the Self, Optimization and the Imaginary of Metrics'. Paper presented at 3rd Seminar of the Research Network for the Anthropology of Technology, *Big Data and the Power of Narrative*, Copenhagen, Danmark.

Leonardi, Paul M., Marleen Huysman, and Charles Steinfield. 2013. 'Enterprise Social Media: Definition, History, and Prospects for the Study of Social Technologies in Organizations'. *Journal of Computer-Mediated Communication* 19 (1): 1–19. doi:10.1111/jcc4.12029.

Lomborg, Stine. 2014. *Social Media, Social Genres: Making Sense of the Ordinary*. Routledge.

Mazmanian, Melissa, Wanda J Orlikowski, and JoAnne Yates. 2013. 'The Autonomy Paradox: The Implications of Mobile Email Devices for Knowledge Professionals'. *Organization Science* 24 (5): 1337–1357. doi:10.1287/orsc.1120.0806.

Milan, Stefania, and Emiliano Treré. 2020. 'The Rise of the Data Poor: The COVID-19 Pandemic Seen From the Margins'. *Social Media + Society* 6 (3): 205630512094823. doi:10.1177/2056305120948233.

Miller, Paul. 2016. 'How Intranets and Related Technologies Are Redefining Internal Communications'. In *Gower Handbook of Internal Communication*, edited by Marc Wright, pp. 189–198. CRC Press.

Moore, Phoebe V. 2018. *The Quantified Self in Precarity: Work, Technology and What Counts*. Routledge Advances in Sociology 1. London: Taylor and Francis. http://www.myilibrary.com?id=1035578.

Natale, Simone, and Emiliano Treré. 2020. 'Vinyl Won't Save Us: Reframing Disconnection as Engagement'. *Media, Culture & Society* 42 (4): 626–633. doi:10.1177/0163443720914027.

Nguyen, Minh Hao, Jonathan Gruber, Jaelle Fuchs, Will Marler, Amanda Hunsaker, and Eszter Hargittai. 2020. 'Changes in Digital Communication During the COVID-19 Global Pandemic: Implications for Digital Inequality and Future Research'. *Social Media + Society* 6 (3): 2056305120948255.

Nippert-Eng, Christena. 1996. 'Calendars and Keys: The Classification of "Home" and "Work"'. In *Sociological Forum* 11: 563–582. https://www.jstor.org/stable /684901.

Oldenburg, Ramon, and Dennis Brissett. 1982. 'The Third Place'. *Qualitative Sociology* 5 (4): 265–284.

Orgad, Shani. 2019. *Heading Home: Motherhood, Work, and the Failed Promise of Equality*. New York: Columbia University Press.

Petersen, Anne Helen. 2020. *Can't Even: How Millennials Became the Burnout Generation*. Boston, MA: Houghton Mifflin Harcourt.

Polson, Erika. 2020. 'The Aspirational Class "Mobility" of Digital Nomads'. In *The Routledge Companion to Media and Class*, edited by Erika Polson, Lynn Schofield Clark, and Radhika Gajjala, 1st edition, pp. 168–179. Routledge.

Portwood-Stacer, Laura. 2013. 'Media Refusal and Conspicuous Non-Consumption: The Performative and Political Dimensions of Facebook Abstention'. *New Media & Society* 15 (7): 1041–1057. doi:10.1177/1461444812465139.

Reagle Jr, Joseph M. Reagle. 2019. *Hacking Life: Systematized Living and Its Discontents*. Cambridge, MA: MIT Press.

Reichelt, Malte, Kinga Makovi, and Anahit Sargsyan. 2021. 'The Impact of COVID-19 on Gender Inequality in the Labor Market and Gender-Role Attitudes'. *European Societies* 23 (sup1): S228–S245. doi:10.1080/14616696.2020.1823010.

Reichenberger, Ina. 2018. 'Digital Nomads–a Quest for Holistic Freedom in Work and Leisure'. *Annals of Leisure Research* 21 (3): 364–380.

Sayers, Janet. 2009. 'Flat Whites: How and Why People Work in Cafés'. *New Zealand Journal of Employment Relations* 34 (2): 77–86.

Squazzoni, Flaminio, Giangiacomo Bravo, Francisco Grimaldo, Daniel García-Costa, Mike Farjam, and Bahar Mehmani. 2020. 'Only Second-Class Tickets for Women in the COVID-19 Race. A Study on Manuscript Submissions and Reviews in 2329 Elsevier Journals'. SSRN Scholarly Paper ID 3712813. Rochester, NY: Social Science Research Network. doi:10.2139/ssrn.3712813.

Syvertsen, Trine. 2017. *Media Resistance: Dislike, Protest, Abstention*. New York: Springer.

Syvertsen, Trine, and Gunn Enli. 2020. 'Digital Detox: Media Resistance and the Promise of Authenticity'. *Convergence* 26 (5–6): 1269–1283. doi:10.1177/1354856519847325.

Thompson, Beverly Yuen. 2019. 'The Digital Nomad Lifestyle:(Remote) Work/ Leisure Balance, Privilege, and Constructed Community'. *International Journal of the Sociology of Leisure* 2 (1–2): 27–42.

Treem, Jeffrey W., and Paul M. Leonardi. 2013. 'Social Media Use in Organizations: Exploring the Affordances of Visibility, Editability, Persistence, and Association'. *Annals of the International Communication Association* 36 (1): 143–189. doi:10.1 080/23808985.2013.11679130.

Turkle, Sherry. 2015. *Reclaiming Conversation: The Power of Talk in a Digital Age*. New York: Penguin Press.

Uysal, Nur. 2016. 'Social Collaboration in Intranets: The Impact of Social Exchange and Group Norms on Internal Communication'. *International Journal of Business Communication* 53 (2): 181–199.

Vaidhyanathan, Siva. 2018. *Antisocial Media: How Facebook Disconnects Us and Undermines Democracy*. Oxford, UK: Oxford University Press.

Woldoff, Rachael, and Robert C. Litchfield. 2021. *Digital Nomads: In Search of Freedom, Community, and Meaningful Work in the New Economy*. New York: Oxford University Press.

World Health Organization. 2020. 'Responding to Community Spread of COVID-19: Interim Guidance, 7 March 2020'. World Health Organization.

Yip, Paul S. F., and Pui Hing Chau. 2020. 'Physical Distancing and Emotional Closeness Amidst COVID-19'. *Crisis* 41 (3): 153–155. doi:10.1027/0227-5910/a000710.

Zhang, Stephen X., Yifei Wang, Andreas Rauch, and Feng Wei. 2020. 'Unprecedented Disruption of Lives and Work: Health, Distress and Life Satisfaction of Working Adults in China One Month into the COVID-19 Outbreak'. *Psychiatry Research* 288 (June): 112958. doi:10.1016/j.psychres.2020.112958.

Zuboff, Shoshana. 2019. *The Age of Surveillance Capitalism: The Fight for the Future at the New Frontier of Power*. London: Profile Books.

Chapter 9

Disconnecting on Two Wheels

Bike Touring, Leisure, and Reimagining networks

Pedro Ferreira and Airi Lampinen

Underlying long-term bicycle touring (also referred to as 'bike touring' or just 'touring'), as with other outdoor experiences, there is an often-expressed desire to disconnect. Broadly speaking, touring involves living on the bicycle for a period of time, ranging from days and weeks to months or even years. While on tour, cyclists can cover distances not commonly thought of as bike-able, and traverse broad geographies. Living on the bicycle typically involves carrying a set of items, such as a tent and cooking gear, depending on the kind of experience that is sought. We draw on interviews with bike tourists to investigate how different desires, needs, and constraints are balanced, on the road, and how they help shine a different light into discussions of disconnection. In a broader investigation of outdoor enthusiasts' activities, we have previously focused on away-ness, the taking of temporary liberties outside of ordinary life, and disconnection as inspiration for design (Helms et al. 2019) as well as on how enthusiasts centre leisure and the escaping of everyday life of work and obligations (Ferreira et al. 2019). In this chapter, we contribute to discussions of disconnection through the investigation of bike touring as an activity that disconnects, focusing particularly on the managing of boundaries between work and leisure.[1]

---

[1] Details on the interview materials we draw upon can be found in Ferreira et al. 2019.

CONNECTIVITY: FROM NECESSITY
TO BURDEN AND BACK

Contemporary discussions around connectivity are multiple and context-dependent. Only recently, connectivity was often framed academically as an issue of 'access', of leaving unconnected people 'behind' (Van Dijk 2006). As Selwyn recounts (2003), the equalizing promise of networks and digital connectivity focused on bridging the digital divide and acted as a driver behind IT developments and interventions. One Laptop Per Child is but one prominent and visible illustration of trying to bring this techno-utopia to the many (Ames 2019). Selwyn (2003) argues that there are many consequences to such drive, namely that it assumes connectivity to be an unquestioned good and a self-evident goal while its absence is seen as a wrong to be righted or a deficiency to be corrected.

The way connectivity is discussed within academia has evolved significantly as a result of ongoing debates around privacy, work–life balance, and data-based discrimination. Perhaps the most striking development is the shift in how disconnection is perceived and discussed. In many ways, we have moved from concerns around equality of access and disconnection as an absence to be corrected, towards debates on the need to disconnect, moral panics of youths' excessive screen time, warnings of techno-exhaustion (prominent during the Covid-19 pandemic as 'Zoom fatigue'[2]), the legal enforcement of work–life balance,[3] and discussions regarding digital addiction and detox (Syvertsen and Enli 2020). People's livelihoods are increasingly dependent on their connectivity, particularly for the most vulnerable workers (Gray and Suri 2019). To disconnect digitally is becoming a luxury that not everyone can afford while it is still upheld as a virtue—a healthy lifestyle—by many. This sentiment is captured well in Portwood-Stacer's (2013) framing of non-use as a form of conspicuous *non*-consumption. As Bollmer suggests (2016), the fight against connectivity is lost and long gone, and we are all constituted as citizens of networks—what he calls 'nodal citizens'—and therefore we can benefit from richer understandings of the diverse networks and connectivities that we belong to.

Responses to the Covid-19 pandemic have further influenced the debate regarding disconnection, for instance, with the normalization of working from home. Technologies for remote work have become everyday tools for many. The rushed effort to move work and life (more fully) online has,

---

[2] From the videoconferencing software of the same name that became popularized at that time.
[3] As an example are the 'right to disconnect' laws of France and other EU countries (Donini et al. 2017), which have also been criticized for their unintended consequences, such as shifting the burden of compliance onto the worker (Hesselberth 2018).

in many instances, come at the cost of a resurgence in digital divides, for instance, when school systems are not equipped to handle online teaching[4] and wealthier parents opt to provide their children with private alternatives, leaving those with lesser resources in even more vulnerable positions. While being able to work from home and socialize with friends and family across distances is a relative privilege, these arrangements are full of challenges that highlight how both connection and disconnection may start feeling like a trap. These reckonings come at a time when scholarship has become more nuanced, largely moving past the connection/disconnection dichotomy (Light 2014; Karppi 2018; Hesselberth 2018). Rather than thinking about connection and disconnection as states one oscillates between, we suggest drawing on Nippert-Eng's scholarship on 'boundary work' and 'boundary play' (Nippert-Eng 2005) to understand how ideas related to (dis)connection are malleably constructed, carefully explored, and tailored to fit changing circumstances.

DISCONNECTING AND BOUNDARIES OF WORK AND LEISURE

Bike touring promotes a shift from academic discussions of 'nomadic work' (Carvalho, Ciolfi, and Gray 2017; Carvalho 2014)—the driver behind much of the early and since critiqued hype of connectivity and working 'anytime/anyplace' (Kleinrock 1996; 1995)[5]—to considering 'nomadic leisure' and the way it shifts our spatial and temporal thinking around digital technologies (Ferreira et al. 2019). This tension between leisure and work is partly informed by leisure studies' understanding of the relationship between work and 'free time' (Rojek 2010). These distinctions are related, and often parallel, to the distinction between connection and disconnection. We draw here on a rather productive mirroring between the complexities in that work with discussions around the boundary work that goes into distinguishing between work and life (Nippert-Eng 2005) as well as the boundary sculpting that has been addressed within the study of digital work (Ciolfi and Lockley 2017; Bødker 2016) and even in support of sustainable tourism (Dickinson et al. 2017). These cut to the core of many concerns regarding the ownership of personal and collective time and our (in)dependence from digital connections. The drive to get away and to be free, that animates bike tourists, can help inform not only scholarship in leisure studies and the design of new forms of connected technologies,

---

[4] This was visible in, for instance. the Bolivian government's decision to cancel the school year (Dube 2020).
[5] For a thoughtful critique, see Gregg (2013).

but also our understanding of what it means to be connected, including the anxieties it involves, and alternative forms of connectivity.

The extreme nature of bike touring as an unusual activity echoes the extreme nature of the Covid-19 pandemic as a state of exception. In light of the pandemic, concerns for a clear separation between work and leisure as well as concerns around too much time spent digitally connected, have largely been thrown out the window. Desired disconnection may feel like a luxury we cannot afford to pursue, while connectivity re-emerges as an issue of social justice. During pandemic times, connectivity is needed not just to enable both work and personal life, but also in our dealings with the state or the corporate sector. While some have voiced concerns over the demands, and exhaustion, of hyperconnectivity, the state of exception geared towards collective survival has reframed connectivity as a bare (and benign) necessity. This has forced an emergency resculpting of boundaries between private and professional spheres, or between leisure and work, throwing into turmoil both academic and lay understandings of how to handle these boundaries. Our more literal pursuits of leisure have come under threat: travel has become increasingly difficult and off-putting, and previously simple social events are now, more often than not, heavily restricted if not outright illegal. In sum, we are experiencing a radical disruption in how we disconnect, and how we utilize our free time (if we still have free time amid the new constellations of obligations the pandemic has brought about).

Phenomena related to connectivity and disconnection are extremely fragmented—and fortunately so, since we are all experiencing these events differently, given the different resources we have and the varied constraints we face in dealing with our circumstances. What is more, from the get-go, we also have very different goals, expectations, and definitions of what disconnection means and when it might be desirable. Focusing on bike touring as a practice, rather than investigating a particular technology in detail, allows us to consider disconnection in light of an endeavour that is desirable yet not without its issues.

Finally, we would like to highlight that leisure activity is complex and rife with asymmetries over who gets to do what, where, and under what conditions (Rojek 2010). We do not wish to romanticize outdoor activities or to cast bike touring, specifically, as inherently more free than everyday endeavours or as equally available for everyone. Engagement with space (Massey 2010) and time (Sharma 2014; Wajcman 2019) is highly gendered, racialized, and structured around the same kinds of privilege that affect society at large. Digital technologies are at the epicentre of these structures of exclusion, with growing discontent regarding its ability to enforce and amplify pre-existing modes of segregation and discrimination (Noble 2018; Benjamin 2019). Discussing disconnection through the prism of bike touring should be considered within the wider frames of how both the outdoors and technology are indissociable from social and societal structures. While such issues have been widely documented when it comes to digital technology, it is worth noting that the outdoors is equally problematic when it comes to how it is made accessible and inaccessible along racial or sex/gender divides (Finney 2014; Pires 2018). In what follows, we document our participants' experiences in working and playing with the boundaries of work and leisure, but we want to point out upfront that our empirical work so far does not allow us to account more fully for the diversity of experiences related to the outdoors. There are necessarily many stories which are not rendered visible in our work. With that caveat in mind, we turn to bike touring to consider disconnection and its relation to the boundaries of work and leisure.

BOUNDARY WORK, PLAY, AND FREEDOM

There are obvious parallels to thinking about connection and disconnection, on the one hand, and scholarship on 'boundary sculpting' between work and home (Ciolfi and Lockley 2017; Bødker 2016; Wajcman et al. 2009), on the other. Unsurprisingly, there are wide-ranging attitudes towards work and leisure as two distinct domains. Nippert-Eng (2005) attributes these distinctions to different 'frames of mind'. She describes how some might like to keep these frames as separate while others would welcome permeability. Aims, motivations, and personal situations all play a role in how 'boundary work', that is, the active practice of shaping, maintaining, or dissolving boundaries, unfolds. Understanding boundary work is central to our inquiry into cyclists' activities while bike touring. Another useful concept from Nippert-Eng is 'boundary play' where the boundary is itself the focus of a playful activity. Play, as understood by Nippert-Eng, is not strictly separated from the concept of work. Rather, it is differentiated in terms of attitudes or 'frames of mind'. Essentially, one is able to engage with boundaries for amusement, because one may feel safe enough in a return to 'the normal', abandoning the transformations explored during play as temporary. Play as separate from ordinary life is in line with Huizinga's idea of a 'magic circle' (Huizinga 1955), and the separation of play as a place away from the demands of ordinary life. This is to say neither that play is unproductive nor that this separation is analytically tenable, as Consalvo reminds us (2009). What it does is offer us a sufficiently safe arena for the kinds of boundary play that helps open up and imagine new possibilities.

In our work, bike touring is seen through the lens of boundary play, meaning that bike touring continuously reshapes the categories of work and leisure as well as connection and disconnection. To quote from an interview with one of our participants, Matt: 'There are no goals in terms of cycling so many miles or so many kilometers. If we're behind, we will happily jump the train or whatever. It's not a challenge. It's just a month of freedom.' This statement of playful freedom further resonates with Nippert-Eng's concept of boundary play as well as with Rojek's point in leisure studies—that underlying the leisurely pursuit in the neoliberal society is the question of 'freedom' (Rojek 2010). As pointed out, this begs the question of 'freedom *from* what?' (Rojek 2010, our emphasis)—but also freedom *for* what? While our participants obviously shared a passion for cycling, there was also a sense of disruption with everyday life. It is through boundary play that we accomplish boundary work, shifting our notions of leisure, work, freedom, and disconnection. By breaking away with the everyday we are able to glimpse at the strategies employed around digital technologies and how they are differently deployed.

METHOD

We draw on a total of 16 in-depth, semi-structured interviews with 11 participants. This is part of a broader research project on outdoor activities (Helms et al. 2019; Ferreira et al. 2019) and a research focus on enjoyment and leisure (Ferreira 2015; Brown and Juhlin 2015). Participants in this study were recruited through a popular internet forum on Reddit dedicated to bike touring. After a first call that attracted almost exclusively a set of male participants, we repeated the call, albeit targeting it specifically towards female bike tourists. Where possible, we interviewed participants both before and after a tour. Others were interviewed opportunistically at either end, or at times during their time on the road. Interview materials were analyzed through multiple iterations of coding and interpretation resulting in distinct and overlapping themes relating to our analytical interests around leisure, disconnection, as well as the lived practice of touring. We invite the reader to look at a previous publication for a more thorough, in-depth, description of our methods (Ferreira et al. 2019). We provide a brief summary of participants in table 9.1.

In this chapter we first look at how disconnection is sought through boundary play and work. We then consider how disconnection is balanced with other demands and finally how bike touring invites us to think about remaking connectivity.

DISCONNECTION AND BOUNDARY PLAY

I run my own business. I work hard. I've got two kids. I've got a mortgage. [. . .] And it's really cool to just be able to go, right, a month, I'm not checking my

Table 9.1 Overview of Participants

Pseudonym	Demographics	Length of Tour	Where	Company
Matt	49, male, British	< 1 month	Europe	1–3 friends/family
Yann	29, male, Polish	4 month + 1 month	Africa/Europe	Solo
Gary	60+, male, United States	1 month	Balkans	Solo
Adrian	30, male, Dutch	1 month	Europe	Girlfriend
Paul	25, male, Brazilian	3 month	United States	Friend
Jeff	27, male, United States	2 month	United States	Solo
Hannah	20+, female, Hungarian	> 1 year	Europe	Boyfriend
Renee	22, female, United States	1 month	United States	Group: Cycling for Multiple Sclerosis
Sophia	30+, female, United States	3 month	South America	Husband
Elina	34, female, Finnish	3×1 month	Europe	Husband
Olivia	25, female, United States	1 month	Europe	Solo

emails. I'm not going on social media. I don't care about what Donald Trump's doing. I'm not going to let the news upset me about Brexit. I'm just going to switch off, drop off the grid. (Matt)

Most bike tourists we interviewed brought up technology, or more precisely a distancing from digital technology, as a key motivation for touring. In fact, bike touring is in many ways perfect for this: the continuous, physical, involvement throughout the day is not easily compatible with checking emails or going on social media. While bike touring is mostly flexible when it comes to achieving daily, or overall predefined, goals, it does require significant amounts of pedalling. In that sense, bike touring itself is a kind of boundary play (Nippert-Eng 2005) in that the regular rhythms of cycling tended to keep the smartphone at bay, continuously forming and shaping the line between the worlds of being on- or offline. While disconnecting was often presented as the end goal, it was through the cycling activity that our interviewees explored, and recreated, boundaries around their use of digital technologies. It should then come as no surprise that when asked about whether he missed being connected, Jeff replied, 'Honestly, it's really nice to get away from so much internet. Yeah. It's really been the opposite. Don't get me wrong, I really like to stay in touch with my friends and hear how everybody's doing, but I prefer not being so reachable.'

Pedro Ferreira and Airi Lampinen

However, boundaries are porous. The ordinary worlds of online media consumption that our participants were purposefully trying to escape made their way back into touring on a regular basis, as Yann expressed reflecting on his smartphone use during downtime: 'I was excessively using it for just surfing mindlessly, like reading Reddit too much.' While his characterizations of spending time online 'excessively' and 'mindlessly' echoes the way social media use is portrayed as a broader societal concern,[6] we take them as expressions of personal concern specifically at odds with his goals of away-ness (Helms et al. 2019)—an act of being unavailable for a restricted time and taking temporary liberties separate from everyday life, including social commitments, professional obligations, and economic constraints. Smartphone use was praised by others for its entertainment potential, a technological 'swiss army knife' to quote Adrian's metaphor, well-suited to the outdoor nature of bike touring. Participants regularly noted that their smartphones allowed them to take an often welcomed break from the desired disconnection, to watch a movie or listen to music. The ability of apps to store content for viewing in offline mode was particularly welcomed given how participants often found themselves outside of network coverage, ironically demonstrating a technological feature that supported efforts to strictly disconnect. While our interviewees, as is commonly the case in outdoor activities, were clearly motivated by the idea of disconnecting, this was not meant in any literal or purist sense of the term. As we have reflected elsewhere, a more productive way to think of our participants' desires was the frame of pointed disconnections (Helms et al. 2019). The kinds of (dis)connection our participants sought were made more pleasant, or even possible, through a more tailored and purposeful approach to connectivity. This is a common aspect in outdoor activities more generally, as illustrated by, for instance, the impact that GPS warning systems such as the Spot Generation 3[7] have in crucially enabling the confidence required to go on long adventurous hikes that one might not otherwise venture into (Helms et al. 2019).

The notion of pointed (dis)connection echoes calls for purposeful use and for taking back control of our digital lives. Such calls have been voiced both in popular literature, such as Cal Newport's self-help book *Digital Minimalism* (2019), and academic writing, most recently in Rob Kitchin and Alistair Fraser's *Slow Computing* (2020). And indeed, our participants' desires to disconnect hint at a discomfort with digital devices. In contrast to everyday life and its habits, bike touring offers a seemingly more straightforward, absorbing activity that is in many ways antithetical to digital connectivity. Taking

[6] We refer here to moral panics around technology use that tend to recreate themselves at different turns (Turkle 2012), and that are also often the target of critique.
[7] https://www.findmespot.com/en-ca/products-services/spot-gen3.

back control of our digital lives, to paraphrase Newport, may thus require a disconnecting act, not as the end goal but as a means. In this sense, our participants experience what Hesselberth (2018) describes as 'media disruption'. Hesselberth sees these approaches to disconnection as limited on the grounds that they often require extra labour and, paradoxically, extra work in terms of the tailoring of connectivity. These paradoxes to disconnection have been highlighted by others such as Light and Cassidy (2014) or Karppi (2018), that argue for more nuanced understandings of what connectivity means. To some extent, there is an argument for an acceptance of the default state of connectivity and focusing rather on modes of resistance—for instance, in what Karppi calls 'paranodal' (2018)—and the generation of new forms of being connected.

Disconnecting, from our participants' perspective, was achieved by exploratively stepping outside the world of everyday routines, radically disrupting one's temporal and spatial engagement with social and technological life. It is in that sense that we see bike touring less as a manifestation of how free/ leisure time is best occupied and more as boundary play through which one explores the relation between work, leisure, and meanings of deliberate (if not total) disconnection. Disruption has been documented by others as an opportunity for technological rearrangements, for instance, in the case of residential mobility (Shklovski and Mainwaring 2005). While bike touring may be seen as extreme in some sense, it offers a relatively safe, low-stakes, and (typically) time-bounded activity that can be productive for participants in exploring and defining their own sense of disconnection, providing the rituals, routines, and relative safety through which boundary play can happen (Nippert-Eng 2008).

BALANCING EVERYDAY DEMANDS AND MAKING TIME

Matt's description of bike touring as 'just a month of freedom' does significant conceptual heavy lifting when it comes to carving out the very possibility of disconnecting, something which might not be readily available to all. Similarly, Yann's 'mindless scrolling' relates closely to the notion of digital detox (Syvertsen and Enli 2020) or broader concerns over what has been termed 'problematic smartphone use' (Elhai et al. 2017). However, upon closer scrutiny, we find that these framings run into conceptual trouble, particularly as digital technologies, and in particular smartphones, are interwoven (and often integral) to most other everyday life activities, from child rearing, work, taking a break or, ironically, finding out about digital detox opportunities. Excessive focus on measurable aspects of technology use, such as 'screen time', maps uncomfortably well to the way tech companies have adopted engagement as the main metric through which our interactions with/through technology are measured and optimized. This narrow framing obscures the broader contexts of everyday life, of which digital technologies are only a component. Our interviews offer us two ways to think about disconnection as an achievement by the participants in (1) balancing everyday demands and (2) making time.

The relationship between bike touring and the world of responsibilities is not an easy one. As Jeff puts it:

A lot of people have children or mortgages or medical stuff, and it's not everybody that can actually just cut away and do it. But even if you only have two weeks, bike travel is a great way to rejuvenate yourself and your lifestyle and your sense of what can be.

As with other leisure activities it tends to both require free time and a possibility for detachment, while simultaneously serving a recuperative function (Rojek 2013). Every one of our participants had to carve out their availability differently, both in terms of responsibilities towards family and work functions:

Once a year, I'd either go off my own or hopefully take a couple of friends and do a two-week trip. I think, one month trips or longer is going to have to wait until my kids are grown up and left and I can convince my wife to come along with me. (Matt)

For someone like Matt, there was a need to carve out time away from work, while balancing it with his family responsibilities, something he hopes might change as his children become more independent. Our interviewees had quite different starting points. For Matt, the ability to, in his own words, 'drop off the grid' was dependent on his ability to remain tethered to his wife and children through WhatsApp, without which disconnecting might not have been possible or justifiable. Tethering ourselves in this way shows the limits of framing digital disconnection, most often vis-à-vis the smartphone, as the issue at stake. On the one hand, a binary focus on disconnection conceals the wider contexts of use and tends to address the taming of technology as a matter of personal discipline (Syvertsen and Enli 2020). Staying in contact with family allowed individuals like Gary, who, despite being retired and therefore a beneficiary of extra free time, needed to appease his partners' concerns when bike touring. For others, like Olivia and Renee, digital technology allowed them to keep their parents equally reassured, reducing familial tensions and maintaining important relationships, even as constant availability was not expected. Generally speaking, our participants restricted smartphone use, for the most part, to specific moments, mainly in the evening. This limited logging on and checking in opened up for an easier acceptance of bike tours and ensured a sense of security both for the participants and for their loved ones.

Disconnecting is thus not just a matter of severing ties in a disciplined manner but rather a careful balancing of the kinds of freedoms that are desired against other obligations, and finding productive ways to do so:

> Being a freelancer, I can just . . . I say to people I'm going to be away for four weeks, so that's how long it takes and that's fine. [. . .] Some of the people I work with did contact me just casually through WhatsApp. But they respected the fact that I wasn't there. [. . .] I think I do tell people that I don't read email on my phone, so the people know that we can chat but we can't really do anything right now. (Adrian)

The way that Adrian tailors his free time for bike touring, allowing that time to remain unperturbed apart from his family and partner who could reach him, was dependent on his job as a freelancer and his longer-term efforts, prior to the activity itself, in aligning with colleagues' expectations.

Another one of our participants, Elina, had a very different, and rather unique, approach to bike touring: at the end of a tour, she would find a safe location for storing her bike and gear, travel back home to address her broader responsibilities, only to pick up the tour where she left off, at the next opportunity. This episodic touring was made possible partly because her work as an online teacher allowed Elina to attend to professional tasks while on the road, with some parallels to working anytime/anyplace and nomadic work discussions:

> I work a lot with a laptop and writing and stuff, so it's a good way to have in a way a complete break from that. Because otherwise, usually, when I have a laptop with me, I'm working at least a bit in a bus or in a train, and if I'm traveling like that. [. . .] But with cycling, it's not possible. That's a good thing, so it's a good way to have a holiday, like a real holiday in a way. [. . .] I wish it would be possible to leave it [the laptop] away, but I think all of the times have been so because I'm teaching also, [. . .] so most of the times I have had an online course going on when I have been on those cycling trips.

For Elina, her ability to bring some work, even if that meant remaining connected in a way that was not necessarily ideal for her, was a key factor in being able to go cycling and, thus, achieving a broader sense of detachment from her usual routines.

The ability to disconnect through bike touring is differently available to participants. These different availabilities reflect not only socio-economic differences, but, more broadly, different abilities to manage and traverse space and time. Here we are inspired by both Massey's work on *power geographies* (2010) and Sharma's subsequent extension of the concept to *power chronographies* (2014). Their work describes how people's ability to manage temporally and spatially are linked and affect each other, rather than merely individually constituted, and are situated in wider social contexts. These different accounts of bike touring help shed light in how these different arrangements and contexts permit varying degrees of spatial and temporal control. This of course echoes earlier discussions over unequal access to leisure (Rojek 2010) as well as of disconnection as a luxury and status symbol (Portwood-Stacer 2013). Alongside other aspects of everyday life, the Covid-19 pandemic has severely reshaped not only our ability to be mobile, but also our ability to connect. We are now reminded daily that our technological engagement is an issue well beyond personal discipline alone, and it might even have become a prerequisite for our jobs with many companies moving exclusively to remote work. And while successful disconnection should be seen as a personal achievement, in that it is never absolute but construed and maintained by the participant, it is of course also a social (and even epidemiological) one, built on a layered world of opportunities and demands—or lack thereof.

RECONNECTING AND REMAKING
FORMS OF CONNECTIVITY

Bike touring and disconnection appear inexorably linked and feeding off of each other, as Jeff showed through his changing attitude towards social media:

> I think when I get to Oregon, I'm planning to get rid of my data and purposely not have any internet in my living space. I'm going to deactivate my Facebook probably, I don't know, probably a week after I get there.

The transient experience of disconnection that bike touring offered, however, revealed both general changes in terms of attitudes towards, and uses of, digital technology and a generalized return to old habits upon returning to one's everyday life after a bike tour. As discussed earlier, disconnecting, here, appears as a breather, a moment of disruption, rather than a straightforward act with clear-cut long-term implications.

During this moment of disruption, bike tourists not only re-evaluate their existing practices but they also discover new platforms and ways of being connected. For instance, for some of our participants, larger hospitality platforms like Airbnb or Booking.com, became overshadowed with more specific alternatives dedicated to this niche activity:

> There's the app called WarmShowers and so I know that that's a good way to meet people who are willing to house you or at least lend you their backyard to camp in. So I think that will be interesting. I guess as a girl and I'm a pretty small girl, it's just a little bit scarier to be out on my own in a very unfamiliar place, but I don't know, I'm just willing to take the risk a little bit more now than I was when I was a little younger.

This quote from Renee highlights the role of platforms like WarmShowers in the very enabling of the experience of bike touring, namely among female bike tourists, by providing a place to sleep in what felt like a safe(r) manner. For others, like Hanna and her boyfriend, there was no predefined plan and they used touring as a learning opportunity, co-constituted via digital platforms:

> We research on the Internet, what looks nice and [. . .] also we use a website [. . .] I don't know if you know it, HelpX, which is similar to WorkAway, so volunteering work. And we register on HelpX and we find places on there. For example, we worked in a permaculture farm in Turkey already for a week, East of Istanbul and we wanted to discover what a farm looks like, but then after a week we realized it's like winter and there's nothing really happening where we can learn stuff.

Platforms such as HelpX or WorkAway provided them with a means of living, with varying degrees of mobility and disconnection. Platforms like HelpX and WarmShowers stand in contrast with the more famous catch-all platforms that aim to serve larger swaths of people, providing opportunities for reconsidering our relationship with digital technologies. As a community-oriented, volunteer-based network, WarmShowers also stands in contrast with pervasive models of platform monetization that have come increasingly under criticism for the pressure placed on workers and unclear uses of personal data. Underlying bike touring, then, are notions of purpose and deliberation, as Jeff put it:

> I want it to be deliberate as opposed to passively being online because it's just like the internet's so distracting. I feel like it's like having candy in your pocket and always checking email and messages and stuff like that. So, it's nice to . . . I like it that when I'm camping it's just there's no way to do it, and then when I come into town, I have a specific list of things. It's like, 'Okay, I want

to communicate with this person,' or, 'I want to send . . . I want to upload these pictures or I want to post something on social media,' or something like that. Then you leave and that's it. You know you're not just on it all day just checking, checking, checking.

While this interplay between temptation, possibility, and control have some undertones reminiscent of digital detox debates mentioned before (Syvertsen and Enli 2020), they speak to a broader sense in which smartphones were instrumental in opening up for the very possibility of bike touring while setting it apart from everyday life, allowing participants to discover ways of connecting differently.

CONCLUSION

Bike touring is well equipped to display some of the tensions, anxieties, and paradoxes of (dis)connection. Through Nippert-Eng's understanding of boundary play we can appreciate disconnection as less of a concrete, definite, state of affairs and more of a 'frame of mind' (Nippert-Eng 2008), that is negotiated and constructed through the cycling activity. The parallel with how leisure and work are separated and maintained allows us to appreciate the limits that everyday obligations and demands impose on these categories, and participants' efforts in creating and maintaining these spaces. The legitimate anxieties and concerns around the need to disconnect express a sense of loss of control that is commonly found in technological critiques. Our analysis shows that digital technologies might, somewhat paradoxically, hold some promise in addressing some of those concerns. On the one hand, this may seem to surrender ontologically to our condition as nodes in a network. On the other hand, it opens up a renewed focus when it comes to technological liberation. Disconnecting, as Bollmer suggests, should not be seen as a return to a pre-cultural state: 'I'm not suggesting that we should strive to free ourselves from the tyranny of social media, discovering a "true" human nature that has been obscured' (2016, 5). Rather, it should be seen as an ongoing and constrained negotiation. It is in this sense that we see bike touring as productively 'paranodal' (Karppi 2018), a site of resistance allowing us to question our 'nodal citizenship'. Unpacking these different, niche, network dynamics can be useful in tackling—or perhaps reframing—issues of problematic smartphone use. Others have shown the potential of digital technologies in promoting, rather than threatening, sustainable tourism and community building (Dickinson et al. 2017).

The Covid-19 pandemic has brought about widespread institution of what Agamben (2005) famously calls a 'state of exception'. According to

Agamben, the curtailing of rights and freedoms is achieved by appealing to the preservation of an essentialized form of 'bare life'. Appealing to essences opens up for a shift in authority, not only on the part of the state, but also in epistemic authority (i.e. Who makes knowledge on essences?). Such attitudes fail to capture the role that technologies play in the co-construction of our '"human nature" at least when we suggest that it is in our nature to desire "connection", is an effect of the ways we use and describe technologies' (Bollmer 2016, 5). Instead, we draw on this drive towards disconnection as a way to rethink 'the metaphors we (often incorrectly) use to describe technology, many of which are best observed in everyday practices and discourses surrounding social media' (Bollmer 2016, 5), and practically address the personal, legitimate concerns around the need to disconnect.

ACKNOWLEDGEMENTS

The materials presented in this chapter are based on fieldwork conducted together with our colleagues Karey Helms and Barry Brown. This work has been supported by the Swedish Foundation for Strategic Research project RIT15-0046 and by Swedish Research Council grant number 2017-05382_3.

REFERENCES

Agamben, Giorgio. 2005. *State of Exception*. The University of Chicago Press.
Ames, Morgan G. 2019. *The Charisma Machine: The Life, Death, and Legacy of One Laptop per Child*. MIT Press.
Benjamin, Ruha. 2019. *Race after Technology: Abolitionist Tools for the New Jim Code*. Pollity.
Bødker, Susanne. 2016. 'Rethinking Technology on the Boundaries of Life and Work'. *Personal and Ubiquitous Computing* 20 (4): 533–544.
Bollmer, Grant. 2016. *Inhuman Networks: Social Media and the Archaeology of Connection*. Bloomsbury Publishing USA.
Carvalho, Aparecido Fabiano Pinatti de. 2014. 'Collaborative Work and Its Relationship to Technologically-Mediated Nomadicity'. In *COOP 2014-Proceedings of the 11th International Conference on the Design of Cooperative Systems*, 209–224. Springer.
Carvalho, Aparecido Fabiano Pinatti de, Luigina Ciolfi, and Breda Gray. 2017. "Detailing a Spectrum of Motivational Forces Shaping Nomadic Practices." In *Proceedings of the 2017 ACM Conference on Computer Supported Cooperative Work and Social Computing*, 962–977. ACM.
Ciolfi, Luigina, and Eleanor Lockley. 2017. 'Work-Life Strategies on the Move: Reconfiguring Boundaries'. *International Reports on Socio-Informatics* (IRSI) 14 (3): 35–40.

Consalvo, Mia. 2009. 'There Is No Magic Circle'. *Games and Culture* 4 (4): 408–417.

Donini, Annamaria, Michele Forlivesi, Anna Rota, and Patrizia Tullini. 2017. 'Towards Collective Protections for Crowdworkers: Italy, Spain and France in the EU Context'. *Transfer: European Review of Labour and Research* 23 (2): 207–223.

Dube, Ryan. 2020. 'Bolivia Decision to Cancel School Because of Covid-19 Upsets Parents'. *Wall Street Journal*, August 4, 2020, sec. World. https://www.wsj.com/articles/bolivia-decision-to-cancel-school-because-of-covid-19-upsets-parents-11596577822.

Elhai, Jon D., Robert D. Dvorak, Jason C. Levine, and Brian J. Hall. 2017. 'Problematic Smartphone Use: A Conceptual Overview and Systematic Review of Relations with Anxiety and Depression Psychopathology'. *Journal of Affective Disorders* 207: 251–259.

Ferreira, Pedro, Karey Helms, Barry Brown, and Airi Lampinen. 2019. 'From Nomadic Work to Nomadic Leisure Practice: A Study of Long-Term Bike Touring'. *Proceedings of the ACM on Human-Computer Interaction* 3 (CSCW), 1–20.

Finney, Carolyn. 2014. *Black Faces, White Spaces: Reimagining the Relationship of African Americans to the Great Outdoors*. UNC Press Books.

Gray, Mary L., and Siddharth Suri. 2019. *Ghost Work: How to Stop Silicon Valley from Building a New Global Underclass*. Eamon Dolan Books.

Gregg, Melissa. 2013. *Work's Intimacy*. John Wiley & Sons.

Helms, Karey, Pedro Ferreira, Barry Brown, and Airi Lampinen. 2019. "Away and (Dis) Connection: Reconsidering the Use of Digital Technologies in Light of Long-Term Outdoor Activities." *Proceedings of the ACM on Human-Computer Interaction* 3 (GROUP), 1–20.

Hesselberth, Pepita. 2018. 'Discourses on Disconnectivity and the Right to Disconnect'. *New Media & Society* 20 (5): 1994–2010.

Huizinga, Johan. 1955. *Homo Ludens: A Study of the Play-Element in Culture*. International Library of Sociology. Routledge.

Karppi, Tero. 2018. *Disconnect: Facebook's Affective Bonds*. University of Minnesota Press.

Kitchin, Rob, and Alistair Fraser. 2020. *Slow Computing: Why We Need Balanced Digital Lives*. Bristol University Press.

Kleinrock, Leonard. 1995. 'Nomadic Computing—An Opportunity'. *ACM SIGCOMM Computer Communication Review* 25 (1): 36–40.

———. 1996. "Nomadicity: Anytime, Anywhere in a Disconnected World." *Mobile Networks and Applications* 1 (4): 351–357.

Light, Ben. 2014. *Disconnecting with Social Networking Sites*. Springer.

Light, Ben, and Elija Cassidy. 2014. 'Strategies for the Suspension and Prevention of Connection: Rendering Disconnection as Socioeconomic Lubricant with Facebook'. *New Media & Society* 16 (7): 1169–1184.

Massey, Doreen. 2010. *A Global Sense of Place*. Aughty.org.

Newport, Cal. 2019. *Digital Minimalism: Choosing a Focused Life in a Noisy World*. Penguin.

Nippert-Eng, Christena. 2005. 'Boundary Play'. *Space and Culture* 8 (3): 302–324.

Noble, Safiya Umoja. 2018. *Algorithms of Oppression: How Search Engines Reinforce Racism*. NYU Press.

Pires, Candice. 2018. '"Bad Things Happen in the Woods": The Anxiety of Hiking While Black'. *The Guardian*, July 13. https://www.theguardian.com/environment/2018/jul/13/hiking-african-american-racism-nature.

Portwood-Stacer, Laura. 2013. 'Media Refusal and Conspicuous Non-Consumption: The Performative and Political Dimensions of Facebook Abstention'. *New Media & Society* 15 (7): 1041–1057.

Rojek, Chris. 2013. 'Is Marx Still Relevant to the Study of Leisure?'. *Leisure Studies* 32 (1): 19–33.

_____ . 2010. *The Labour of Leisure: The Culture of Free Time*. Sage.

Selwyn, Neil. 2003. 'Apart from Technology: Understanding People's Non-Use of Information and Communication Technologies in Everyday Life'. *Technology in Society* 25 (1): 99–116.

Sharma, Sarah. 2014. *In the Meantime: Temporality and Cultural Politics*. Durham, NC: Duke University Press.

Shklovski, Irina A., and Scott D. Mainwaring. 2005. 'Exploring Technology Adoption and Use Through the Lens of Residential Mobility'. In *Proceedings of the SIGCHI Conference on Human Factors in Computing Systems*, 621–630. CHI '05. New York, NY, USA: ACM. doi:10.1145/1054972.1055058.

Syvertsen, Trine, and Gunn Enli. 2020. 'Digital Detox: Media Resistance and the Promise of Authenticity'. *Convergence* 26 (5–6): 1269–1283. doi:10.1177/1354856519847225.

Van Dijk, Jan AGM. 2006. 'Digital Divide Research, Achievements and Shortcomings'. *Poetics* 34 (4): 221–235.

Wajcman, Judy. 2019. 'How Silicon Valley Sets Time'. *New Media & Society* 21 (6): 1272–1289. doi:10.1177/1461444818820073.

Wajcman, Judy, Michael Bittman, Jude Brown, Michael Bittman, and Jude Brown. 2009. 'Intimate Connections: The Impact of the Mobile Phone on Work/Life Boundaries'. In *Mobile Technologies: From Telecommunications to Media*, edited by Gerard Goggin and Larissa Hjorth, 9–22. London: Routledge.

Chapter 10

Analogue Nostalgia

Examining Critiques of Social Media

Clara Wieghorst

As digital connection becomes an ever larger part of their day, [young people] risk ending up with lives of less.

(Turkle 2015, 22)

This quote by sociologist Sherry Turkle is symptomatic of a kind of nostalgic media critique. In the age of the techlash, analogue nostalgia can be found not only in academic critiques of social media but as a widespread phenomenon. In the documentary *The Social Dilemma* (Orlowski 2020), former tech enthusiasts like Tristan Harris and Jaron Lanier suggest that we have fallen victim to the addictive nature of social media. According to these critics, instead of engaging with our fellow human beings like we used to, we spend our time on our phones comparing our bodies with those of Instagram influencers and consuming news provided by algorithms that stir up prejudice and hate. The phenomenal success of the Netflix documentary—within the first four weeks of release it was watched in 38,000,000 homes (Moore 2021)—indicates that it has touched a nerve. Social media are no longer seen as convenient tools to connect with friends and family but as a threat to our mental health and political system. These popular modes of critiquing social media mobilize a longing for former times. This longing extends beyond social issue documentaries into the arts and popular culture, where a nostalgia for old media like analogue cameras, vinyl records, and typewriters can be interpreted as an epiphenomenon of the advent of digital media (Marks 2002; Schrey 2014). Examining this analogue nostalgia for old media contextualizes analogue nostalgia in critiques of social media. I will begin by examining the notion of media nostalgia, then move to describing nostalgia for analogue media as a specific relation. Then, I will focus on two critiques of social media by two distinguished media scholars. The first is Sherry Turkle's book *Reclaiming Conversation* and the second is *The Culture of Connectivity* by José Van Dijck. While their approaches differ significantly, I argue that both works are analogous in the ways in which they rely on analogue nostalgia when constructing their criticism of social media. In other words, I propose that analogue nostalgia can not only be found in critique that focuses on the effects of social media on individuals but also be found in critique that focuses on the social media itself, even though it is more prevalent in the former than in the latter.

The aim of this chapter is not to criticize Turkle's and Van Dijck's approaches but to consider their texts as symptomatic of analogue nostalgia in critiques of social media. At the same time, I suggest an alternative mode of criticizing social media. I argue that practices of remediation (Bolter and Grusin 2000) in which analogue aesthetics are imitated digitally (Bartholeyns 2014) and the temporal contingency of trends point to the fact that we have not moved from an analogue age to a digital one but live 'in several times at once' (Rancière 2012, 37). This also means embracing the fact that social media have become part of human lives. Even if we live in a culture of connectivity and social media sites have been standardized in the interest of platform companies, it is still possible to meaningfully interact on (and off) social media. As a consequence, and as an alternative to the techlash, I suggest focusing on the socio-technological processes of disconnection (Karppi 2018) instead of presuming a state of disconnectivity associated with conversation, connectedness, and the analogue as opposed to a state of connectivity associated with technology, standardization, and the digital.

MEDIA NOSTALGIA

Originally, nostalgia means homesickness. The term is derived etymologically from the Greek words *nóstos (νόστος*, returning home) and *álgos (ἄλγος*, longing). The term was coined in the doctoral dissertation of Johannes Hofer, which was published in Basel in 1688. Hofer observed a painful desire to return home among Swiss mercenaries, which manifested itself in various physical and psychological complaints ranging from loss of appetite to hallucinations to schizophrenia (Niemeyer 2014, 7–8).

Svetlana Boym (2001) distinguishes between restorative and reflective nostalgia. Whereas the former focuses on *nóstos*, attempting to reconstruct the lost home, the latter form of nostalgia stresses *algós*, the longing itself. Thus, nostalgia cannot be understood as a merely reactionary phenomenon but as an ambivalent practice between mourning what has been lost and creating the present by preserving the past. According to Katharina Niemeyer, nostalgia is 'related to a way of living, imagining and sometimes exploiting or (re)inventing the past, present and future' (2014, 2). She claims that nostalgia 'has always been an affair of mediated processes' (2014, 7). Media, especially new technologies, could serve as a platform and instrument to express nostalgia (Cook 2005). Sometimes, however, outdated media themselves, like vinyl records or analogue cameras, become objects of nostalgia.[1] In a study on generational media experience, Göran Bolin (2016) distinguishes between three different media-related types of nostalgia, namely 'technostalgia' (ibid., 256), 'nostalgia as a loss of childhood' (ibid., 258), and 'nostalgia as the (im)possibility of intergenerational experience' (ibid., 259).

Technostalgia differs from the other two modes of nostalgia by the fact that it is the only one that can be 'cured' because it refers to media objects that are still there. Following Boym's distinction between restorative and reflective nostalgia, technostalgia is the only one of the three nostalgia forms that works restoratively. It is not possible for the interviewees in Bolin's study to become children again and it is only partially possible to share the feeling of one's own youth with one's own children, which can be a painful realization. However, the interviewees can maintain their record collections and listen to old, home-made mixtapes in their car cassette recorders. When nostalgia is directed at objects, these objects can not only represent the past but also evoke it. At least for a moment, old media allow 'a lustful revival of this past' (Böhn 2007, 144).

If media nostalgia serves to evoke past times, it can be assumed that the concrete character of the longed-for media object does not matter. Any outdated media could become the object of nostalgic longing, whether analogue or digital. Still, the analogue vinyl record seems to be more suitable for nostalgic charge than the digital Compact Disc (CD). Tellingly, the German company 'Newtro' (New but Retro) produces sound systems that include a phonograph, a CD player, and a cassette deck. Their looks imitate old radios (Newtro 2020). Even though CDs are outdated and—according to the logic of technostalgia—could serve to evoke memories of a childhood in the 1990s and early 2000s, a CD player only seems to be suitable for nostalgic charge when combined with a phonograph and the look of an old radio. So, the question arises: From a nostalgic perspective, what is it that distinguishes analogue media objects from digital media objects?

One of the main points of every kind of nostalgic media criticism seems to be that something of that which is mediated gets lost in the process of its mediation. Plato was the first known media critic who feared that the 'being' or 'life' of a statement would be lost through its mediation. He was of the

---

[1] See (Böhn 2007) for the self-referentiality of media nostalgia, which he diagnoses when nostalgia for outdated media is produced in media.

opinion that the written word was less alive than the spoken word (Sterne 2006, 338). Another prominent figure in this tradition of thinking is Walter Benjamin. He famously notes (2010 [1935], 15) that the 'aura' of a work of art is 'always depreciated' by its technological reproduction.[2] In a similar way, Régis Debray (1996, 26) distinguishes between the logosphere (characterized by writing), the graphosphere (when printed text was the main means of diffusion), and the videosphere (referring to audiovisual media). Against these metaphysical perspectives, Hartmut Böhme (2010) promotes a pragmatic evaluation of media technologies. He argues that classifications like Debray's rely on the cultural critical model of a transition from a literate culture to an audiovisual culture in the process of which a *'desubstantialization of reality'* (Böhme 2010, 30; my translation, emphasis in original) has taken place. Böhme notes that Debray's model presupposes a 'secret metaphysics of writing' (2010, 30; my translation) and states that writing is a pragmatic cultural technique among others that does not have any privileged access to reality or truth. So, there is a type of media critique that builds on something like a competition of media. The representatives of this critique state that their preferred medium is more capable of transferring the truth or reality than other media. They believe in some inner truth of that which is mediated, which risks getting lost if mediated by the 'wrong' medium.

Nostalgia for Analogue Media

This type of media critique is also characteristic of nostalgia for analogue media. As Benjamin outlines the loss of the artwork's 'aura' if it is technically reproduced, so the analogue nostalgists think that 'the essence' or 'life' of the music would be lost if it is digitally recorded. The discontinuous code of zeros and ones that is allegedly the base of digital recording causes anxiety for analogue nostalgists who prefer the allegedly continuous mode of analogue recording. Jonathan Sterne (2006, 338) writes polemically, 'For many years now, critics have written of digital audio recording—in its myriad forms—as less "live" or less "natural" than analogue recording. By implication, these critics suggest that digital audio is closer to death.' Similar to Böhme, Sterne suggests judging recording technologies by less metaphysical and more pragmatic criteria. Since digital audio files are easy to share and easy to listen to in noisy environments, 'where critics have found the chasm of death in the spaces between frames of digital recording, they should have found vivacious life instead' (ibid., 346).

---

[2] Benjamin's perspective on this development is not merely cultural critical but ambivalent. Technical reproduction leads to new forms of perception which can be emancipatory. For an extensive discussion of Benjamin's concept of the aura see Bratu Hansen (2008).

However, for analogue nostalgists, life is not vivid but *imperfect*. British radio icon John Peel emphatically sums up this celebration of the imperfect: 'Somebody was trying to tell me that CDs are better than vinyl because they don't have any surface noise. I said, "Listen, mate, life has surface noise"' (Chasanoff 2012 quoted in Schrey 2014, 32). This topos of the digital as perfect and the analogue as imperfect is not only found in the statements of analogue nostalgists, but also in the scientific literature that reflects the phenomenon. According to Dominik Schrey, the term 'analogue nostalgia' first appeared in 2002 in Laura Marks's book *Touch: Sensuous Theory and Multisensory Media* (Schrey 2014, 34). Marks (2002) uses the term to describe artistic practices that produce an analogue aesthetic in the digital age, a trend that Claire Bishop (2012) also identifies. Analogue nostalgia in artistic practices always seems to be a matter of countering the perfect, virtual world of the digital with something concrete, physical, imperfect. Marks writes as follows:

In the high-fidelity medium of digital video, where each generation can be as imperviously perfect as the one before, artists are importing images of electronic dropout and decay, 'TV snow' and the random colors of unrecorded tape, in a sort of longing for analog physicality. Interestingly, analog nostalgia seems especially prevalent among works by students who started learning video production when it was fully digital. Related to analog nostalgia is the brave attempt to re-create immediate experience in an age when most experience is rendered as information. (2002, 152–3)

Marks contrasts the perfect impenetrability of digital video with the error-proneness of analogue video, which shows signs of wear and tear and is subject to an aging process that makes it more physical than digital video. She attests that film-makers grown up after the advent of digital media have a special longing for the immediate, physical experience that seems to distinguish analogue film from digital film. The analogue can create an immediacy that has been lost in the information age.

Bishop (2012), like Marks, states that the digital age constitutes a nostalgic use of analogue media in contemporary art: 'Today, film's soft warmth feels intimate compared with the cold, hard digital image, with its excess of visual information (each still contains far more detail than the human eye could ever need)' (ibid., 436). Bishop stresses that in his earliest texts on relational aesthetics, curator Nicolas Bourriaud contrasted the 'artists' desire for face-to-face relations' with 'the disembodiment of the Internet'. She states that Bourriaud pitched 'the physical and the social [. . .] against the virtual and representational' (2012, 437). Against this background, she concludes that artists are indeed, in the spirit of Benjamin, afraid for the aura of their art, which they see as endangered by its digital distribution. There is, for Bishop, a crucial difference between digital media and earlier emergences of new media, such as photography and film in the 1920s and video in the late 1960s: While these formats were based on images, the digital is based on code and therefore is

> inherently alien to human perception. It is, at base, a linguistic model. Convert any .jpg file to .txt and you will find its ingredients: a garbled recipe of numbers and letters, meaningless to the average viewer. Is there a sense of fear underlying visual art's disavowal of new media? Faced with the infinite multiplicity of digital files, the uniqueness of the art object needs to be reasserted in the face of its infinite, uncontrollable dissemination via Instagram, Facebook, Tumblr etc. (ibid., 441)

Due to new distribution capacities and a general shift in the creative process itself, today's artists fear that the uniqueness of their works of art is threatened. For, as Bishop notes, the art form of the twenty-first century is sampling, the artful assembly of what already exists, 'Questions of originality and authorship are no longer the point: instead, the emphasis is on a meaningful recontextualization of existing artifacts' (ibid., 438). As every computer user is able to archive and create constellations, the artists see their obsolescence approaching with concern. They counter this fear by clinging to concrete, material objects that can be touched. The figure of the creative artist, who with their genius creates something genuinely new, seems threatened. As a reaction to this, works of art are created that captivate by their tactile qualities and whose production requires great effort in terms of craftsmanship. Bishop speaks of 'the pressures that current regimes of technology and communication have placed on the object, which becomes increasingly fragile and provisional, as if to assert subjectivity (and tactility) against the sealed, impregnable surface of the screen' (ibid.).

Bishop's deliberations on analogue nostalgia among artists hint to the fact that there is an overlap in pondering digital technology and social media. Both are seen as threatening the uniqueness and immediacy of artistic creation in particular, as well as subjectivity and vivid interactions in general. Artists face these developments by steering towards old analogue media, which, in opposition to new digital media, are seen as imperfect and personal. The characteristics described here not only refer to the functioning of particular media technologies but rather describe general modes. The digital encompasses everything computerized and is associated with the information age, impenetrable screens, and discontinuous code whereas the analogue stands for imperfection, decay, continuity, and immediacy. In this context, the digital is seen as a hypermediated mode, whereas the analogue spills over from denoting old media into denoting a mode of non-media: having an analogue conversation does not mean chatting via an analogue telephone but talking face to face without the usage of any media.

There are two characteristics of nostalgia in general and analogue nostalgia in particular that are especially important for my further analysis: first, analogue nostalgia builds on dualistic distinctions. One mode is seen as superior to the other because it is closer to nature and therefore more capable of conveying immediacy. Second, nostalgia is directed towards the past without being merely reactionary. In what follows, I would like to use these two categories to both analyse Van Dijck's and Turkle's critiques and to suggest alternative modes of reckoning with social media.

(NOT) THINKING IN DUALISMS

I argue that critiques of social media in the techlash are built around ideas and ideals that resonate with that of nostalgia for old media. In the critiques, the contemporary moment is measured against an idealized past. This idealized past is seen to be closer to human nature. This relation of closeness is characterized often by the absence of automation. I would like to present some passages from Turkle's *Reclaiming Conversation* and Van Dijck's distinction between connectedness and connectivity as symptomatic of this way of reckoning with social media. While Turkle has general objections against communicating via digital short messages and checking social media instead of engaging with friends face to face, Van Dijck's critique focuses on the history of social media in the context of platform capitalism. Thus, only Turkle is nostalgic for 'the analogue', understood as a state free of digital media. However, in order to understand how Van Dijck's critique works, the concept of analogue nostalgia is equally helpful as it points to the dualistic distinction between a 'natural' and a 'more artificial' mode, which she reproduces by distinguishing between connectedness and connectivity. It is important to note that I don't read Turkle and Van Dijck as the creators of analogue nostalgia in critiques of social media but use passages of one each of their respective books in order to analyse how analogue nostalgia works in critiques of social media. This means that I consider these passages as symptomatic of prevalent analogue nostalgia in the techlash.

Conversation versus Connection (Turkle)

Human relationships are rich, messy, and demanding. When we clean them up with technology, we move from conversation to the efficiencies of mere connection. I fear we forget the difference.

(Turkle 2015, 21)

To conceive humanity and technology as polar is to wish away humanity:
we are sociotechnical animals, and each human interaction is sociotechnical.

(Latour 1994, 64)

Turkle describes human relationships as imperfect—'messy', but at the same time 'rich' and 'demanding'. Technology is able to purge these human relationships through efficiency, which is not seen as positive, but rather as threatening. Turkle's book is a plea for human conversation. Her goal is to salvage the richness of human interactions against the threat of connecting via modern technology. In Turkle's dichotomy, human beings are vulnerable (ibid., 27), hesitating (ibid., 23), fallible (ibid., 49), bored, and afraid (ibid., 38). Usage of technology serves to control these weaknesses. According to Turkle, we prefer to send perfectly edited text messages because we are afraid to face an interaction situation in real life where we might reveal our imperfect, vulnerable self by making a slip of the tongue, and because we are afraid that the conversation might take a course we did not anticipate.

The digital age causes us to be overwhelmed with emotions—both our own and those of others. At the same time, we unlearn to be alone with ourselves. Instead of enduring boredom, we turn to the smartphone: 'We use technology to "dial down" human contact, to titrate its nature and extent. People avoid face-to-face conversation but are comforted by being in touch with people—and sometimes with a lot of people—who are emotionally kept at bay' (ibid., 29). We must, however, relearn, according to Turkle, to endure the spontaneity of human relationships, and above all, in order to be able to face our fellow human beings, we must relearn to be alone in order to reflect upon ourselves:

> In order to feel more, and to feel more like ourselves, we connect. But in our rush to connect, we flee solitude. In time, our ability to be separate and gather ourselves is diminished. If we don't know who we are when we are alone, we turn to other people to support our sense of self. (ibid., 47)

The idea of an autonomous, authentic subject that must rely on its inwardness to meet its fellow human beings is a necessary premise for Turkle's critique of technology. In her critique of digital communication, Turkle romanticizes the human self in a way that has been challenged not only by a number of science and technology studies (STS) approaches but also by more classical sociological perspectives of the twentieth century. For if one thinks, for example, of Simmel's (1995 [1903]) analysis of the blasé attitude as a necessary mechanism for survival in the big city, of Goffman's (1980 [1956]) reference to the theatrical character of every interaction situation, or of Luhmann's theory of communication (1991 [1981]), it becomes clear that sociology approaches the question of social order without the assumption of an authentic self with anthropologically constant needs—in fact, sociology constantly destabilizes this notion. Simmel explains that it is essential to keep our fellow human beings emotionally at bay in order to survive in modern society—a mechanism that Turkle denounces. Goffman shows that in interactions we are constantly busy 'managing' the impression we make on others (even before Instagram), and Luhmann argues that the problem of communication should be approached through its improbability rather than through normative claims.

Instead of assuming that society consists of ready-made subjects who somehow interact with each other, these authors raise the question of the emergence of social order. This goes hand in hand with not ontologizing identity, but rather focusing on the never-ending processes that are necessary to create an intelligible identity that allows one to act (Butler 2015 [1990]). According to Latour, who criticizes thinking about the relation of humanity and technology as polar in the context of STS, these processes always involve non-human actors, because the human cannot be conceived as inherently free from technology. He writes, 'Even the shape of humans, our very body, is composed in large parts of sociotechnical negotiations and artifacts' (Latour 1994, 64). In referring to the debate on restricting the sale of guns in the United States, Latour demonstrates the fallacies of both technological determinism ('guns kill people') and anthropocentrism ('guns don't kill people; people do) and instead suggests accounting for distributed agency by acknowledging the existence of a new actant that emerges when a citizen holds a gun or when a gun finds itself in the hands of an angry citizen—the 'citizen-gun' or 'gun-citizen' (1994, 32). This principle of symmetry implies the jettisoning of the dichotomy between human subjects who have certain ends and non-human objects that function as means to obtain these ends. It seems that Turkle is very keen on upholding this exact dichotomy. She fears that technology is no longer simply a tool for us humans, but that it exercises a power over us that we must resist. In fact, the result of her qualitative research is that many people feel addicted to their phones.[3] Young people in particular complain that they cannot resist the constant impulse to check their smartphones. One of Turkle's students claims that 'we are not as strong as technology's pull' (Turkle 2015, 31). She feels bad because she is not able to not look at her cell phone during a seminar, although she finds the seminar

---

[3] As psychological studies prove hardly any tangible correlation between mental health issues and time spent online—the effect of social media on depression has been measured to be about as high as eating potatoes (Orben and Przybylski 2019, quoted after Sutton 2020)—Theodora Sutton (2020) suggests framing digital addiction not as a medical condition but as a social fact.

very interesting and feels obliged to pay attention. To escape the dangerous enchantment of social media technologies, Turkle preaches moderation. She sees our health and emotional well-being are endangered by technology and demands that the latter serves our human purposes again. She calls upon both consumers and companies for moderate, conscious smartphone consumption. In this sense, Turkle's thinking is perfectly in line with the claims of Tristan Harris, whom I introduced in the opening of this chapter as one of the main figures of *The Social Dilemma* and thus as one of the popular critics of social media beyond academia.

Nathan Jurgenson (2013) uses the term 'digital austerity discourse' to describe this widespread conviction that we need to cut down our screen time in order to re-engage in human interactions. Instead of assuming a 'digital dualism', he argues for the notion of 'augmented reality', in which we do not assume a healthy, natural, authentic self threatened by social media technologies. Instead, he suggests seeing ourselves as a 'Haraway-like cyborg self comprised of a physical body as well as our digital profile, acting in constant dialogue' (2011). Those who, like Turkle, denounce excessive smartphone use as unhealthy, he accuses, following Foucault, of defining a new realm of the normal, the healthy, the natural. Within this logic, a neoliberal sensitization of the individual takes place, and the individual's health becomes their own responsibility. To meet this responsibility, everyone can 'consume ethically', for example, by booking expensive digital detox vacations. Jurgenson (2013) writes, 'The true narcissism of social media isn't self-love but instead our collective preoccupation with regulating these rituals of connectivity.' He thus transfers Foucault's (1998 [1976]) argument, according to whom the regulation of sexuality takes place through its discursivation, to the discursivation of smartphone use, as promoted by Turkle. By talking about our inability to stay away from our phones, by tracking our screen time, or by announcing an intention to spend less time with our devices in the future (e.g. as a New Year's resolution), we set up a new realm of the healthy and normal. This discursivation is accompanied by a devaluation of those who do not see themselves in position to resist and moderate the pull of digital media. Turkle does not express this devaluation with overt aggression, but rather with concern about her interviewees who succumb to the smartphone drug and therefore lose touch with their fellow human beings: 'Every time you check your phone in company, what you gain is a hit of stimulation, a neurochemical shot, and what you lose is what a friend, teacher, parent, lover, or co-worker just said, meant, felt' (2015, 40). It follows from this logic that those who, like Turkle, have recognized the dangers of digital communication and are able to deliberately deal with technology are in a morally superior position and also lead a richer life because they are able to understand the feelings of their fellow human beings.

Turkle's argument relies on assuming a dichotomy between human and technology. In this classification, technology is to serve as a means for obtaining human ends. These ends, however, must not consist of keeping fellow humans at bay; rather, Turkle praises the immediacy of human interactions in which humans show their imperfections and weaknesses. In regulating their smartphone use, however, humans are to be not weak but powerful in resisting the addictive nature of their mobile devices. Even though Turkle does not explicitly use the word 'analogue', referring her argument to analogue nostalgia helps to understand how it works. Digital technology is construed as 'artificial' against an idealized past that was 'more natural' and therefore closer to human nature and more capable of conveying immediacy. In this logic, which can be traced back to Plato, it is not called into question that the purpose of media is to transport as much immediacy of the non-mediated as possible. Hence, for Turkle, it is reprehensible to dial down the intensity of an interaction by sending a text instead of making a call. In the 'digital age' the power of talk must be reclaimed.[4]

Connectedness versus Connectivity (Van Dijck)

Compared to Turkle, Van Dijck puts less emphasis on the individual and makes a less normative argument. Furthermore, she does not dismiss technology altogether but assumes that there used to be a desirable form of connecting on the internet. She analyses how the early Web 2.0 has been taken over by big companies. Nonetheless, her *Critical History of Social Media* relies on dualistic distinctions. The main distinction Van Dijck makes is between connectedness and connectivity. The former describes the original need of users to connect with their peers. Van Dijck writes, 'Originally, the need for *connectedness* is what drove many users to [social media] sites' (2013, 4, emphasis in original). The latter is what corporate platforms made out of connectedness. By the means of coding technologies, they commodify the behavioural and profiling data users produce unintentionally while connecting on the internet. I argue that by distinguishing between connectedness and connectivity, Van Dijck creates two opposing realms—the former comprising innocent users, citizens, and old media and the latter comprising owners, corporate agents, and new media (ibid., 131). Although Van Dijck emphasizes that, in reference to Latour, she understands the platforms she investigates as socio-technological assemblages (ibid., 26–28), she always makes a strict distinction between 'human' and 'automated'. She analyses critically how CEOs cultivate the 'conflation of human connectedness and

---

[4] The subtitle of *Reclaiming Conversation* is *The Power of Talk in a Digital Age*.

automated connectivity' (ibid., 13). The goal of her book is to 'deconstruct [. . .] what meanings developers *impute* to their platforms' goals, and functions—meanings that peculiarly reflect rhetorical attempts to absorb utopian Web 2.0 connotations into corporate missions' (ibid., 11, emphasis in original). It seems as though Van Dijck wants to disentangle the conflation between connectedness and connectivity. Again referring to Latour (2005), at the end of her book, she writes of the necessity to 'reassemble the social', implying that in the culture of connectivity, the utopian visions of the early Web 2.0 era need to be reinforced at the expense of corporate interests (ibid., 175). This gesture of salvaging a former, more natural mode resonates with analogue nostalgia and is hardly compatible with a Latourian perspective, for Latour explicitly wants to refrain from such romanticizing ideas of the social. In his demand to 'reassemble the social', the social is not a normative term referring to the realm of human interactions. Rather, he demands that we trace back the associations needed for any entity to exist and act—be it human or non-human. In this framework, the world cannot be categorized into realms such as the social or the economy but it consists of various heterogeneous actor–networks. From this perspective, the power of corporate platforms consists of their ability to produce more connections than other actors and a way to curtail their power could be to redistribute this ability more equally. But criticizing social media, be it the way it influences our communication or the way it has been commodified and standardized, should be done without presupposing pristine humanness or pristine sociality that risks getting lost because of digitization since, as the next section will show, digitization cannot be regarded as a linear process in which we are moving further away from a purportedly more natural condition.

NOSTALGIA'S TEMPORALITIES

By shedding nostalgia for a past that was more inherently connected to nature, we free ourselves to imagine new ways—and revivify dormant and alternative traditions—of connecting nature, culture, history, and technology.

(Sterne 2016, 42)

Media nostalgia in general and analogue nostalgia in particular seem to have a peculiar temporal structure: on the one hand, as expressed by Bishop, the clinging to physicality seems to rely on a concept of time as linear and progressing. In the course of advancing digitization, the object 'becomes increasingly fragile and provisional' (Bishop 2012, 438). On the other hand, analogue nostalgia seems to be a trend whose occurrence might last for only a short period of time and whose function is limited to questions of habitus and distinction. Listening to vinyl and wearing an analogue camera around the neck do not necessarily imply the intention to take a stand against digital media but can be mere decisions of style that might serve to show the belongingness to a certain group of people at a certain point in time.

Introducing a media-theoretical anthology on the analogue/digital distinction in 2004, German media theorist Jens Schröter notes that soon after the advent of the CD in 1982 and digital photography in 1989 'the pessimistic cultural voices' that lamented the loss of authenticity were 'silenced' (Schröter 2020, 9). In 2004, Schröter diagnoses the triumph of digital euphoria over analogue nostalgia, whereas today, in the age of the techlash, analogue nostalgia seems to have reappeared. Thus, in examining analogue nostalgia two different temporal structures can be found: a continuous one and a multi-layered one that does not assume linear progress or linear decline but accounts for discontinuities. The first concept of time is in line with what Jacques Rancière calls the 'thesis of the homogeneity of time' (2012, 24). Instead, he advocates a 'heterochrony' (ibid., 36) that accounts for discontinuities and for the simultaneity of different times. I argue that both Van Dijck and Turkle tend to presuppose the first homogenous concept of time, which is symptomatic of the techlash. Van Dijck describes an evolution from connectedness to connectivity. According to her, 'the transformation from networked communication to "platformed" sociality, and from a participatory culture to a culture of connectivity, took place in a relatively short time span of ten years' (2013, 4–5). In this evolutionary story, the utopian spirit of the early Web 2.0 that was characterized by connectedness and participation has evolved into the culture of connectivity in which the profit of big companies is the main focus. For Turkle, it seems clear that current technologies of communication deprive us of 'real' connections. Whereas in former times, we had to talk to each other in order to communicate, today, we tend to keep each other at bay by connecting via short messages.

Turkle presents a study whose goal is to investigate which media enable the best connection among people. Four different ways of communicating were tested: face-to-face conversations, video chat, audio chat, and the exchange of online short messages. The results are clear: the study participants, old college friends who had not seen each other for a long time, felt closest to each other when they talked face to face. The connection was least intense when they chatted online via text messaging (the intensity of the connection was measured by how the friends interact with each other and by asking how they felt after communicating with each other). Turkle writes that attempts by the test persons to 'warm up' their online messages with emoticons, laughter ('hahaha'), or writing in capital letters failed. Turkle sums up: 'It is where we see each other's faces and hear each other's voices that we become most human to each other' (ibid., 23). Here, Turkle sets up a hierarchy between the different communication media. Text messages score the worst, because they are the 'coldest'. The 'warmest', insofar as it creates the most intense connection, is the immediate, non-mediated face-to-face conversation. When we see our faces and hear our voices, we become more human to each other, whereas text messages are not able to bring us close.

This hierarchization provides interesting information about how analogue nostalgia works. The matter of warmth is also of great importance in nostalgia for analogue recording and playback media: analogue films and analogue photography are considered warmer than digital photography, and the sound of a record is considered somehow warmer and more alive than the sound of a CD. Turkle now uses the argument of warmth for communication media. It does not matter whether a particular medium is based on analogue signals or on digital code, but the question is how we become most human to each other. Thus, Turkle's nostalgia refers to the analogue as a mode of non-media. Interestingly, Turkle now establishes a hierarchy that describes how this mode of non-media, that is, the human voice or human facial expression, can best be conveyed through media: if we cannot meet in real life to talk to each other, which is undoubtedly the best form of communication, it is better to talk on the phone than to write short messages because on the phone we hear the voice of our counterpart and speak for ourselves. This hierarchization once again points to the ambivalence of 'analogue', for the paradoxical question underlying Turkle's description of the experiment is, 'How can we convey the real, the human—yes, the immediate—through media?' This question is posed with the fear that the immediate might be lost in the process of mediation. The goal is to prevent this loss by conveying as much immediacy as possible, for example, by speaking on the phone using our natural voices. According to Turkle, we succeed least in conveying the immediate in digital short messages.

She describes communication by short messages in a way that is reminiscent of the discrete form of digital data transmission—Turkle describes digital communication as 'connecting in sips' (ibid., 35). This form of communication

> may work for gathering discrete bits of information or for saying 'I am thinking about you'. Or even for saying 'I love you'. But connecting in sips doesn't work so well for an apology. It doesn't work so well when we are called upon to see things from another's point of view. In these cases, we have to listen. We have to respond in real time. In these exchanges we show our temperament and character. We build trust. Face-to-face conversation unfolds slowly. It teaches patience. We attend to tone and nuance. (ibid., 35)

Here, Turkle is referring not to the working of digital data transmission, but rather to the fact that we exchange short messages that are deprived of the information needed to conduct a 'real' conversation—an argument that is also found among analogue nostalgists who fear that the discrete digital signals of CDs will deprive the music of something that can only be conveyed by the continuous signals of analogue audio. It remains ominous what this 'something' is—in both cases it seems to be something natural that is threatened by the digital. Turkle argues that only with our natural voice, in the spoken word, can we show our 'temperament' and 'character'. At best, the voice is accompanied by our facial expressions in face-to-face conversations—if this is not possible, a telephone call is preferable to a written message because it can transport the human voice. Further reasons for Turkle's dismissal of short messages are their speed and their brevity. Digital communication makes us impatient—instead of having continuous conversations in which we look at each other, listen to each other, and thereby engage with each other, we get used to a state of constant interruption.

Without using the word 'analogue' and without talking about media technology data transfer, Turkle reproduces the characteristics of 'analogue' and 'digital'. The non-media face-to-face conversation is the most 'real' and 'warmest' form of communication, because it is the one that can convey our 'character' and 'temperament'. The exchange of digital short messages, on the other hand, deprives our communication of this liveliness. Face-to-face conversations are characterized by their continuity. Turkle describes them in a way that is reminiscent of analogue data transmission, while digital communication is presented as constantly interrupted, that is, discontinuous.

CONCLUSION: A HETEROCHRONIC PERSPECTIVE ON THE PROCESSES OF DISCONNECTION

The binary between continuity and discontinuity can be found on two different levels: first, on the level of describing the workings of analogue versus digital data transmission and second, on the level of conceptualizing time. On both levels, Turkle stands on the side of continuity. She argues for continuous conversation instead of discontinuous connection and tells a linear story of decline in which humans have unlearned how to talk to each other because of digital technology. Van Dijck makes no case for continuous transmission, but by presuming the distinction between connectedness and connectivity and by describing an evolution from the former to the latter, she is in line with the thesis of the homogeneity of time and thus conceptualizes time continuously. This homogenous concept of time is symptomatic of the techlash. It can be challenged by considering analogue nostalgia as a trend phenomenon that only lasts for a short period of time and can disappear and reappear. The fallacy of presentism, which consists of presupposing linear decline in the case of cultural pessimism and linear progress in the case of digital euphoria, can be obviated by historicizing analogue nostalgia.

Far from being sober media technological terms, 'analogue' and 'digital' tend to be charged with all kinds of meanings. As Jonathan Sterne (2016) shows, referring to different historical entries from the *Oxford English Dictionary*, starting from the 1950s, 'analogue' begins to signal everything 'outside computers' (ibid, 37). In the second half of the twentieth century, the digital and the analogue have become 'imaginable as . . . cultural condition[s]' (ibid., 38). However, instead of assuming that we have moved from analogue times to digital times and eventually start 'being digital', as Nicholas Negroponte (1995) famously predicted in 1995, a heterochronic perspective on social media allows for the simultaneity of the analogue and the digital. This also means jettisoning the idea that the analogue is superior to the digital because it is closer to nature or reality, as it has been claimed not only by fans of vinyl records but also by media theorists such as Kittler (1999, 35 quoted after Sterne 2016, 38), Massumi (2002, 135 quoted after Sterne 2016, 39), and Galloway (2017). Benjamin Peters suggests that 'the digital and the analogue are non-oppositional modes of indexing the world' (2016, 101). Sterne claims that 'reality is just as analogue as it is digital; and conversely, that it is just as non-digital as it is not-analogue' (2016, 41). Similar to Latour, he adds the following:

> This goes back to an old argument, one made well by the last generation of technology scholars . . . including Kittler and Massumi at other points in their writings: technology is part of the domain of human existence, not something outside it. (ibid.)

As Stäheli and Stoltenberg (2020 quoted after Stäheli 2021, 433) show in their research on digital detox tourism, there is no such thing as a natural state free of any (media) technology. In order to produce the analogue space of a digital detox camp, practices of analogization are needed, including the use of old media like VHS cassettes and typewriters. Ironically, in the camp, new forms of media like the Google search engine are imitated 'analogically': when people want to know something, they can write down their questions on a piece of paper, put it in a box, and hope that someone knows the answer to their questions and writes it down themselves. This example shows that presuming a homogenous time is mistaken: we are not living in an age where we have become digital and processes of remediation necessarily mean that analogue media are imitated digitally. It is more complicated: the ubiquity of digital media produces a longing for 'the analogue' as a purportedly media-free state. It turns out that such a thing does not exist but needs to be produced by the usage of media. The media used to create the analogue are not exclusively old media but, like the human search engine, new media that are remediated 'analogically'.

The first consequence for a critique of social media that is different from analogue nostalgia in the techlash is thus to account for what Rancière calls a 'heterochrony', a perception of time that is multi-layered and discontinuous.[5] It follows, second, not to presume that there is a realm free of technology and one flawed by technology. There is not only 'nothing to disconnect from' (Bucher 2020) but neither, as Bucher also makes clear by pointing out that a temporal disconnection produces meaningful data points, nothing to disconnect *to*. We cannot go back to an innocent state of connectedness and we have to accept that our communication relies heavily on media technologies. As Bucher writes with reference to Nancy (2000 quoted in Bucher 2020), we are always singular plural. Similar to what I have pointed out in reference to Latour, Bucher states, '[This] being-with . . . is not exclusively between human beings, but a mode of being-together that includes the more-than-human as well' (615). For reckoning with social media, this means neither focusing on the state of being disconnected nor equating this state with the analogue or some former purportedly more natural mode, but on the processes of 'undoing networks' (Karppi et al. 2021) that include humans and non-humans.

REFERENCES

Bartholeyns, Gil. 2014. "The Instant Past: Nostalgia and Digital Retro Photography." In *Media and Nostalgia: Yearning for the Past, Present and Future*, edited by Katharina Niemeyer, 51–69. Basingstoke, Hampshire; New York: Palgrave Macmillan.

Benjamin, Walter. 2010 [1935]. *The Work of Art in the Age of Mechanical Reproduction*. Lexington: Prism Key Press.

Bishop, Claire. 2012. "Digital Divide." *Artforum*, September, 51 (1): 435–441.

Böhme, Hartmut. 2010. "Der Wettstreit der Medien im Andenken der Toten." In *Gedächtnisparagone—intermediale Konstellationen*, edited by Sabine Heiser and Christiane Holm, 25–46. Göttingen: V & R Unipress.

Böhn, Andreas. 2007. "Nostalgia of the Media / in the Media." In *Self-Reference in the Media*, edited by Winfried Nöth and Nina Bishara, 143–153. Berlin: de Gruyter.

Bolin, Göran. 2016. "Passion and Nostalgia in Generational Media Experiences." *European Journal of Cultural Studies* 19(3): 250–264. doi:10.1177/1367549415609327.

---

[5] This goes hand in hand with historicizing disconnection, as advocated (2018b) and done (2018a) by Pepita Hesselberth. For a historicizing approach to digital disconnection see also Syvertsen (2020).

Bolter, Jay David, and Richard Grusin. 2000. *Remediation: Understanding New Media*. Cambridge, MA: MIT Press.

Boym, Svetlana. 2001. *The Future of Nostalgia*. New York: Basic Books.

Bratu Hansen, Miriam. 2008. "Benjamin's Aura." *Critical Inquiry* 34(2): 336–375. doi:10.1086/529060.

Bucher, Taina. 2020. "Nothing to Disconnect from? Being Singular Plural in an Age of Machine Learning." *Media, Culture & Society* 42(4): 610–617. doi:10.1177/0163443720914028.

Butler, Judith. 2015 [1990]. *Gender Trouble: Feminism and the Subversion of Identity*. New York: Routledge.

Cook, Pam. 2005. *Screening the Past: Memory and Nostalgia in Cinema*. London; New York: Routledge.

Debray, Régis. 1996. *Media Manifestos: On the Technological Transmission of Cultural Forms*. London; New York: Verso.

Foucault, Michel. 1998 [1976]. *The Will to Knowledge*. London: Penguin Books.

Galloway, Alexander R. 2017. "What Is the Analog?". Last modified December 29, 2017. Accessed April 14, 2021. http://cultureandcommunication.org/galloway/what-is-the-analog.

Goffman, Erving. 1980 [1956]. *The Presentation of Self in Everyday Life*. Harmondsworth: Penguin Books.

Hesselberth, Pepita. 2018a. "Connect, Disconnect, Reconnect: Historicizing the Current Gesture towards Disconnectivity, from the Plug-in Drug to the Digital Detox." *Cinéma & Cie* XVIII, 30: 105–114.

———. 2018b. "Discourses on Disconnectivity and the Right to Disconnect." *New Media & Society* 20(5): 1994–2010. doi:10.1177/1461444817711449.

Jurgenson, Nathan. 2011. "Digital Dualism versus Augmented Reality". *Cyborgology*. Last modified February 24, 2011. Accessed April 14, 2021. https://thesocietypages.org/cyborgology/2011/02/24/digital-dualism-versus-augmented-reality/.

———. 2013. "The Disconnectionists". *The New Inquiry*. Last modified November 13, 2013. Accessed April 14, 2021. https://thenewinquiry.com/the-disconnectionists/.

Karppi, Tero. 2018. *Disconnect: Facebook's Affective Bonds*. Minneapolis, MN: University of Minnesota Press.

Karppi, Tero, Urs Stäheli, Clara Wieghorst and Lea Zierott. 2021. *Undoing Networks*. Minneapolis/Lüneburg: Meson Press, MN: University of Minnesota Press.

Latour, Bruno. 1994. "On Technical Mediation." *Common Knowledge* 3(2): 29–64.

———. 2005. *Reassembling the Social: An Introduction to Actor-Network-Theory*. Oxford: Oxford University Press.

Luhmann, Niklas. 1991 [1981]. "Die Unwahrscheinlichkeit der Kommunikation". In *Soziales System, Gesellschaft, Organisation*, 25–34. Opladen: Westdt. Verl.

Marks, Laura U. 2002. *Touch: Sensuous Theory and Multisensory Media*. Minneapolis, MN: University of Minnesota Press.

Moore, Kasey. 2021. "Every Viewing Statistic Netflix Has Released So Far (February 2021)." *What's on Netflix*. Accessed April 14, 2021. https://www.whats-on-netflix.com/news/every-viewing-statistic-netflix-has-released-so-far-february-2021/.

Negroponte, Nicholas. 1995. *Being Digital*. London: Hodder & Stoughton.

Newtro. 2021. "Newtro Website." Accessed April 14, 2021. https://www.newtro.de/produkte.

Niemeyer, Katharina. 2014. "Introduction: Media and Nostalgia." In *Media and Nostalgia: Yearning for the Past, Present and Future*, edited by Katharina Niemeyer, 1–23. Basingstoke, Hampshire; New York: Palgrave Macmillan.

Orlowski, Jeff, dir. 2020. *The Social Dilemma*. Netflix. Accessed April 14, 2021. https://www.netflix.com/pt/title/81254224.

Peters, Benjamin. 2016. "Digital.' In *Digital Keywords: A Vocabulary of Information Society and Culture*, edited by Benjamin Peters, 93–108. Princeton, NJ: Princeton University Press.

Rancière, Jacques. 2012. "In What Time Do We Live?" In *The State of Things*, edited by Marta Kuzma, Pablo Lafuente and Peter Osborne, 9–37. Oslo: Office for Contemporary Art Norway.

Schrey, Dominik. 2014. "Analogue Nostalgia and the Aesthetics of Digital Remediation." In *Media and Nostalgia: Yearning for the Past, Present and Future*, edited by Katharina Niemeyer, 27–38. Basingstoke, Hampshire; New York: Palgrave Macmillan.

Schröter, Jens. 2020. "Analogue / Digital—Opposition or Continuum?" Preprint. MediArXiv. doi:10.33767/osf.io/x7eq3.

Simmel, Georg. 1995 [1903]. "The Metropolis and Mental Life." In *Metropolis*, edited by Philip Kasinitz, 30–45. London: Palgrave Macmillan.

Stäheli, Urs. 2021. *Soziologie der Entnetzung*. Berlin: Suhrkamp.

Sterne, Jonathan. 2006. "The Death and Life of Digital Audio." *Interdisciplinary Science Reviews* 31(4): 338–348. doi:10.1179/030801806X143277.

———. 2016. "Analog." In *Digital Keywords: A Vocabulary of Information Society and Culture*, edited by Benjamin Peters, 31–44. Princeton, NJ: Princeton University Press.

Sutton, Theodora. 2020. "Digital Harm and Addiction: An Anthropological View." *Anthropology Today* 36(1): 17–22. doi:10.1111/1467-8322.12553.

Syvertsen, Trine. 2020. *Digital Detox. The Politics of Disconnecting*. Bingley: Emerald Publishing.

Turkle, Sherry. 2015. *Reclaiming Conversation: The Power of Talk in a Digital Age*. New York: Penguin Press.

Van Dijck, José. 2013. *The Culture of Connectivity: A Critical History of Social Media*. Oxford; New York: Oxford University Press.

Index

echo, 43–44, 54–55

echolocation: background of theory of, 40–41; in bats, 54; definition of, 39; dislocation through, 53; ontological security from, 39; ping and echo in, 45; relationality of, 55; Self and, 4, 39; social, 39, 57

echosorting, 44

economic livelihood, 112–13

Edenius, Mats, 129

Ehrenberg, Alain, 149

elite disrupters, 29

emotional labour, 68

emotions, 214

energy-drains, 96

Enterprise Social Media (ESM), 168–69, 173–74

entrepreneurialism, 74

Envelope, 139–41

Eriksson Lundström, Jenny, 129

ESM. *See* Enterprise Social Media

Estée Lauder, 73–74

ethics, of technology: during Covid-19 pandemic, 170; experimentation in, 129–33; Hollier driven by, 130; in Silicon Valley, 130; techlash responded to by, 128; virtue, 22–23; in world-building, 141

everyday life: balance of, 197–200; home centralized in, 175–76; Workplace in, 178–79

exclusion, 15

Exit, Voice, and Loyalty (Hirschman), 116

experimentation: in disconnection, 141–43; in ethics, 129–33; norms reinforced by, 141; sensorial networks and, 140; tech ethics and, 129–33; techlash responded to with, 139, 143. *See also* Google Digital Wellbeing Experiments

Facebook, 28, 88, 88n1, 98, 113, 114; ambivalence with, 86; data misuse by, 92–93; digital detox from, 94; familial commitment

in, 112; happiness displayed on, 97; Instagram owned by, 104; Workplace from, 168–69, 173–74, 183

face-to-face conversation, 220, 221

facial recognition, 43–44, *44*, 45

fake sociality, 97–99

Falconer, Venetia, 74

fallacies, 215

familial commitment, 112

fear, 41, 47, 52–53, 112, 154

fear of missing out (FOMO), 41, 47, 112

feature phone, 129

feedback, *42*, 42–43, *43*, 45, 55

feelings, 38–39, 41

Feldman, Zeena, 6, 136

Felix, Levi, 160–61

Ferragni, Chiara, 73–74

Ferrer, Christian, 159

Filho, Freire, 151n5

Fish, Adam, 161

followers, 67

FOMO. *See* fear of missing out

food influencers, 71

forced disconnection, 167; boundaries during, 184; coding analyzing, 170; communicative context in, 178–80; in Covid-19 pandemic, 168–69, 170–71, 174–75; description of, 174; home-home conflict, digital media encroachment and, 180–83; of knowledge workers, 180; overcoming of, 183; reconnection, digital media and, 172–74; research methodology for, 168–71; sociability and, 180; spatiality in, 175–77; temporality in, 177–78. *See also* lockdown

Foucault, Michel, 148, 216

@48HourChallenge, 74

Fraser, Alistair, 22, 196

freedom: in disconnection, 197–99; play, boundary work and, 193–94

Froh, Paul, 47

About the Contributors

Christoffer Bagger is a PhD fellow at the Department of Communication, University of Copenhagen. His thesis project empirically explores how digital media traverse the boundary between personal and professional life. His work is particularly interested in enterprise social media. He is part of the research project 'Personalizing the Professional'.

Alex Beattie is a research fellow at the Center for Science in Society, Te Herenga Waka—Victoria University of Wellington. He researches science communication and the relationship between new media technologies and disconnecting from the internet. Alex has featured in *Convergence* and *Science, Technology, & Human Values* and is a contributing author of *Making Time for Digital Lives: Beyond Chronotopia* (Rowman & Littlefield).

Aleena Chia is lecturer of media, communications, and cultural studies at Goldsmiths, University of London. Her previous appointments include assistant professor at the School of Communication in Simon Fraser University. She researches cultures of creativity in digital game production, social media disconnection, and Silicon Valley spiritual subcultures. Her work has been published in the *Internet Policy Review*, *Journal of Fandom Studies*, *Television and New Media*, and *American Behavioral Scientist*.

Zeena Feldman is senior lecturer in digital culture in the Department of Digital Humanities, King's College London. Her research examines the ways digital communication technologies impact understandings and performances of offline concepts—for instance, belonging, sharing, mental health, and food. She has published widely, including in *Information, Communication &*

Society, Celebrity Studies, TripleC, The Independent, OpenDemocracy, and *The Conversation.*

Marianna Ferreira Jorge holds a master's and a doctorate degree in communication from Fluminense Federal University where she is currently a postdoctoral fellow. Her main research topics are Contemporary Subjectivities, Digital Technologies, Malaise, Medicalization, and Neoliberalism. She is author of the book *Desempenho tarja preta: medicalização da vida e espírito empresarial na sociedade contemporânea* (*Prescription Performance: Medicalisation of Life and the Entrepreneurial Spirit in Contemporary Society*) (Eduff, 2021).

Pedro Ferreira is an associate professor at the IT University of Copenhagen, Denmark. His research interests include leisure, play, international development, postcolonialism, and the digital infrastructuring of everyday life. Ferreira holds a PhD in Human–Computer Interaction from the Royal Institute of Technology (KTH) in Stockholm, Sweden, and a MSc and BSc in Computer Science from the Technical University of Lisbon, Portugal.

Ana Jorge is a research coordinator at CICANT and associate professor at Lusófona University. Ana is a Media and Cultural Studies scholar and researches children, youth and media, audiences, celebrity culture, and digital culture. Her scholarship appears in journals such as *Celebrity Studies, Social Media and Society, Journal of Children and Media,* and *European Journal of Cultural Studies.*

Magdalena Kania-Lundholm, PhD, is a senior lecturer in sociology at Dalarna University, Sweden. Her research combines sociology of communications and media, cultural sociology, critical internet studies, social theory, and qualitative methods. Recent work focuses on questions of technology (non-)use, digital inequalities, and practices and experiences of digital disconnection. Her work has been featured in journals such as *Sociology Compass, Journal of Aging Studies,* and *Media, Culture & Society.*

Tero Karppi is associate professor at the University of Toronto. He teaches at the Institute of Communication, Culture, Information, and Technology and the Faculty of Information. He is the author of *Disconnect: Facebook's Affective Bonds* (University of Minnesota Press 2018) and his research has been published in journals such as *Theory, Culture & Society, Social Media + Society,* and *New Media & Society.*

Airi Lampinen is an associate professor of human–computer interaction at the Computer and Systems Sciences Department at Stockholm University,

Sweden, and a docent of Social Psychology at the University of Helsinki, Finland. Her research interests include exchange platforms, algorithmic systems, and the interweaving of interpersonal and economic encounters. She holds a PhD in Social Psychology from the University of Helsinki and a BSc (Eng.) from Aalto University's Information Networks degree programme.

Stine Lomborg is PhD and associate professor at the Department of Communication, University of Copenhagen. Her work, grounded in empirical studies of the uses of digital media, centres on understanding the implications of communication for the good life. She is particularly interested in current regimes of tracking of the self as they unfold across key contexts of everyday life.

Annette N. Markham is professor of media and communication and co-director of the Digital Ethnography Research Center (DERC) at RMIT University in Melbourne, Australia, and professor MSO (on leave) of Information Studies at Aarhus University, Denmark. She is well known for her research on identity and cultural formations in digitally saturated sociotechnical contexts, as well as her transformations of models for innovative and ethical modes of studying people in digital contexts.

Marco Pedroni is an associate professor of sociology of culture and communication at the University of Ferrara, Italy. He researches, teaches, and writes about fashion, media, and cultural industries. He is a co-editor of the *International Journal of Fashion Studies* published by Intellect Books. His articles have appeared in journals such as *Poetics*; *Fashion Theory*; *Film, Fashion and Consumption*; and *Journal of Public Policy*.

Julia Salgado holds a master's and a doctorate degree in communication and culture from Rio de Janeiro Federal University where she was also a postdoctoral fellow. Her main research topics are youth culture, consumer culture, entrepreneurship, motherhood and entrepreneurship, neoliberalism and the media. She is author of the book *Entre solitários e solidários: o empreendedor como trabalhador ideal* (*Between Solitary and Solidary: The Entrepreneur as the Ideal Worker*) (Appris, 2020).

Trine Syvertsen is professor of media studies at the University of Oslo. She has published on media policy, history, public broadcasting, television, and digital media. Her books include *Media Resistance: Protest, Dislike, Abstention* (2017) and *Digital Detox: The Politics of Disconnecting* (2020). She chairs the project 'Intrusive Media, Ambivalent Users and Digital Detox (Digitox)', funded by the Norwegian Research Council (2019–2023).

Clara Wieghorst is a PhD candidate at the Center for Digital Cultures at Leuphana University of Lüneburg, Germany. Since 2018, she works as a research associate in the project 'Disconnectivity. Imaginaries, Media Technologies, Politics', funded by the German Research Foundation. She holds a master's degree in sociology. Together with Tero Karppi, Urs Stäheli, and Lea Zierott she has co-authored *Undoing Networks* (University of Minnesota Press, 2021).

Brita Ytre-Arne is professor of media studies at the University of Bergen, and an expert in qualitative media use research. She has published extensively on news audiences, social media, smartphone use, and media in everyday life, and co-edited the book *The Future of Audiences* (with Ranjana Das). She has currently guest-edited (with Stine Lomborg) a special issue of *Convergence* titled 'Advancing Digital Disconnection Research'.

www.ingramcontent.com/pod-product-compliance
Lightning Source LLC
Chambersburg PA
CBHW030647270326
41929CB00007B/243